I0797435

BISON
BOOKS

Nourishing Growth and Suffocating Life

Water, Politics, and Infrastructure in Urban Oklahoma

DANIEL MAINS

UNIVERSITY OF NEBRASKA PRESS
Lincoln

The University of Nebraska Press is part of a land-grant institution with campuses and programs on the past, present, and future homelands of the Pawnee, Ponca, Otoe-Missouria, Omaha, Dakota, Lakota, Kaw, Cheyenne, and Arapaho Peoples, as well as those of the relocated Ho-Chunk, Sac and Fox, and Iowa Peoples.

For customers in the EU with safety/GPSR concerns, contact:
gpsr@mare-nostrum.co.uk
Mare Nostrum Group BV
Mauritskade 21D
1091 GC Amsterdam
The Netherlands

LIBRARY OF CONGRESS CONTROL NUMBER: 2025011322

Designed and set in Garamond Premier Pro by Katrina Noble.

CONTENTS

ILLUSTRATIONS

Photographs

Maps

ACKNOWLEDGMENTS

This book would not have been possible without the willingness of dozens of Norman residents to share their thoughts and experiences about water and politics. In particular, I want to thank Amanda Nairn, who shared her wealth of contacts with people in the world of water. These contacts provided the essential foundation I needed to begin my research. Amanda was always available to meet and discuss the project, even when our viewpoints on water and Norman diverged. John Hancock graciously shared a tub of documents related to Norman Citizens for Civic Responsibility that he inherited from Larry Wood. The staff and city council members of the City of Norman were always quick to respond to emails and take time out of their busy schedule to meet.

I am grateful to the many colleagues who provided critical feedback on early drafts of this book. I am fortunate to have outstanding colleagues at the University of Oklahoma Honors College. Ben Alpers, Marie Dallam, Julia Ehrhardt, Rich Hamerla, Brian Johnson, Bob Lifset, Mandy Minks, Carolyn Morgan, Andreana Prichard, David Song, and Sarah Tracy all provided generous comments on chapter drafts. Darcie DeAngelo, Lori Jervis, Kim Marshall, Claire Nicholas, Camilo Sanz, and Elyse Singer all participated in OU's sociocultural anthropology writing group and commented on multiple chapter drafts. I appreciated regular meetings with Lucas Bessire at The Library bar and grill to discuss research, writing, and publishing. Laurel Smith offered valuable suggestions on chapter drafts. I thank Traci Brynne Voyles for connecting me with the University of Nebraska Press. Bruce O'Neill, Derek Pardue, and Jed Stevenson all offered much-needed anthropological critiques from outside the state of Oklahoma. Aaron Quinn read an early version of the entire book and provided valuable feedback that guided revisions. Two anonymous reviewers provided useful suggestions for revisions.

The University of Oklahoma Honors College provided the funding to complete much of the research and writing necessary for this project. A Social Sciences, Humanities, and Arts Seed Grant from OU's vice president for Research and Partnerships supported the project. The staff at OU's Carl Albert Center were very helpful in directing me toward resources related to the history of Lake Thunderbird. David Levy was generous in suggesting archival sources related to my work. Grace Benham was my undergraduate research assistant during the early stages of the project and provided valuable help exploring Facebook discussions of stormwater policy.

The Alexander von Humboldt Foundation provided a Grant for Renewed Research Stay that allowed me to spend June 2023 at the Rachel Carson Center in Munich, Germany, where I finalized the manuscript. Funding to support production of this book was provided by the University of Oklahoma Libraries' Open Access Fund.

My editor at University of Nebraska Press, Bridget Barry, has been amazing. She closely read the entire manuscript and offered detailed suggestions for edits.

Thank you to everyone who joined me for a creek walk, a bicycle ride, or a casual discussion of Norman's political ecology. The members of Soccer Tuesday United were essential for maintaining my mental health and sense of humor over the past six years. I thank my parents for letting me explore "Way Back There" as a child. Alise Osis has been there throughout this project, joining me for walks, reading chapter drafts, and providing me with the space I need to work. This book is dedicated to my kids, Iris and Gus. Walking in Norman's creeks with Iris and Gus was the initial inspiration for this project. I wish them a future of lots of creek walks and clean water.

NOURISHING GROWTH
AND SUFFOCATING LIFE

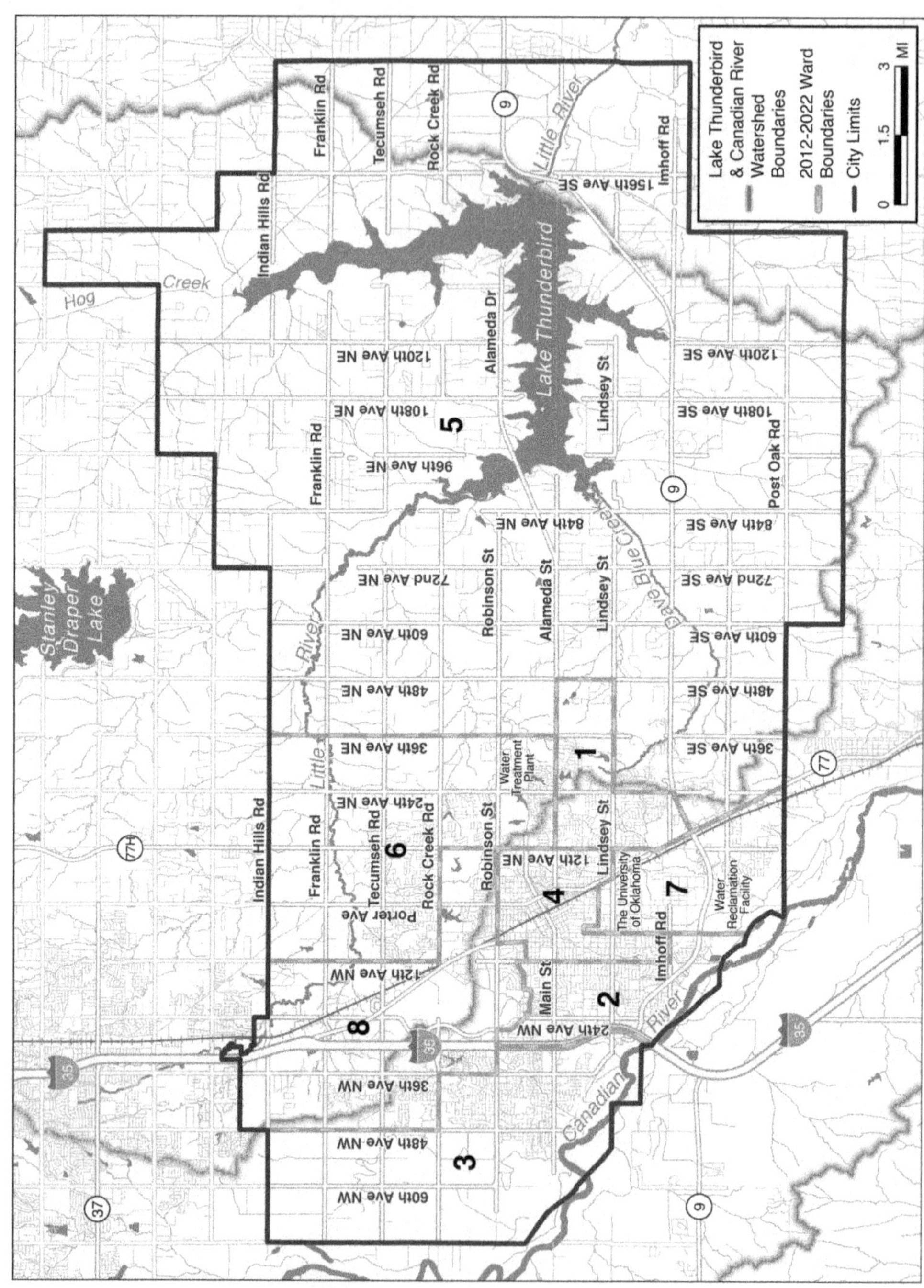

Map 1. City of Norman. Created by Todd Fagin.

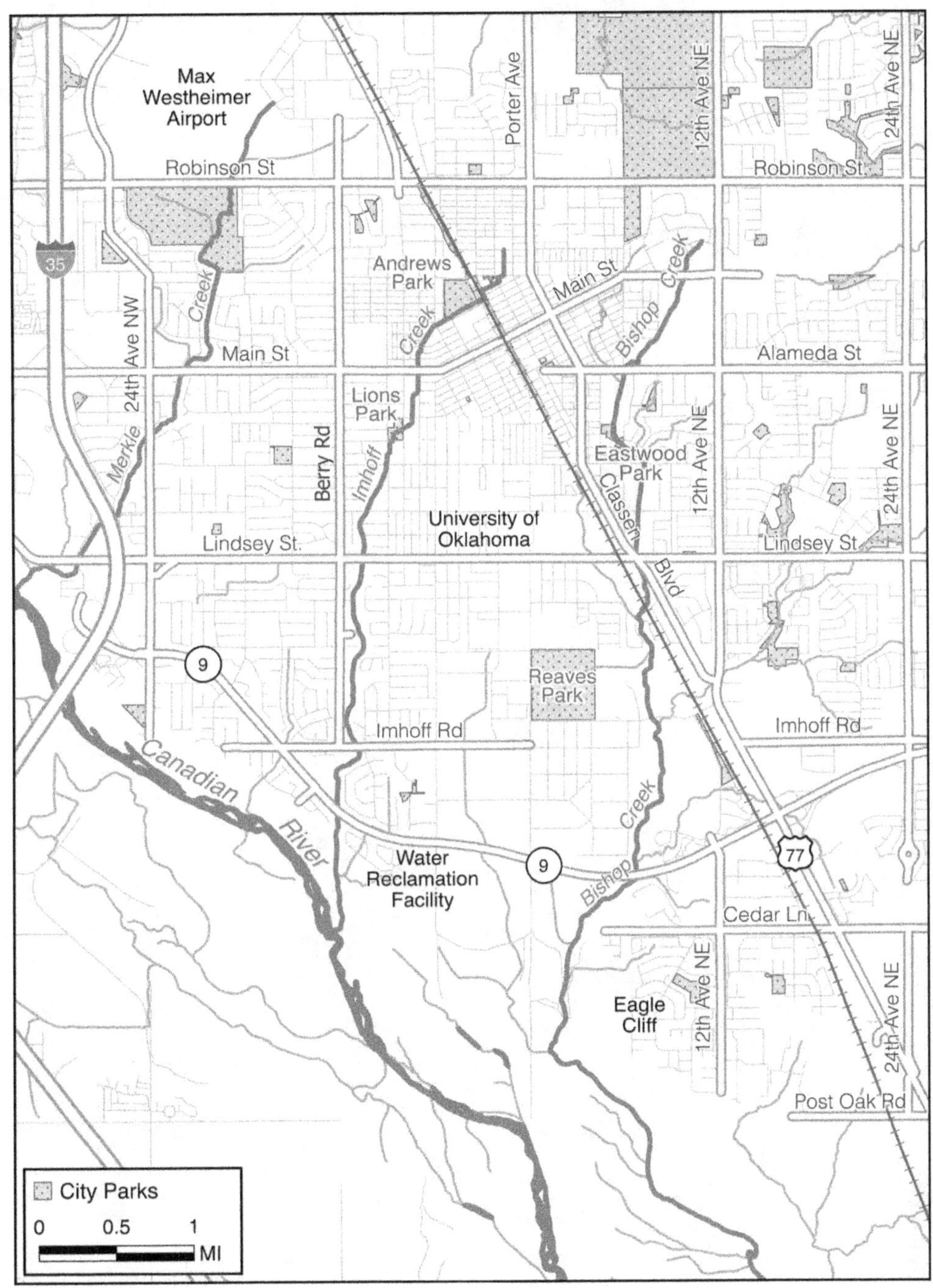

Map 2. Central Urban Norman. Created by Todd Fagin.

Introduction

Eutrophication, Creeks, Conspiracy, and Citizenship

NORMAN, OKLAHOMA, is a pleasant college town filled with affordable homes on quiet tree-lined streets. Despite its relatively small population of 130,000, as home to the University of Oklahoma, Norman hosts major sporting events, monthly downtown art walks, and a thriving music scene. It is often included on lists of the best places to live in the United States.[1] Memories of my first days in Norman, however, are forever shaped by the city's water. My first taste of Norman tap water was something terrible, perhaps the worst tap water I have ever tasted. The smell hit me first—a cocktail of mold, dirt, and algae. The taste even cut through a strong cup of coffee. I have never been a bottled water drinker, but I immediately went out and bought a gallon jug.

I had driven to Norman from Maine in my blue 1995 Honda Odyssey minivan; my family would meet me later. For now, I was alone in the house we had bought a few blocks from the university where I would soon begin my first tenure-track job. It was August 2011, a summer of record-breaking heat in Oklahoma, endless days of temperatures above 100. My movers laughed when they unloaded the cross-country skis, snow shovel, and sleds that had been essential during my family's two years in Maine.

Alone in the house, slowly unpacking boxes, I had to get out and do something. I looked at a map and saw there was a lake just east of town. I got into the minivan and drove. Even with the air-conditioning blasting, I could feel the heat radiating through the windows. After only two or three miles, the housing developments began to thin out and the road opened onto rolling hills, sprawling lawns, and patchy forests of oak and red cedar. A few miles more and I saw a small parking lot near the lake with people swimming in the murky red-brown water. I drove on until a sign announced I had reached a state park. I pulled off the road and walked to where the water met the red soil to form a beach. Though the sun was setting, the heat was still intense. I took off my shoes and waded into the opaque, lukewarm water, letting the muddy lake bottom squish between my toes.

I did not know it at the time, but I had driven to the source of my tap water—Lake Thunderbird. I eventually learned that the bad taste of my water was a result of eutrophication, a term that comes from the Greek for "well-nourished." People in this part of the world like thick green lawns, but grass does not grow easily here, so urban Oklahomans frequently apply fertilizers containing phosphorous.[2] It doesn't often rain in central Oklahoma, but when it does, the rain comes down hard, washing the lawn fertilizers into creeks that eventually make their way to Lake Thunderbird. All those nutrients cause explosions of algae growth.[3] The algae die and are decomposed by bacteria, consuming large amounts of oxygen in the process. The lack of oxygen then kills fish and other aquatic life. Lake Thunderbird was created in 1965 to provide the drinking water necessary for Norman's population of forty-five thousand to nearly triple in about sixty years. That same growth, and the resulting increase in rainwater runoff, produced the well-nourished waters of Lake Thunderbird that suffocate life.

The eutrophication in Lake Thunderbird is a small version of what is happening throughout the United States, perhaps most famously in the Gulf of Mexico. The creeks and rivers that fill Lake Thunderbird are just one fraction of the Mississippi River watershed that captures water from more than one million square miles. The Mississippi River eventually carries enough nutrients into the Atlantic Ocean to create an oxygen-deprived dead zone that sometimes grows to more than eight thousand square miles.[4] Eutrophication is a form of self-devouring growth.[5] The massive dead zone in the Gulf of Mexico is a result of the overly nourished life in the United States. There is something inherently pleasurable about nourishing growth, but the United States is often nourished in terms of quantity, not quality. Outside of power plants, the top two carbon emitters in Oklahoma are fertilizer producers.[6]

These fertilizers, which make their way into the Mississippi River, nourish industrialized farming and monocrops like soy and corn. It is a food system that certainly supports growth, but not human health.

Eutrophication often occurs far from the source of the nutrients. Farmers and consumers of the food they produce rarely experience the dead zones that fertilizers have created. I had lived in the overly nourished nation of the United States for nearly forty years when I moved to Oklahoma, but it was there that I tasted eutrophication for the first time. I was sensing the death that comes from nourishing growth, and I could not wash that taste out of my mouth.

Why does nourishing growth often lead to the suffocation of life, not just through eutrophication in bodies of water but through urban development more broadly? Using public funds to subsidize growth that primarily benefits the wealthy has self-destructive consequences. Contrary to the myth of the free market, public subsidies for growth are essential to capitalism. Water infrastructure is one of the key methods through which urban growth is subsidized and as such offers an ideal site for understanding the intersection between government and markets. Infrastructure is so effective as a means of redistributing wealth because it is often invisible and outside the realm of popular discussion.

Growth is destructive when it is associated with exclusive forms of citizenship. By citizenship, I refer not just to formal rights but to practice. Substantive citizenship describes one's ability to engage in politics and achieve one's goals.[7] Urban residents often have identical legal rights but vastly different abilities to put those rights into practice and make claims on public institutions. It is these differences in citizenship that cause subsidized growth to reproduce power hierarchies and generate a kind of government welfare for the rich. Differences in substantive citizenship in Norman have at times been enforced with racial and gender-based violence. More commonly, the power of people at the political and economic center of the city to enact their visions for the future creates its own opposition and destabilizes planning and governance.

The processes that I examine in Norman are not unique. Cities throughout the United States struggle with tensions over infrastructure and subsidized growth. Politically, Norman is a microcosm of the nation. The city boundaries contain a predominantly liberal central urban core, a strong contingent of conservative suburbanites, and many libertarian and right wing–leaning rural residents. Norman's political diversity makes reaching a consensus on policy solutions to the challenges of water and urban growth particularly difficult. These battles over water infrastructure and growth allow us to rethink the current political moment and how urban residents throughout the United States engage in local policy making.

Creeks

Following urban creeks led me to this book. I never expected to live in Norman, Oklahoma, and I certainly did not expect to write a book about the city. I came to the University of Oklahoma to teach about African studies, cultural anthropology, and international development. Walking in Norman's creeks began as a way to get outside with my kids, and it gradually became something of an obsession, as I discovered that creeks are winding paths into and out of eutrophication and the politics of growth.

The chemicals that nourish aquatic plant life in Lake Thunderbird and the Gulf of Mexico begin their journey in creeks, many of which are fed by rain. Stormwater that runs off the land comes together to form small creeks that merge into larger creeks and rivers that eventually reach Lake Thunderbird and Norman's drinking water. But in the city's urban core, creeks perform a different function. The roads, parking lots, houses, and stores—all the physical structures that make up a city—depend on creeks to drain stormwater out of the city and prevent flooding.

When a friend told me about a bridge east of town where I could access Dave Blue Creek, I was eager to check it out.[8] Norman is divided between an urban area, where most of the creeks flow into the Canadian River, and the geographically larger but sparsely populated rural area where creeks like the Dave Blue flow into Lake Thunderbird. Fortunately, the intense August heat finally broke the day I visited Dave Blue Creek. Cloudy skies and temperatures in the low eighties made for a pleasant afternoon. There had been a little rain in the morning, the first precipitation in a couple of weeks, but there was no flow in the creek. It was broken into pools separated by a mix of rock and cement. Bridges are popular dumping sites and spending time in a creek provides insights into the local material culture. Pages of the *Norman Transcript* and a box of business cards were scattered in the water. The wheels of a half-buried tractor poked out from the red dirt. A discarded container from a cannabis dispensary and empty cans of light beer served as indications of popular creek-side pastimes. Despite the trash, it was easy to spot small fish flitting about in the pools. Just downstream from the bridge, I was struck by the beauty of the contrast between the exposed red dirt of the creek bed and the deep green of the overhanging mature oaks.

Urban creeks break down the binary between technology and nature. The City of Norman is slowly moving forward with plans to channel treated sewage water to Lake Thunderbird. Dave Blue Creek will be the channel that connects the Water Reclamation Facility to the lake. Drinking treated wastewater strikes me as the stuff of science fiction, something out of Frank Herbert's *Dune*, but this innovative technology depends on something decidedly low-tech—creeks. In moving water in and out of the city, creeks are transformed. Old tractors and beer cans fouling creeks are easy to see, but treated wastewater will bring what the U.S. Environmental Protection Agency calls contaminants of emerging concern to Dave Blue Creek.[9] These contaminants are not usually regulated or measured, but they may have significant impacts on human and aquatic life.

Spending time in creeks is a method for seeing the city differently.[10] The evening of my visit to Dave Blue Creek my family took advantage of the cool weather to walk along Imhoff Creek, near our home. The Imhoff Creek watershed is home to many university faculty and contains much of Norman's historic center. When we turned off from the sidewalk into the creek at a bridge, we entered another world. The bridge forms a cool grotto that is a popular spot for adolescents, and the graffiti reflects their interests—crude drawings of breasts and genitalia, 666, 69, 420, all of the sacred numbers. We walked slowly upstream along Imhoff's paved channel. Large shade trees overhang the creek. It is a pleasure to walk where cars cannot travel, and the creek offers a perspective on the city that is not visible from the road. On one side of the creek are backyards; on the other side an overgrown pecan orchard in the flood plain creates a dense forest that obscures the houses. On the forested side the only visible structure is a dilapidated wooden boat that someone has painted with the words "Norman Yacht Club."

Urban creeks like Imhoff are surrounded by hard surfaces that do not absorb water. Whereas forests and pastures soaked up much of the day's rain before it could reach Dave Blue Creek, Imhoff was flowing freely for the first time in weeks. Surfaces that are impervious to water convey fluids from the entire creek watershed. After only a few minutes we reached a pedestrian bridge that spans the creek. There we saw a bright red fluid draining into it from a pipe, like it was flowing with blood. I later learned that the brilliant red came from the iron-rich red Oklahoma clay that a landscaping crew washed from their tools a few blocks from the creek. Particularly after heavy rains, creeks make connections between different parts of the city visible.

There is trash in the creek, sometimes a lot of trash. Long grasses and brush catch plastic bags and Styrofoam cups. But there is also wildlife. A fox once followed me along this section of the creek, always staying around twenty yards behind. My kids and I spotted a snapping turtle paddling downstream. On a warm summer evening, returning from a free concert at Lions Park, we heard a hooting in the trees and looked up to see a barred owl peering down at us. Each of these unexpected encounters with nature in the city become stories to be shared and remembered.

Creeks are one more vantage point on the consequences of nourishing growth, but they also demonstrate that the outcome of growth is not necessarily eutrophication and the suffocation of life. Just as creeks channel the water and trash that run off from the city's ever-expanding asphalt and concrete, they nurture new and surprising forms of life—the red fox that burrows under Imhoff Creek's concrete banks, the insect larvae luxuriating in warm pools, and the children playing beneath the bridge.[11] Even when they are confined to concrete channels, creeks create unexpected spaces within the city and fracture narratives of self-devouring growth.[12]

Particularly when eutrophication seems inevitable, creeks have been a valuable research method for disrupting my assumptions. Around every bend in the creek something new is revealed. Continually returning to this unique ecosystem generates surprising insights. It is not just creeks; spending time at Lake Thunderbird or the digital ecosystem of Norman's public neighborhood Facebook pages always leaves me surprised and increasingly aware of the cracks in overly deterministic relationships between capitalism and eutrophication.

Creeks have much to teach us. In October 2022 Central Oklahoma was in an extreme drought. We endured the fifth driest September in more than 120 years.[13] But the rain finally came just before midnight on October 15. I left my bedroom window open so I could hear the storm roar as I fell asleep. We got nearly ¾ of an inch of rain. Not enough to impact the drought, but it filled the creeks.

My interest in creeks led me to monitor Bishop Creek for Blue Thumb, a volunteer citizen-science organization administered by the Oklahoma Conservation Commission. Bishop Creek flows north to south, draining neighborhoods on the east side of the university. The watershed encompasses homeless camps, well-kept historic homes, and low-income apartment complexes. Every month I collect a water sample from Bishop Creek and run a half-dozen chemical tests. Monitoring the creek after rain allowed for comparison with the usual dry conditions. The chloride test is one of my favorites. I add the chloride reagent to 23 milliliters of my sample water and then add drops of silver nitrate until the sample turns blood orange. Counting the drops of silver nitrate tells me how much chloride is in the water. Usually, my sample is high in chloride, close to 160 milligrams per liter, but after the storm it was only 15 milligrams per liter. It is likely that the rain diluted the water in the creek. This means that high levels of chloride in my sample probably occur naturally. Salts in the soil increase from east to west across Oklahoma. People visit the Great Salt Plains in Western Oklahoma to dig for large salt crystals in the sandy plains. The rain helped me determine that chloride, one of the major contaminants in Bishop Creek, probably comes from the soil rather than pollution generated by humans.

While the chloride levels went down after the storm other levels went up. Nitrate, nitrite, and orthophosphate levels in my sample were all higher than usual. These are all chemicals found in fertilizers. This told me that the rain most likely washed fertilizers into the creek. This is how eutrophication begins. Simple but powerful connections and processes can be observed at times of change, like after a rainstorm. This is true of social life as well—times of change and instability can clarify social dynamics.

Conspiracy

The summer of 2020 was a time of change. I was still in the early stages of conducting research for this book when the COVID-19 pandemic erupted. That summer a political movement, Unite Norman, formed and attempted to recall city councilors and the mayor because of policies related to COVID-19 and alleged attempts to defund the police. Journalists for national news outlets described a progressive college town in one of the reddest states in the nation torn apart by debates over policing, race, and COVID-19 policy.[14] Norman became a microcosm of the nation's division and anger.

I spent much of the summer sitting at a table on my backyard deck, poring over a plastic tub of newspaper clippings documenting a time in the 1970s when Norman was also torn apart, but over seemingly mundane debates concerning lift stations. In most of Norman, sewage flows downhill to the sewage treatment plant, or as it is called today, the Wastewater Reclamation Facility. If sewage pipes are uphill from a neighborhood, a lift station is needed to pump sewage from homes to a point in the system where it can flow downhill the rest of the way. Lift stations are excellent examples of the mundane and invisible infrastructures that are essential for managing water in cities.[15]

Why were sewage lift stations topics of such heated debates? Because lift stations are essential for nourishing urban growth. As cities expand, lift stations are needed to connect new neighborhoods with the infrastructural grid that moves sewage to treatment plants. A home with no way to get rid of sewage has very little value. Proponents of growth argued that new homeowners in Norman generate tax revenues the city needs to pay for police, fire departments, public parks, and everything else urban residents depend on for a high quality of life.

In contrast, critics of new lift stations connected them to environmental preservation and economic equity. Rainwater in Norman flows to two destinations. In much of the city, including nearly all the neighborhoods developed prior to the 1970s, rainwater flows into the Canadian River. In the rest of the city, it flows into creeks and rivers that eventually reach Lake Thunderbird, which is the source of more than two-thirds of Norman's drinking water. Much of the Lake Thunderbird watershed is on the far side of a ridge from Norman's Water Reclamation Facility. To build new houses in this area, lift stations are necessary. New homes mean that among other materials, dirt from construction sites, chemicals from lawns, and feces from dogs will all be washed into the source of Norman's drinking water every time it rains. As developers and investors use publicly funded infrastructure to support growth, eutrophication results. Activists who sought to limit growth in the Lake Thunderbird watershed in the 1970s understood the lake has struggled with excessive amounts of sediment, phosphorous, and nitrates since it was created in 1965.[16] Subsidized growth destroys water—the source of life. Opposing lift stations was a way of limiting growth in the Lake Thunderbird watershed and protecting the quality of Norman's drinking water.

Larry Hill was one of the many Norman residents who wrote letters to the *Norman Transcript* during the summer of 1974 in opposition to the construction of new lift stations. At the time Hill was a political science professor at the University of Oklahoma. In one of his letters he wrote, "I for one am not willing to have my utility bill increased to subsidize the developers."[17]

When I shared a chapter draft with a colleague, I was surprised to learn from her that Larry Hill still resided in central Norman. My colleague connected us, and soon Hill and I were sitting in the shady backyard of his modern ranch-style house, just a couple blocks from Imhoff Creek. It was a warm October afternoon in 2020, and I followed Hill's lead and wore a surgical mask as we chatted about growth in Norman. In the early 1970s Hill often took his sons fishing in Lake Thunderbird, and it was the planned development in the watershed that led him to attend city council meetings and pay attention to city politics. Hill explained, "I knew how politics works here, which is the same way it works in most all of these sun belt areas. There's an ongoing conspiracy between the bankers, the developers, and the chamber of commerce that really runs all these towns . . . When I say it's an ongoing conspiracy that's what it is." The conspiracy of developers is a way of nourishing growth, but with money rather than fertilizer. Lift stations are expensive.

When cities use public funds to build lift stations, they are subsidizing development by giving value to new homes that developers sell for a significant profit. In other words, developers can sell new homes because they are connected to publicly funded infrastructure for moving sewage.[18] In this sense, lift stations not only move sewage but also transfer wealth from residents to developers.

Hill noted that blocking the lift stations in 1975 may have been a small victory, but it did not defeat the conspiracy. In Norman, real estate developers are usually the top donors of campaign funds to city councilmembers. Developers hire attorneys to lobby for their interests. They have the power to continually fight to advance their agenda, even if they occasionally lose an election. Like eutrophication, "conspiracy of developers" describes an empirical process, but it also functions as a metaphor for broader dynamics—the use of public funds to stimulate economic growth. The conspiracy of developers is an essential dimension of capitalism—owners of capital rely on the state to subsidize growth, often through urban infrastructure.[19] Capitalism is based in collusion and plotting, and the same conditions that produce the conspiracy of developers generate conspiracy theories and an overwhelming sense of doubt.[20] The relationship between conspiracy and capitalism is partially responsible for the proliferation of conspiracy theories that may or may not be grounded in reality.[21]

In many cases market forces would slow growth if not for state intervention.[22] Without government-built networks of roads extending from city centers, it is unlikely that so many middle-class Americans could have afforded suburban homes during the mid-twentieth century.[23] If developers are responsible for the costs of roads, water, and sewage, then housing developments that are far from established infrastructure will be more expensive. Many consumers will choose housing options that don't require new roads, lift stations, and pipes. Government subsidies for growth also push development into areas where there are environmental constraints, like dangers from wildfires or coastal storms.[24] This is not an argument against the construction of new housing, rather it is a critique of subsidizing certain types of growth.

A successful conspiracy depends on invisibility. Infrastructures like sewage lift stations allow conspiracies to hide in plain sight. Most of us do not literally see lift stations, and we do not mentally connect them with economic inequality. Like dams, lift stations are ideal technologies of conspiracy because they redistribute wealth in ways that are difficult to identify. Lift stations are boring and easily forgotten. Norman residents like Larry Hill sought to make lift stations visible so that people see how they redistribute wealth and contribute to eutrophication. The conspiracy of developers is undermined when the relationship between infrastructure, growth, and inequality is brought into the open.

In Norman, the belief that developers conspire with city officials to subsidize growth has not disappeared in the fifty years since the lift station battle. During the rise of Unite Norman in 2020, some Norman residents encouraged others to "connect the dots" to identify a relationship between developers and Unite Norman. Some dots are easier to connect than others. At times it seemed that Unite Norman cofounder Sassan Moghadam was trying to personify a caricature of the fat cat capitalist developer. The website for his real estate development business listed international big game hunting as one of his hobbies, and his display room of taxidermized African mammals is an object of local fascination.[25] In his video messages to Unite Norman members he often sipped top shelf liquor and smoked a cigar. He has long lobbied the city government to make building and development easier in Norman. Critics of Unite Norman immediately claimed that arguments about policing and COVID-19 policy were simply a smokescreen to advance the interests of real estate developers. Unite Norman's efforts to recall the mayor and city council members failed, but in 2021 Unite Norman supported candidates in every city council election, winning two seats. Unite Norman candidates throughout the city received substantial campaign donations from developers. The triumvirate of Norman's three favorite local celebrities—former University of Oklahoma football coaches Barry Switzer and Bob Stoops and country music star Toby Keith—was featured on fliers for all but one Unite Norman candidate.[26] The Unite Norman council members consistently voted in favor of developer friendly policies, supporting requests for rezoning and limiting fees associated with building new homes. The conspiracy of developers that Larry Hill identified in the 1970s was alive and well fifty years later.

Citizenship

Conspiracy, however, implies a plot that hides behind a set of false claims and narratives. Debates over race and policing are not simply an ideological smokescreen that covers more fundamental issues of political economy. In a city like Norman that emerged out of the dispossession of Indigenous land and was a racially segregated "sundown town" until the late 1960s, race, community membership, and growth are always connected. The smokescreen is just as real as the plot.

Rather than race and policing obscuring battles about development, in some cases arguments about water infrastructure are really about race and policing. In 2022 Larry Heikkila defeated Breea Clark to become the first self-proclaimed "conservative" to be elected as mayor of Norman in more than a decade. After taking office Heikkila called for more "fiscally conservative, pro-growth, pro-business, pro-citizen" voices on the city council.[27] I met Heikkila in his city hall office in November, a few months after he took office. When I asked why Norman residents voted "no" on a 2022 water rate increase, despite overwhelmingly approving a rate increase in 2015, he immediately responded, "Not trusting in council. That was a spit in the face of council vote."[28] Why didn't the voters trust city council, I asked. "First off council defunded police," he told me, referring to city council decisions in the summer of 2020. In other words, water infrastructure necessary for the city's growth was withheld because of policy decisions related to race and policing.

In Norman, like most of the United States, 2020 was a time of intense division over seemingly endless issues—COVID-19 policies, Donald Trump, homelessness, mental health, gun violence, education policy, LGBTQ+ rights, and immigration to name a few. In this time of division, the intersection between policing and race emerged as a symbolically potent issue that united all other conflicts and motivated many Norman residents to march with Black Lives Matter banners or wear "thin blue line" T-shirts and attempt to recall city councilmembers.

The June 16, 2020, city council meeting that Mayor Heikkila claimed had destroyed public trust was held only weeks after police officers murdered George Floyd in Minneapolis. Whereas much of the country was still isolating to prevent the spread of COVID-19, in Norman by June the city council had returned to in-person meetings.[29] The primary goal of the June 16 meeting was to approve the city's annual budget, but from the beginning it was clear that in many ways the budget was secondary to discussions about policing and race. The meeting began at 6 p.m. and ran for more than ten hours. After an opening two hours of discussion and questions from council members for the police chief, it was time to introduce amendments to the city budget. The amendments, which provided funds for different projects, all passed unanimously. Then Alex Scott, Ward 8's councilmember, introduced an amendment that appeared to take the rest of council by surprise. The amendment would decrease the police budget by $4.5 million and allocate those funds to the construction of a new fire station in rural Norman, stormwater projects, an audit of the city, and sensitivity training for the police. The city manager clarified that a cut of this size would eliminate positions for sixty-four police officers, more than one third of the department. Scott, a young woman finishing her first and only term on council, noted that she did not expect the amendment to pass. Rather, she hoped it would start a conversation.

After hours and hours of discussion and listening to voices from the community, Norman's city council did not defund the police. Instead, $865,000, most but not all of the Norman Police Department's requested budget increase, was reallocated.[30] At three in the morning many councilors were visibly exhausted and at times confused as they discussed how to reallocate an amount that matched the salaries of police officer positions that were currently unfilled. Ultimately, most of the funds were to be directed toward a mobile mental health crisis unit, which has yet to be created. It was this policy decision that generated the anger and mistrust that led to the rise of Unite Norman, and, according to Mayor Heikkila, caused voters to reject the 2022 water rate increase. Some residents were angered by the "defund the police" rhetoric, but the city council's decision generated such backlash in part because it raised broader questions about who is served by public institutions.

Citizenship was at the crux of battles over policing and race in Norman and elsewhere in the United States. Formal citizenship refers to legally guaranteed rights.[31] For example, as a result of battles over lift stations in the 1970s, Norman residents gained the right to vote on any increase in utility fees, thus expanding the reach of formal citizenship in Norman. This was a change in the rights of all Norman residents. In contrast, substantive citizenship is based in practice.[32] To what degree can all Norman residents put their rights into practice? How do social differences shape residents' ability to influence policy? In practice the possibility of shaping city policy varies with race, class, gender, and education among other factors, but acknowledging this dynamic is extremely contentious.

The June 2020 debate on policing asked if, in practice, all residents were protected by the police, regardless of race. Advocates of police reform believed that the Norman Police Department denied substantive citizenship for people of color. In contrast, to rationalize police violence or claim that incidents of violence are isolated and caused by bad cops was to deny the existence of systemic racism. From this perspective, differences in substantive citizenship do not exist. Battles over policing and race were so potent in part because they represented a broader debate over the fundamentals of equality. Differences in substantive citizenship demonstrate the presence of a major inequality that many Norman residents found highly unsettling.

Following the June 16 meeting, Councilmember Alex Scott, who introduced the amendment to cut $4.5 million from NPD's budget, was attacked on social media. Norman police officers used social media to publicly circulate Scott's address. Alex Scott lived in a duplex. On June 27, 2020, the woman who lived in the other half of the duplex was attacked and raped. The rapist apparently thought he was attacking Scott. On a social media post Scott wrote, "Her rapist dug his elbow into her neck, pushed her into the wall, and told her 'Maybe next time you'll learn your lesson.' He threw her on the ground and raped her."[33] The rapist has not been caught. The attack on Alex Scott's neighbor was intended to simultaneously silence discussions of racism and place limits on the substantive power of women leaders. Other women councilmembers received anonymous threats of sexual violence.[34]

In Norman's past, race was continually used to legitimize the theft of resources and determine who could participate in discussions on the distribution of the benefits of water infrastructure and growth. Race continues to shape the claims that residents can make on public goods like police protection and water infrastructure, but it is not the only factor impacting substantive citizenship in Norman. Gender, sexuality, class, mental health, and housing status all influence one's ability to shape city policy.

Violent exclusion from citizenship is an important theme of this book, but much of my focus is on a different aspect of citizenship, the privilege to shape policy.[35] This is a privilege that I share with other people like me—white urban professionals who often identify as politically liberal. I live around the corner from an idyllic tree-lined street that ends in a cul-de-sac, bordered on one side by Imhoff Creek. A local developer purchased lots near a few homes on the cul-de-sac. One of the lots was zoned only for residential use. The developer requested that the zoning be changed to commercial so that he could build a strip mall. My neighbors were not happy with this plan. They did not want the increased light, noise, and car exhaust polluting their backyard.

The battle over the strip mall dragged on for years. My neighbors fought the plan at every step by lobbying city councilmembers and speaking at city meetings. The developers' attorney did the same. I was proud of my friends and neighbors as they stood before the council and explained their opposition to the proposed rezoning and strip mall. One of my neighbors is an engineer and he presented a powerful slide show that used extensive evidence to pull apart claims made by the developers' attorney. We won! The only councilmembers voting in favor of the developer were the two men recently elected with heavy support from the Unite Norman movement. My neighbors and I signed a card and delivered it with flowers to our councilmember.

Like most cases of nimbyism, controlling what happens in our backyard is rooted in the privilege of an expansive substantive citizenship.[36] Although our formal citizenship is the same as that of others, in practice my neighbors and I have the power to exert significant influence over what happens in our backyards. The fact that we all have backyards is a form of privilege. As a professor writing a book about growth and water infrastructure, I am well positioned to voice my concerns, and I am not alone. My neighborhood is full of university faculty and other professionals who at the very least can make time to attend meetings and make sure their concerns are heard.

The privilege of substantive citizenship works invisibly because it feels so natural. Of course, my neighbors and I don't want a strip mall in our back yard. Of course, we are going to use our time and skills to stop it from happening. But we don't succeed without our privilege. Privilege allows us to safely ride bikes in the middle of the street. Privilege allows our kids to walk alone up and down the creeks through private property. Successfully fighting a development in my backyard and trespassing on private property without fear of violence are expressions of the expansive nature of my citizenship. It is difficult to see this privilege because it feels so natural.

This book is a story of division that in many ways mirrors the United States. It is not, however, primarily a story of conservative Americans. Although many Oklahomans take pride in living in the reddest of red states, Norman is different. It is a place where conservatives and liberals continually encounter each other. I examine the people at the center of Norman—political moderates and liberals who embrace the expertise of urban planners, engineers, and university researchers. This includes people like me, who can influence city politics and take control of their own backyards, as well as those with even more power who can afford to hire attorneys to advance their interests. I argue that the power of those at the center ultimately erodes community and trust in ways that perpetuate cycles of self-devouring growth.

Each chapter examines the interplay between eutrophication, creeks, conspiracy, and citizenship. After a brief interlude on Norman's early history, I explore the creation of Lake Thunderbird and argue that eutrophication has its roots in racial violence. The second chapter examines a grassroots antigrowth movement that reformed city politics in the 1970s through expanding citizen control over water infrastructure. I then dive into Norman's creeks and explore how they function as a commons that mediates some of the destructive consequences of urban growth. The fourth chapter examines shifting conceptions of truth in relation to debates over stormwater policy that played out on Facebook. Finally, I examine the importance of trust in relation to hexavalent chromium in Norman's drinking water supply and long-term plans for achieving water security by channeling treated wastewater into Lake Thunderbird.

Historical Interlude

Boomers, Sooners, and a Conspiracy of Developers

OKLAHOMA WAS FOUNDED on the intersection between eutrophication, the conspiracy of developers, and citizenship.[1] When I moved to Norman, I had no idea why fans of the University of Oklahoma Sooners chanted "Boomer, Sooner!" at sporting events. I did not know what a Sooner was. Eventually I learned the chant was a celebration of the 1889 land run that opened what was then Indian Territory to white settlers. The story told in children's books is that settlers lined up at the border and waited for the sound of a gunshot at noon on April 22. Thousands flooded across the border on foot, horseback, and horse-drawn wagons. They raced into the supposedly unoccupied territory and staked out land claims. The boomers were those who boomed loudly and continuously, advocating for the opening of Indian Territory to settlement.[2] The sooners were settlers who cheated and snuck into Indian Territory early to stake their claims.

Children in Oklahoma's elementary schools sometimes reenacted the story, lining up on the playground field and then racing to claim their land. In some cases, in a misguided attempt to make the reenactments more realistic, Native American students were placed on the land to be opened, where they faced an onslaught of screaming children in this reenactment of historical trauma. A friend who works in Native American education told me about the endless conversations she had with school administrators about stopping this practice, only to have the reenactments begin again when new teachers arrived.

What is now Oklahoma was designated as Indian Territory in the early nineteenth century. In the 1830s and 1840s, Oklahoma was where the trails of tears ended for the Cherokee, Choctaw, Chickasaw, Seminole, and Muscogee (Creek) Indians. The U.S. government forcibly relocated these groups, collectively known as the Five Tribes, from the southeastern United States to Indian Territory.[3] From 1855 through the 1870s reservations were established for more than thirty other tribes, some whom the U.S. government moved from elsewhere in the United States and others from what is now Oklahoma. In some cases, the federal government leased land from the Five Tribes to create new reservations. Land was also taken from the Five Tribes as a sort of punishment for their alliance with the Confederacy during the U.S. Civil War.[4] The U.S. government forced the Seminole Nation to sell more than 2.1 million acres of land at the low price of fifteen cents per acre, and then buy one hundred thousand acres of this land back for fifty cents an acre.[5] Land taken from the Five Tribes and not assigned to other Native Americans was classified as "unassigned land." Yet, although the U.S. government may not have "assigned" this land, it had been occupied and used for thousands of years. The Caddo Nation and Wichita and Affiliated Tribes lived in the area where Norman is today. Among others, the Apache, Comanche, Kiowa, and Osage nations all made use of the Norman area for migration, trade, and hunting.

The first land run, in 1889, was on this so-called unassigned land. It was here that Norman and Oklahoma City would be established. During the 1889 land run the boomers were frequently sooners. A *Harper's Weekly* journalist who was present at the land run told the story of boomers arriving by train:

> Hardly had the train slackened its speed when the impatient boomers began to leap from the cars and run up the slope. Men jumped from the roofs of the moving cars at the risk of their lives . . . I ran with the first of the crowd to get a good point of view from which to see the rush. When I had time to look around me I found that I was standing beside a tent, near which a man was leisurely chopping holes in the sod with a new axe.
>
> "Where did you come from, that you have already pitched your tent?" I asked.

"Oh, I was here," said he.
"How was that?"
"Why, I was a deputy United States marshal."[6]

It was illegal for a government employee to take up a lot, but there was no authority present to enforce this law.

Sam Anderson's *Boom Town* describes William Couch's role in establishing Oklahoma City.[7] Couch was one of the leaders of the boomers and he spent years leading illegal expeditions into the unassigned lands in Indian Territory and lobbying politicians to open the land for settlement. Couch was one of the founders of the Seminole Town and Improvement Company, an organization that drew up plans for Oklahoma City and other cities. As Anderson explains, the organization did not include Seminole Indians: "Having stolen tribal land, white businessmen were now stealing tribal names."[8] At noon on April 22, 1889, many of the men who emerged from bushes and trees to claim land in Oklahoma City were boomers and members of Couch's Seminole Town and Improvement Company.[9] The boomers were also sooners. These boomers had designed Oklahoma City's plan, so they had no trouble staking out the most valuable real estate. Couch's Seminole Company supporters pushed for him to become mayor, and with their power consolidated, their town survey and land claims were legitimized.[10] Even the best conspiracies, however, rarely work as planned. Couch staked his claim on the outskirts of Oklahoma City, but it was occupied by squatters while he was busy trying to run the city. When Couch returned to his claim in 1890, one of the squatters shot him in the knee, and Couch died from the complications.[11]

Norman was just twenty miles to the south, or two railroad stops from Oklahoma City. It takes its name from Abner Norman, who led the survey of the land that includes the present-day location of the town.[12] Abner Norman chaired the government survey of the area from 1871 until the work was completed in 1873. It is not clear if he actually visited the future townsite, but the words "Norman's Camp" were burned into a large elm tree near a spring where the survey party camped.[13] A little over ten years later, Norman's Camp served as the base for another group of surveyors planning a railroad line that would cut through the "unassigned lands" that the U.S. government had acquired from the Seminoles and Muscogee. In another case of subsidized growth, the U.S. government purchased land from the Seminoles so that it could be given to the railroad.[14] Legislation passed in 1884 authorized the rail line and granted 13½ acres for a station for every ten miles of track. One of these station grounds was not far from Norman's Camp, and railroad tracks reached what was then christened as Norman in 1887.[15] Santa Fe Railway trains began running on the track by June 1887, creating a line that extended from Galveston, Texas, to Kansas City, Missouri.[16]

If Oklahoma City grew in a series of booms and busts, Norman's development was slow and steady. Many of the Santa Fe Railway officials had connections with the Seminole Company and they came together to organize the Norman Townsite Company, which mapped out Norman prior to April 22.[17] On the day of the land run, members of the Norman Townsite Company arrived on the first train and immediately began staking out key pieces of real estate. Just as in Oklahoma City, the boomers who pushed to open the unassigned lands determined Norman's spatial layout and then sought to be the first ones on the ground to claim choice plots of land.

The land run was in many ways another conspiracy of developers. Boomers used surveys and plans to control local governance and determine the value of land. With the land mapped some boomers became sooners, illegally arriving early to stake out the most valuable land for themselves. The U.S. government played an essential role in supporting this conspiracy, first taking land from the Five Tribes, and then opening it for settlement. The benefits of public resources and government intervention were directed primarily toward white men and their families.

Although the land run of 1889 has been memorialized in Oklahoma popular culture, it was just the first of many land runs and land lotteries that opened Indian Territory to settlers. The U.S. government acquired land largely through the General Allotment (or Dawes) Act of 1887.[18] Most of the tribes in Oklahoma held their land in common, meaning ownership was not assigned to particular individuals.[19] Through the Allotment Act the U.S. government allotted land to individual tribal members in parcels of 40, 80, or 160 acres.[20] Any land left over after allotment was considered unassigned and opened to runs and lotteries.[21] Rather than unoccupied prairie, settlers encountered a patchwork of land that could be staked out among Native American allotments. Through allotment the U.S. government enclosed the commons and subsidized growth, transferring two-thirds of Indian lands to settlers between 1887 and 1934.[22]

Allotment and settlement were based in an ideology of growth, a belief that the United States had a moral obligation to make land as productive as possible, which could only be achieved by smallholder farming, organized around nuclear families.[23] The numerous tribes that made homes in Indian Territory during the nineteenth century had diverse ways of living and negotiating land tenure, but for many, shared common land for grazing, hunting, foraging, farming, travel, and meeting was essential. Their way of life became increasingly threatened, as surveys, often for railroads, measured land so that it could be transformed from commons to an allotment that may be assigned, bought, and sold.[24] Not only did allotments create unassigned land that could be distributed through land runs—they made it possible for individual Native Americans to sell their newly allotted land, thereby becoming completely dispossessed from it. From the perspective of the U.S. government, if allotments failed to improve Native Americans' quality of life, this was the fault of Native Americans, not a result of the intentional destruction of a way of life based on commonly held land. In supporting the allotments and the slaughter of bison, the railroad devoured Native American lives to support new settler communities. This was different from the eutrophication that nourishes growth until it suffocates life. Coupled with the mass slaughter of bison, dispossession through allotments comprised attempted genocide, rather than suffocation caused by one's own waste. The self-devouring dimensions of this instance of subsidized growth emerged later as settlers plowed up the prairie and created the Dust Bowl, one of worst ecological disasters of the twentieth century.[25]

Conspiracy is intended to deceive. The dispossession of Native American land, however, sometimes relied on force rather than deception.[26] Deceit is reserved for those who possess membership in a shared community. Native Americans throughout Indian Territory resisted allotment, but they had few options aside from losing their land without compensation.[27] In 1901 Chitty

Harjo led a rebellion of Muscogee who refused to accept allotments. The federal government responded by imprisoning nearly one hundred Muscogee resisters.[28] The arrest of one hundred people was not a hidden plot; rather, dispossession of commonly held land was accomplished by force. Racism and ethnocentrism erased the need for conspiracy, and power operated with little concealment. This is a recurring theme in Norman's history. Those deemed to lack substantive citizenship, often for reasons of race, were simply excluded from debates concerning infrastructure and the redistribution of resources.

University on the Prairie

Pieces of the history of the 1889 land run and Native American dispossession are told on Norman's Legacy Trail. The Legacy Trail is a wide sidewalk that follows the railroad tracks cutting through the center of town. The trail is lined with metal signs fixed to polished blocks of stone that tell Norman's history. One of the plazas includes a table with a cast iron, three-dimensional, bird's-eye view map of Norman, circa 1907. Seemingly every structure in Norman is included on the map. My kids and I sometimes stare at the map, trying to locate where our home would eventually be built, fifty years later. The first two signs on the trail are titled "Indian Territory" and "Native Oklahoma." Maps ostensibly displaying the regions occupied by different tribes accompany the signs, but very little information is given about Native peoples. Rather, much of the Native Oklahoma sign is devoted to describing instances when whites passed through what is now Norman prior to the city's existence.

Further north along the Legacy Trail, there is a far more detailed installation, "University on the Prairie." Individual signs are devoted to each of the first five decades of the university's history. Almost from its founding, Norman has been a university town. After the land run, Norman's boosters immediately began advocating for the territory's university to be placed in Norman. To receive the university, the territorial government required Cleveland County, where Norman is located, to present the territory with $15,000 worth of bonds and donate forty acres of land within a half-mile of downtown for the university's construction.[29] County residents voted to approve the bond in May 1891. Overwhelming support from Norman residents outweighed the general disapproval for the bond from the rest of the county residents. The logic behind investing in the university was articulated by the *Norman Transcript* editors, who wrote, "No farmer who has the good of the people and the progress of the country at heart, will refuse to vote the bonds necessary to secure the University here. It means dollars instead of cents in their pockets in the future."[30] In other words, the university would bring economic growth and increased property values. The *Norman Transcript*'s support for growth and development would rarely waver during the coming century.

Oklahoma City went from a railway stop to a city of ten thousand in a day, but Norman's growth was far slower. It was months before all the lots in the Norman Townsite were claimed.[31] A year after the 1889 land run, Norman's population was still less than one thousand, and it was not until 1900 that it finally reached two thousand.[32] The city grew together with the university. When the university opened in 1892 there were just fifty-seven students and a handful of faculty members. Nearly thirty years later the student population had increased to thirty-six hundred and the city population was five thousand. Today, Norman is Oklahoma's third most populous city after Oklahoma City and Tulsa.

The first commercial oil well in Oklahoma was completed in 1897 and by the time of statehood in 1907 some called Oklahoma the "largest oil-producing entity in the world."[33] Although Norman's growth has not followed the oil industry's boom and bust cycle, the University of Oklahoma and Norman are not independent of the industry. My livelihood as a professor largely depends on oil and gas.

My position at OU was created when Wick Cary left more than $11 million to the university in 2009. Logan Wickliffe "Wick" Cary Jr. was born in Oklahoma City and earned a degree from Yale. Cary was a lifelong bachelor and lived much of his life in an apartment on St. Charles Avenue in New Orleans, while working as a geological consultant for the petroleum industry.[34] His gift to the university was used for athletics, the geology department, and faculty lines in Constitutional Studies, the College of International Studies, and the Honors College, where I was hired for my expertise in African studies and international development. I never would have written this book without Wick Cary donating millions to the university.

The Honors College where I teach was named for Aubrey McClendon's parents in 2008 after McClendon, the cofounder and former CEO of Chesapeake Energy, promised millions of dollars in donations to OU.[35] McClendon's Chesapeake Energy was an industry leader in fracking—injecting liquids at extremely high pressures into the earth to get at previously inaccessible oil and gas. McClendon amassed rights to more than 16 million acres of shale that could be tapped with explosives and horizontal drilling. In another form of self-devouring growth, fracking caused unprecedented earthquakes in Oklahoma. Under McClendon, Chesapeake accumulated massive debts, totaling $13 billion in 2010. That same year Chesapeake paid McClendon a $75 million bonus. McClendon died early in the morning when the car he was driving slammed into a concrete underpass, the day after the U.S. Department of Justice's Antitrust Division filed criminal charges against him.[36]

This is the power of economic growth. Particularly for a white, male American like me, growth supports jobs, universities, grants, and numerous other opportunities. My dependence on oil and gas means that I am complicit in everything I critique. In the chapters that follow, I explore both the creative potential and destructive powers of nourishing growth. In many cases, growth benefits some, often people like me, while simultaneously suffocating life for others. Although many of us are complicit in nourishing the growth that ultimately suffocates life, complicity should not lead to complacency.

1 Tasting Growth and White Supremacy in a "Progressive, Wholesome City"

AT A BLACK LIVES MATTER rally at Norman's Andrew's Park on a sweltering day during the summer of 2020, a local activist and member of the Absentee Shawnee Tribe asked the audience if they know where their water comes from. The city of Norman as it exists today is a direct result of Absentee Shawnee displacement, she explained. Lake Thunderbird, the primary source of Norman's drinking water, displaced thirty Absentee Shawnee families and destroyed burial grounds when it was built in the early 1960s.[1] For the Absentee Shawnee, the construction of Lake Thunderbird was one more act of forced displacement. Absentee Shawnee held more than thirty-two hundred of the four thousand acres that became Lake Thunderbird and the state parks on the shoreline.[2] It was not simply eutrophication and growth that I was tasting in Norman's tap water. I was tasting a history of dispossession of Indigenous land and white supremacy in the well-nourished waters of Lake Thunderbird.[3]

When we look at a map, Lake Thunderbird resembles the gaping mouth of a crocodile. Each of the jaws is perhaps three or four miles in length. The upper jaw points north while the lower jaw points west toward Norman's urban core. The tips of the jaws are where tributaries meet the lake—Hog Creek in the north, Little River and Dave Blue Creek in the west. The teeth that line the jaws are small creeks, many of them nameless, that create inlets and miniature bays where they meet the lake. The crocodile's jaws capture everything, all the water, but also red dirt, fertilizers, and trash. The water in Lake Thunderbird is only taking a break on its journey to the Gulf of Mexico.

Some of it will pass through the dam where it becomes the Little River again before reaching the Canadian River. Some water will be absorbed into the soil beneath the lake. Even more water will evaporate. And every day nearly ten million gallons of water will be piped west from the lake, back toward Norman's urban core to the water treatment plant.

I keep returning to that tip of the crocodile's lower jaw where Thunderbird's primary tributary, the Little River, enters the lake. Pale skeletons of trees drowned by the lake are visible reminders of what was once here. I like to walk the banks on winter days when the lake is low and heat from the sun reflecting off the murky water is welcome. The banks are not sandy, more of a fine orange-red dirt. They are covered with driftwood, everything from stout tree trunks to small branches. Trash is mixed with the wood—endless beverage containers, old tires, a set of football pads half-buried in the dirt like discarded armor. The trash becomes thickest where the banks meet the oak forest. A shaggy dog wanders out of the forest and follows me on my walk, occasionally stopping to drink from the lake. When I pause to sit on a log and write, the dog sits calmly at my feet. I need to consciously focus my attention away from the trash to see the herons stalking small fish and the waterfowl skimming over the lake's surface. The lake, birds, fish, and trash are all part of a complex ecosystem that would not exist without Norman's need for water.

Just as the newly created Lake Thunderbird watershed pooled numerous creeks and rivers, it brought together disparate groups of people. In the nearly sixty years since the dam was completed, everyone who has consumed the city's water has participated in the community created by the watershed. When my family and I drink the rainwater that flowed off a pasture into the lake, we are connected with farmers in east Norman. The watershed creates temporal connections as well, linking me with the racially segregated community of the 1960s that displaced Absentee Shawnee families to create drinking water for a growing city.

Infrastructures are technologies that redistribute wealth. Money is pooled to build that which is beyond the capacity of individuals and small groups. Costs are shared because in theory infrastructures will benefit all, but the relationship between who pays for infrastructure and who benefits from it is never simple. Communities build infrastructures, and those infrastructures reproduce community in ways that include and exclude.

Building Dams and Subsidizing Growth

Oklahoma is a land of human-made lakes.[4] There are no naturally occurring lakes in Oklahoma, but through the work of the Army Corps of Engineers and the Bureau of Reclamation, during the twentieth century the state came to have more than forty-seven hundred dams, the fifth most in the United States.[5] Each of these lakes represents the use of public funds to generate growth. It is unlikely that Oklahoma could support anything close to its current population of four million without these reservoirs, which create communities through the conservation and redistribution of water.

The construction of a watershed community begins with the questions of who pays and who benefits. *The Oklahoman*'s Washington DC correspondent, Allan Cromley, described the legislation that financed Lake Thunderbird as "a 19-million-dollar tail that wagged a billion-dollar dog."[6] Lake Thunderbird was the tail, and dams in the Upper Colorado River Basin were the dog. Oklahoma's congressional representatives pushed hard for the Bureau of Reclamation to finance Lake Thunderbird. To gather support for the relatively small Norman project, Congress passed a bill in 1960 that amended the Colorado River Storage Project Act (1956) to change the way interest was calculated for projects in the Upper Colorado River Basin.[7] In practice, this reduced interest rates by nearly 1½ percent for loans connected to a billion-dollar system of reservoirs on the Upper Colorado River Basin.[8] The relatively insignificant Thunderbird project allowed a change in interest rates that made the sale of hydropower from big dams in the Upper Colorado River Basin profitable enough to repay loans from the federal government and complete reclamation projects like those in the Curecanti National Recreation Area on the Gunnison River in Colorado.

The story of the Bureau of Reclamation is the story of what is perhaps the most significant case of state subsidized growth in the history of the United States. Capitalism depends on state intervention to create the conditions in which growth is possible.[9] In the United States, this has often meant ecological transformation. Billions were invested in "reclaiming" the arid West. The Bureau of Reclamation remade the ecology so that it could support large human populations, irrigation-based agriculture, and commerce.[10] Although Lake Thunderbird is a very different kind of project, from its beginnings it was linked to subsidized growth in the West.

In *Cadillac Desert* Mark Reisner argued that with the Reclamation Act of 1902, "the American West quietly became the first and most durable example of the modern welfare state."[11] During the twentieth century the Bureau of Reclamation and the Army Corps of Engineers used public funds to build the water infrastructure necessary for explosive growth in cities like Phoenix and Los Angeles. Public funds were used to support private interests by building dams to generate electricity and support irrigation-based agriculture. Farming in much of the West could be profitable only with the massive subsidy provided by publicly funded dams and irrigation. If the cost of dams was included, the real cost of irrigating land in the arid West was incredibly high. In some cases, it was necessary to invest $2000 per acre to produce crops that would be sold for $150 per acre.[12] This cost was justified with cash register dams that generated hydropower. Unprofitable irrigation projects, therefore, required that more dams be built in the same river basin to offset losses with the sale of hydropower.

Glen Canyon Dam was one of these cash register dams completed with assistance from the Colorado River Storage Project Act amendment that funded Lake Thunderbird. Glen Canyon Dam provides power to nearly 5 million customers, but in 2022, in the midst of the worst drought in more than twelve hundred years, water levels were low enough to threaten power generation.[13] With each passing year of drought, Rebecca Solnit's description of the Glen Canyon Dam as a 710-foot monument to overconfidence becomes increasingly accurate.[14] The combination of drought and climate change led the U.S. Secretary of the Interior to declare in 2022 the first-ever Tier 1 water shortage for Colorado River operations, and nearly 18 percent of Arizona's Colorado River supply was cut.[15] This process resembles eutrophication. Dams are the fertilizers that have nourished the growth of American consumer lifestyles. The waste from this growth is carbon dioxide, which contributes to the climate change that brings drought, the disappearing Colorado River, and perhaps the eventual destruction of the human communities that were once nourished by those dams.

We know from the many stories about water and power in Los Angeles that water follows money, even if that means it flows uphill.[16] Private capital can be used to control the flow of water, but damming and redirecting rivers is not cheap, even for the extremely wealthy. In the mid-twentieth century few people or organizations were better positioned to build mega dams than the U.S. government. If the government could be convinced to build a dam, then the cost of accessing water could be shared by millions of taxpayers. The power to direct that water created endless possibilities for profit. Socializing the cost of controlling water, while privatizing water's benefits, was extremely lucrative but depended on control of the government.

The Colorado River Storage Act was in many ways a conspiracy of developers. Conspiracy takes us beyond the notion of a modern welfare state in the sense that it implies a plot to benefit a few at the expense of many. Public money was used to build dams that allowed small groups of people to control the distribution of water and electricity. Dams are technologies of conspiracy because they concentrate power in the hands of a few; they have been used to export the conspiracy of developers around the world, from the Omo River in Ethiopia to the Narmada River in India.[17]

Lake Thunderbird provided a spark that helped sustain dam-building fever in the West during the 1960s, but in many ways, it differed from massive projects like the Glen Canyon Dam. Norman is east of the 100th Meridian, the rough boundary marking where the arid Great Plains begin and farming without irrigation is impossible. In contrast to the arid west, Norman receives substantial, if irregular, rain fall.[18] Rather than following Oklahoma City's model and piping in water from more than one hundred miles away, the City of Norman dammed the aptly named Little River to capture rainwater from local sources. The Colorado River Basin dams supported extensive networks of irrigation and hydropower for millions of people. Lake Thunderbird was essential for Norman's growth, but even today it provides water for fewer than one hundred thousand people. Thunderbird had the potential to be a very different model of growth, one that minimizes self-destructive consequences and does not magnify the inequalities associated with the conspiracy of developers. The Colorado dams placed immense quantities of water and electricity in the hands of a few, but in theory Lake Thunderbird's drinking water should have benefited Norman residents equally. The possibility of equitable sharing, however, was corrupted by watershed communities built on exclusion.

The most effective conspiracies hide in plain sight. Public interest is the perfect camouflage for conspiracy. In the mid-twentieth century the value of schemes to encourage economic development by controlling nature was rarely questioned.[19] Subsidizing growth appears to be natural and legitimate when it serves the interests of the public. Those same subsidies are often declared illegitimate when they only benefit a few already powerful individuals. To the extent that growth and economic development are perceived as intrinsically valuable, questions of conspiracy and water are effectively hidden. At the time of Lake Thunderbird's creation, there was little opposition because it appeared to be in the interests of the community.

Water for a "Progressive, Wholesome City"

The decision to subsidize growth is based in an ideology of progress, a firm belief that growth represents a path to a better and more desirable future. Norman would not exist in its current form without Lake Thunderbird. For many years Norman relied on wells drilled into the Garber-Wellington aquifer to supply its water. The city's population boomed in the mid-twentieth century, increasing from around twenty-seven thousand in 1950 to nearly thirty-nine thousand in 1960. During the 1950s close to three thousand new homes were built there.[20] More houses, lawns, and people lowered the water table in the aquifer by nearly sixty feet between 1947 and 1954, and like other cities in the region, Norman needed new sources of water.[21]

In 1954 a plan for a reservoir on the Little River was approved by the Bureau of Reclamation.[22] From the beginning, Lake Thunderbird's boosters justified its construction in terms of growth.[23] Visions for the reservoir were not limited to water. Politicians and engineers imagined that by the 1970s Lake Thunderbird would be a "virtual seaport," connecting to a series of canals and navigable rivers that would eventually lead to the Mississippi

River and the Gulf of Mexico.[24] Leaders also envisioned a different navigable canal that would bring water from southeastern Oklahoma and "supply 2 billion gallons a day to central Oklahoma."[25]

When it came time for Norman residents to vote to approve the financing and construction of the dam in May of 1961, the *Norman Transcript* was full of advertisements and editorials encouraging a "yes" vote. An announcement paid for by "Interested Citizens and Taxpayers" claimed, "Norman was founded by far-sighted men and women who staked a claim to a new life here in 1889. These pioneers were looking to the future and liked what they saw—a fertile, verdant valley, rolling hills and they knew the water was good!"[26] The settler mentality is clear. 1889 references the land run that opened Oklahoma to white settlement. The "pioneers" possessed a vision that was focused firmly on the future. They did not see the people who already lived here; rather, their vision was filled with land and good water. Progress and growth were part of this vision from the very beginning. The "pioneers," the announcement implies, were not interested in temporary personal gain. Their goal was to build a city that could be enjoyed by future generations. The announcement continued, "They [the settlers] envisioned the progressive, wholesome city Norman is today—and took immediate steps to build what they wanted. Trees had to be planted, schools and churches organized, local government perfected, sidewalks laid, streets paved, a municipal waterworks constructed—all of these things we enjoy today are ours because progressive men and women took the right steps at the right time with unerring good judgment. We must be faithful to this heritage and look ahead now."[27] "Progressive" in this context refers to a desire for progress, not to the contemporary association with liberal politics. The progressive, wholesome city of Norman was based on infrastructure. Sidewalks, paved streets, and municipal waterworks were necessary for progress. Rather than a vision of rugged individualism, this is a story of a cohesive group with common values whose members build goods to be shared among themselves. References to the past build trust that a shared vision will be realized once again.[28]

Given the power of this imagined past and future, it is perhaps not surprising that there was little organized opposition to the dam. In an open letter to Norman residents the mayor and city council wrote, "We are convinced of the soundness of the conclusions of the many engineers, geologists and experts who have told us that we are foolish to rely now or in the future upon wells for our water."[29] If Norman did not act now to secure its water, many argued that it would ultimately be stuck purchasing water from Oklahoma City and be dependent on the larger city's willingness to sell the resource.[30] Norman residents approved construction of the reservoir by a margin of more than thirteen to one.[31] They had spoken and clearly advocated for a future of growth that relied on water from a new reservoir. Subsidizing growth was a logical move for a community that trusted leaders to guide them toward a better future.

A two-acre observation area was cleared so Norman residents could enjoy the spectacle of the dam's construction.[32] In 1965, when the dam was completed, the *Norman Transcript* began publishing weekly reports on the lake's rising water levels. Former *Norman Transcript* editor Andy Rieger told me that residents packed picnics and drove east on Alameda Avenue on Sunday afternoons to watch the waters slowly rise and submerge a section of road. Each week the water was a little higher. At first, they could wade across, then swimming was possible, and then the expanse of water was far too wide to be crossed. There was something sublime about watching the rising waters of the lake gradually erase well-known landscapes. In the years that followed, Lake Thunderbird was not just a source of Norman's water. It was a place for family cookouts, swimming, boating, and fishing.

The story of Norman and Lake Thunderbird is typical of U.S. cities during the twentieth century. A city invests money to meet a shared community need. Central planning and good governance are essential to this process. Through the foresight of community leaders, water is secured. Water allows growth in population and commerce. Growth generates more revenue, which is reinvested in the city to support further growth and improvements in quality of life. The cycle of growth is a form of progress, each step is better than the last. People are justifiably proud of their ability to plan for water that will nourish future generations. An ample supply of clean water is the foundation for so much of what makes life good.

The self-devouring tendencies of growth, however, were built into the very sense of community that made long-term planning possible. This process was based in shared interests. The city could invest in a project like Lake Thunderbird because there was a shared interest in its outcome—the vast majority of residents would benefit from investing in a long-term water source. Community, however, is never this simple. Just as sharing is essential to infrastructure, so is drawing boundaries. At the time of Lake Thunderbird's creation, Norman was decidedly not an open and inclusive community. People were directly excluded from the city and its new supply of water, primarily based on race. Exclusion combined with ideologies of progress to contaminate the cycle of nourishing growth, leading to eutrophication and the suffocation of life.

Absentee Shawnee Displacement

Absentee Shawnee Tribe members have not forgotten the loss of five square miles of tribal land, the displacement of more than thirty families, and the destruction of burial grounds that resulted from Lake Thunderbird's creation.[33] Absentee Shawnee drew attention to Lake Thunderbird's history in 2016 when they joined protests in North Dakota against the construction of the Keystone XL Oil Pipeline that would threaten the Standing Rock Sioux's primary water source and damage sacred sites.[34] In the early 1960s, however, Absentee Shawnee voices were almost entirely excluded from the planning and construction process.[35] A 1962 article in the *Daily Oklahoman* describes a conversation with Mrs. Little Jim, wife of an Absentee Shawnee leader. The author claims that "the Indians know, however, that the dam and its lake will be beneficial to the area. They do not even desire to protest, she [Mrs. Little Jim] said. They will accept this as their people have accepted uprootings in the past."[36]

Although the Shawnee were uprooted many times in the past, they certainly did not accept forced relocation without resistance. In the late eighteenth century, groups of Shawnee moved westward from what is now Ohio to avoid white settler aggression and came to the Cape Girardeau area of Missouri. Among this group was a young man named Tecumseh, who would later seek to unite tribes to resist colonialism and create a self-ruled Native American confederacy.[37] Tecumseh eventually led an army of more than twenty-five hundred warriors, fighting together with the British against the

Americans during the War of 1812.[38] Tecumseh's image comprises the logo for the Absentee Shawnee Tribe.

The story of the Absentee Shawnee is one of continual movement and searching for autonomy. Between 1825 and the early 1830s, many Shawnees moved from Missouri and Ohio to a 1.6 million acre reservation in Kansas. Other Shawnees, however, moved to southeast Texas, which at the time was part of Mexico, and to Indian Territory near the confluence of the Canadian River and Little River. After Texas achieved independence in 1836, the Shawnees residing there were forced to leave and many moved north to join others in Indian Territory, not far from Norman's present location.[39] The Shawnees living in Indian Territory did not participate in the 1854 meeting in which much of the 1.6-million-acre Shawnee reservation in Kansas was ceded to the U.S. government, and thus took the name Absentee Shawnee. The Shawnees in Kansas retained two hundred thousand acres of land that was allotted to individual families, but the Absentee Shawnee never received these allotments.[40]

The Absentee Shawnee in Indian Territory returned to Kansas during the Civil War to escape pressure from the Confederate Army and then came back to the banks of the Little River after the war's end. Upon return, the Absentee Shawnee found that the federal government had granted much of the land they had occupied in Indian Territory to the Citizen Potawatomi tribe as a reservation.[41] An 1867 treaty granting this land to the Absentee Shawnee was never ratified by the U.S. Senate.[42] Even before the 1889 land run, after years of removals space was at a premium among the tribes in Indian Territory. Despite decades of movement the Absentee Shawnee prepared for a future in the Little River Valley and planted orchards and built log houses. The U.S. government sought to solve the problem of conflicting Absentee Shawnee and Citizen Potawatomi land claims with an 1872 Act of Congress that gave land allotments to both tribes.[43] Many Absentee Shawnee opposed these allotments, both because they did not want to share the area with the Citizen Potawatomi and because they wished to maintain practices rooted in common land ownership.[44] The Office of Indian Affairs blamed the refusal to take allotments on "the influence of the chiefs and the superstition of some of the non-progressive Indians."[45] Advocates of allotments among the Absentee

Shawnee described a division between "progressive" and "non-progressive" leaders.[46] Big Jim was one of the "non-progressive" leaders who tried to prevent allotments by refusing to give the names of his followers for allotment rolls. Thomas Wildcat Alford, one of only a few Absentee Shawnee who were educated in boarding schools at the time, secretly collected names and passed them on to government officials so that allotments could be made. Alford assisted with the survey necessary for allotments, and in his autobiography he wrote that Big Jim and followers "pulled up my corner stakes as fast as I could establish them."[47]

In the hopes of maintaining common land and avoiding allotments, members of the Big Jim band traveled on horseback to Mexico in 1900, but most of the members of this group, including Big Jim himself, perished after an encounter with smallpox. Under the leadership of Big Jim's son, Little Jim, many Absentee Shawnee remained living along the Little River, near the intersection with Hog Creek.[48] This unique ecosystem of intersecting rivers and creeks would soon be flooded by Lake Thunderbird. Interviews were conducted with Absentee Shawnee after the dam was completed in the context of the Doris Duke project, in which American Indians were interviewed between 1967 and 1972 about their history and culture. Web Little Jim, grandson of Absentee Shawnee leader Big Jim, explained in 1969 how the Absentee Shawnee arrived in the area and then were forced to move:

> He [Big Jim] brought the tribe back to where we are now—between the South Canadian and the North Canadian. Brought us into these blackjack [oak] hills. He thought he would pick out the poorest land so the white people would never want it and we would never have to move again. But we were moved—by the dam—Thunderbird dam. Sometimes I don't think the Indians have a chance. Settle on the sorriest land there was and they come and move us out.[49]

Clifton Blanchard offered a similar perspective in a 1968 interview:

> Big Jim was the one that brought Absentee Shawnee down in here where we are now. He told the government that he been pushed enough

> so if they would give him and his people the worst land in Oklahoma, then no white man would want it anymore. So here we are on sand hills, red dirt, and still they put in that Thunderbird Lake and take our land. I live on ½ acre of land. I used to have 160 acres but it's all under water now, and the government give me $40 an acre. Real generous of them.[50]

The interviewer noted that this last sentence was said sarcastically. Absentee Shawnee landowners received less than 15 percent of their land's market value.[51]

Rather than the vague references to a fertile, verdant valley with good water praised by dam boosters, Web Little Jim and Clifton Blanchard described the specific characteristics of extremely poor land—blackjack oaks that thrive in poor soil, red dirt, and sand hills. In contrast to the dam boosters' "progressive" visions of pioneers settling lands, for the Absentee Shawnee the Little River Valley was perhaps an end to their search for refuge from white settler colonialism and ideologies of progress. The choice to settle in the Little River Valley came from a desire to maintain commonly held land and tribal sovereignty.

Clifton Blanchard told his interviewer,

> I'm glad you're interested in Indian ways. But white man cheat the Indian a lot. I been learning English so I could get along, but I look at past to see future. I have my land taken away by the Lake and I don't even know what they were doing. I thought they wanted to borrow it. That's the way it sound when they told me, but now I never get it back unless I want to swim down to the bottom of the lake and see it.[52]

Blanchard compared the Lake Thunderbird case to the arrival of whites in the Americas. In both cases American Indians were cheated out of their land. Lake Thunderbird was one more case of loss.

> White man always take land from Shawnee. We start out in Mississippi. Then they push us into Missouri, then they push us into Kansas. They

> they [*sic*] push us into Oklahoma Territory now they flooding us with that lake . . . We have bad land now, but I don't know where the white man going to push us next. A lot of these old people think that white man is trying to kill all the Sahwnee [*sic*] out real slow so nobody will notice it.[53]

The narratives from Web Little Jim and Clifton Blanchard demonstrate the limits of Norman's progressive community. The displacement of the Absentee Shawnee was not a conspiracy, it was done openly. The overwhelming support for the dam was largely a result of an extremely narrow definition of citizenship, both legally and symbolically. At the time, Norman's city limits did not yet encompass the rural area where the lake would be built. Absentee Shawnee and others in the area were not permitted to vote on the dam. Civically, symbolically, and geographically the Absentee Shawnee were erased. Media coverage of the dam made little mention of the people who would be displaced or the burial grounds that would be flooded. Rather, the figure of the "pioneer" extended the colonial mentality of settling an uninhabited land from the past to the present. Building a dam to support growth in Norman was an easy decision when those who would lose their land were excluded from the discussion.

Many of the Absentee Shawnee who were displaced by Lake Thunderbird moved to the Little Axe community, on the eastern edge of the lake. Although Little Axe is more than seventeen miles from Norman's City Hall, it is still within Norman's current municipal boundaries. Like other east Norman residents, the Absentee Shawnee living in Little Axe do not receive water from Lake Thunderbird and the City of Norman. For better or for worse, they must access water on their own.

Dams, pipelines, and railroads are forms of Wiindigo infrastructure that entrench settler colonialism.[54] In Anishinaabe legends, the Wiindigo is a cannibalistic monster. Winona LaDuke and Debora Cowen argue that "Wiindigo economics is cannibal economics, it destroys the source of its own wealth, Earth."[55] It is estimated that dams have inundated more than one million acres of tribal land in the continental United States.[56] In contrast to the self-devouring growth of eutrophication, the cannibal economics of

Wiindigo infrastructure do not always devour the self.[57] In Norman, Lake Thunderbird produced growth by devouring not the self (the white pioneer) but the other (Absentee Shawnee). The descendants of white settlers would eventually experience other forms of self-devouring growth, but at least initially growth depended on devouring others.

Cannibalistic dams are not unique to the United States. In Ethiopia, where I have conducted research for many years, hydropower dams have destroyed the livelihoods of hundreds of thousands of already marginalized pastoralists. Like the Lake Thunderbird dam, in Ethiopia and elsewhere, the destructive power of dams has been masked with visions of progress.[58] Destruction in the present is justified with promises of a better life in the future. With Wiindigo infrastructure, however, some will eat, and others will be eaten.

Once the monster has been created, it is very difficult to kill. In the United States the twenty-first century has seen efforts to remove dams, but the process is highly complex and filled with unexpected challenges.[59] Settler colonialism is built into material infrastructures, and even when ideologies change Wiindigo infrastructures persist.[60]

Sundown Town

The community that built Lake Thunderbird practiced other forms of racial exclusion. When Dr. George Henderson and his family moved to Norman in 1967, two years after the Lake Thunderbird dam was completed, they became the first Black people to own property in the town. At that time there were fewer than one hundred African Americans living in Norman.[61] It was extremely difficult for Black people to even rent housing there. In 1967 a Black graduate student hoping to rent an apartment in Norman was turned down twenty-eight times.[62] In the late 1960s and early 1970s the few Black people living in in the city were harassed and threatened with violence at bars, in restaurants, and on the streets. A good deal of this abuse came from the police.[63]

Norman was one of thousands of sundown towns in the United States, located primarily outside of the traditional South.[64] Sundown towns were jurisdictions that prohibited Black people from residing within their borders. They ranged in population from just a few thousand to well over one hundred thousand. Black people could often enter sundown towns for the workday but faced violence and harassment if they stayed beyond that.

The city of Norman was formally incorporated in 1891 and Black residents were driven out in 1892. An African American barber received a note warning, "You are hereby notified to leave this town in the next ten days . . . We give you timely warning to get your things and 'git' or you must stand the consequences."[65] Whites who sought to violate the sundown rule also faced violence. In 1898 the mayor of Norman and others beat up a white man, J. J. Wallace, who hired a Black roofer named George Rogan. When faced with a mob Wallace explained that Rogan possessed skills that he could not find among the local white laborers. The mob beat Wallace and Rogan, and Rogan was forced to walk the railroad tracks eighteen miles back to Oklahoma City. Wallace lost the sight in his left eye after the attack and sued the city of Norman, but the court ruled that the government could not be expected to do anything about local sentiment.[66] In 1922 a mob of more than five hundred people armed with clubs, guns, and ropes attacked a dance hall at the University of Oklahoma where an African American band had been invited to play. Police and university students escorted the musicians to the train station, from which they escaped to Oklahoma City.[67]

Many of Norman's leaders during the first half of the twentieth century were active supporters of segregation and racial terrorism. Edwin De Barr was one of the first faculty members at the University of Oklahoma and a university leader from 1892 to 1923. He was dean of the School of Pharmacy, chair of the Department of Chemistry, and a university vice president. He was also the Grand Dragon of the Oklahoma Ku Klux Klan and was later named Imperial Kludd, the Klan's national chaplain.[68] De Barr was pushed out of the university in 1923 because of his affiliation with the KKK and an anti-Catholic commencement speech he gave at an Oklahoma high school.[69] He was, however, allowed to maintain his lab at the university and shortly before his death served as the 1950 homecoming parade marshal.[70] OU's chemistry building was named for De Barr until 1988 when students led an effort to have his name removed.[71] Almost thirty more years passed before a street near campus bearing his name was rechristened after months of intense debate.[72]

This was the environment that Dr. Henderson found when he moved to Norman from Detroit where he had been a professor at Wayne State University. Black people were actively excluded—denied housing, threatened, and attacked verbally and physically. George Henderson and his wife, Barbara Henderson, were experienced community activists, and they consciously sought to desegregate Norman. The Hendersons struggled to find a homeowner who would sell to them.[73] After Sallies Real Estate finally found them a home, the realtor faced death threats. Henderson writes, "It took six years after the bigots had blacklisted it for the agency to go out of business."[74] Vandals repeatedly left garbage in Henderson's yard. Racial slurs were frequently shouted from passing cars. Police regularly stopped Henderson near his home, asking him why he was in the neighborhood. Twice, during Henderson's first years at OU, a bullet was fired through the window of buildings hosting Black student organizations.[75] Henderson explains, "Racism was an abhorrent truth that most people in the University and the residents of Norman chose to ignore in public. The punishment for talking about it was meted out through silence, stares, glares, chiding, or ostracism."[76] Many white families welcomed Henderson and his family into their homes and circle of friends, but the topic of racism was carefully avoided.

This was the "progressive, wholesome city" that built Lake Thunderbird. During the 1950s and 1960s Norman was a haven for families from Oklahoma City who did not want their children attending desegregated schools. When the residents of Norman came together in 1961 to fund Lake Thunderbird, it was with the understanding that future beneficiaries would be white. Norman residents were following in the steps of the progressive men and women who founded the town in 1891. They were building a community founded on white supremacy, in which progress was intended for a racially segregated population. The social obligation to share is rooted in part in physical presence.[77] Regardless of other factors, anthropologists have demonstrated that people generally share with those who are physically present, and often presence implies being seen.[78] Sundown towns like Norman excluded Black people from citizenship in a community that shared the benefits of infrastructure.

Watersheds create communities, and much of Dr. Henderson's work was fundamentally about expanding inclusion in the new community that emerged from the Lake Thunderbird watershed. Like Lake Thunderbird, the University of Oklahoma was ostensibly a public good but African Americans faced severe barriers to accessing it. Henderson was a leader in founding the Afro American Student Union (ASU) and supported students as they fought back against institutionalized racism. He pushed his students to investigate discrimination in access to housing at the university and in Norman more broadly. Henderson's struggle against racism created more expansive forms of substantive citizenship in which Black people were better positioned to fight for access to housing, education, and other public goods, as he worked against forms of nourishing growth that only benefited the few.

Annexing the Lake Thunderbird Watershed

With the creation of Lake Thunderbird, all the creeks and rivers that flow into the lake became part of a single watershed that Norman's municipal government sought to control by annexing more than 170 square miles of rural land in 1961. The move increased Norman's population by more than three thousand.[79] In terms of area, the annexation gave Norman the odd distinction of being the largest city in the United States with a population less than 250,000.[80]

The annexation was a surprise for most Norman residents, and it occurred without the consent of people living on much of the annexed land. Stanley Draper and other members of the Oklahoma City Chamber of Commerce called Norman's mayor, Earl Sneed, to a meeting and told him in a "forceful but friendly manner," that if he did not act immediately, Oklahoma City would annex the area.[81] Oklahoma City was highly interested in controlling Lake Thunderbird, in part to secure access to the imagined future canal to southeastern Oklahoma.[82] Mayor Sneed claimed he received information from a source he could not reveal that Oklahoma City was on the verge of annexing and days later Norman made its move and annexed the land.[83]

Many rural residents did not wish to be incorporated into Norman. In late 1961 and early 1962 a debate played out in the pages of the *Norman Transcript* between the *Transcript*'s editorial board and rural residents who were angry about the annexation. The *Transcript* consistently supported the city leaders' agenda. The editorial board directly rebutted those who opposed annexation, often countering the arguments of individuals quoted in the day's news. If this editorializing was not enough, the *Transcript* published a two-part, multiple page article by Norman mayor Earl Sneed, supporting the annexation.

The outcry in response to the October 1961 annexation was sustained and vocal. O. S. Boyd, who ran a dairy farm in the area that was annexed, was among the leadership of the opposition. Boyd explained, "This thing took us by surprise, but there is going to be something done . . . I've talked to a lot of lawyers, and they all say there's nothing legal about it. That's the way Hitler operated and the way Khrushchev is operating now. I thought we lived in America."[84] Boyd was not the only rural Norman resident to compare the city's leaders to Hitler. In a letter to the editor Jeff Cox noted, "It seems that this is what we fought World War II about. Hitler was on an annexation spree, and if we had not gone to war we might be a part of Germany now."[85]

On October 19, 1961, the day the annexation was announced, the *Norman Transcript* ran an editorial announcing, "City, Landowners Will Both Benefit."[86] Although the *Transcript* had made no mention of the plans for annexation in the preceding weeks, the editors offered up a careful defense of Norman's expansion. The editors explained, "If Norman had notified all landowners in advance of its plans, a lot of discussion would have followed, there would have been some holdouts, and Norman's plans might have been defeated. That is why the City Commission had to get the project in shape and take action immediately."[87] The following day the *Transcript* ran another editorial titled, "Well Done, City Officials," which stated, "Norman city officials merit a sincere vote of thanks from the citizenship of Norman for their strenuous, persistent efforts of the last few weeks in getting things in shape for the annexation action taken Wednesday night."[88] Editors appeared to have been aware of all the work city officials were doing to prepare for the annexation, indicating that they knew what was coming but chose not to report it.

Two days after the *Transcript* ran the story quoting Boyd, the editors offered a rebuttal: "It is pure nonsense to charge that the action smacks of the tactics of Hitler and Khrushchev." Rather, the city's objectives "are sincere and above suspicion from every standpoint."[89] The editors raised issues of community and self-interest that would return as sources of division between urban and rural Norman residents for years to come:

> It would be selfish of an owner to want to share in all the good things that come from city growth, construction of a lake, and other progress and not join in steps to protect homes, maintain health and sanity [*sic*] standards and have an attractive area from every standpoint. Further down the road, if not now, every landowner in the Norman and lake area who has any regard for the common welfare will thank Norman for its wise course in assuring orderly, desirable development.[90]

Here, the editors imply that welfare is common to all Norman residents. In other words, residents share the same needs and interests and therefore they should agree to support orderly development. Consequently, to oppose annexation is to oppose common welfare.

Tensions came to a head once more in February 1962 when a group of rural landowners filed a suit against the City of Norman in the U.S. District Court in Oklahoma City.[91] A gathering of the Cleveland County De-Annexation Association drew nearly three hundred people on a Saturday afternoon. Attendees were urged not to vote in city elections or pay taxes.[92] Former state senator E. B. George referenced World War II to describe rural Norman as under attack: "Pearl Harbor had her sneak attack and we've had ours."[93] George went on to say, "They [the City of Norman] are broke and they know it. They need taxpayers to impose taxes on everybody they can, to pay their commitments, pave their streets and build city halls."[94] Senator George called the City of Norman's claims of shared community false. Rather than shared welfare, George argued that the city was trying to take from rural residents through the imposition of taxes. If all are members of the same community, then equal taxation appears to be legitimate, but if the city is equated to an attacking army, then these taxes do not come from a single community. The taxes will pay for *their* streets, not *ours*. In opposing annexation, rural residents were opposing an expanded community and opting out of urban citizenship. It was a refusal to pay for *their* infrastructure, but also a statement that "us" and "them" would not become a *we*.

The conflict was fundamentally about membership in a community with shared interests. The *Transcript*'s references to zoning, subdivisions, regulations, and development used images of well-organized change to establish common interests. Who could stand in the way of a "nice residential area with a beautiful park"? Together with city leaders, the *Transcript* editorial board attempted to erase difference and speak for everyone as a singular community. The interests of dairy farmers like O. S. Boyd and urban residents, however, were not the same. City leaders' expertise did not encompass the specific conditions faced by rural farmers.[95] Associating the City of Norman with Adolf Hitler was a clear statement of difference. Indeed, the construction of community is often based on the erasure of other perspectives. Annexation was intended to protect and control Norman's water source for its urban residents, but water from Lake Thunderbird would not be delivered to rural residents. Orderly development through shared management of infrastructure only works if there is a common interest in that infrastructure. References to Hitler and Pearl Harbor demonstrate a fundamental desire for rural autonomy. Where a shared vision of the past and future among Norman residents supported the dam project, in this case clear differences in interests undermined the possibility of trust.

During one of the weeks that the *Transcript* was filled with debates over rural annexation, a much shorter article appeared regarding the removal of Absentee Shawnee graves.[96] If the conflict over annexation was about community membership, such a question was completely absent when it came to the Absentee Shawnee. The article simply announced the removal of graves and families, without any indication of a possible conflict. Where the possible imposition of new taxes for rural residents was equated to Hitler and the attack on Pearl Harbor, real violence in the form of Absentee Shawnee displacement and loss of land was met with silence. In framing the annexation as an invasion, white rural residents naturalized their occupation of the land and constructed themselves as indigenous.

Although white rural and urban residents had significant differences, at a deeper level they shared citizenship in a broader community that was defined largely by race. White rural residents were able to compare annexation to Pearl Harbor and Hitler's attacks in Europe because there was no question of shared community membership with residents of the white sundown-town of Norman. Responses to rural critiques are evidence of this shared community. Earl Sneed wrote a lengthy defense of annexation published in the *Norman Transcript*. The mayor felt the need to defend his decision to community members. Rural residents' World War II references were far from literal. They shared a system of governance with Mayor Earl Sneed that allowed for debates to play out in the pages of the local newspaper. In contrast, the Absentee Shawnee tribe was forced to give up land to support a racist sundown town. This was a direct attack by one group on another that reflects differences in substantive citizenship and the ability to make claims on public institutions.

Only rural whites had the privilege to question the false assumptions of those at the center of their community in a public forum. Their opposition to annexation did not contest Wiindigo infrastructure and the self-devouring tendencies of growth. White landowners exerted their expansive substantive citizenship, like connections with former state senator George, to protect their private property. This was an individual rather than a systemic solution to the problem of growth, intended to protect collective interests primarily tied to the ownership of property. When the editors of the *Norman Transcript* wrote of "common welfare," rural white landowners were included in that shared community, even if they disliked how urban leaders defined their welfare. White landowners did not want to be part of the city, but they did have the option of inclusion. African Americans and Native Americans were entirely excluded from the discussion.

Erasing the Taste of Growth

In the years since Lake Thunderbird's creation, parts of the watershed have gradually urbanized. The headwaters for Lake Thunderbird's primary tributary, the Little River, are found north of Norman in the city of Moore, near multiplex cinemas, big box stores, strip malls, and the sprawling Little River Park. Moore does not rely on Lake Thunderbird for water, but it is part of the lake's watershed. A sign in Little River Park notes that a 2013 tornado destroyed nearly forty-five hundred of the park's trees and I longed for their shade when I visited in early June. It was only midmorning, but the sun and humidity made for intense heat. Within the park the river is broken up by ponds. A clear line of woody debris mixed with Styrofoam and plastic drink containers evidenced recent flooding on a mostly bare plain between the river and the sidewalk. Near the north end of the park, I escaped the sun and followed a dirt path through the forest along the river. Here the river had dug a deep canyon into the red earth. Based on flood lines, recent storms may have raised the river to depths of nearly thirty feet, but today just a few inches of clear water ran over rocky riffles. When the Little River leaves the park, it passes by strip malls and big box stores before traveling under the Interstate 35 freeway and moving south and then east through rural Norman toward Lake Thunderbird.

My daughter, Iris, and I once investigated the other end of the Little River, where it empties into Lake Thunderbird. Iris loves the water, and she was eager to join me in exploring the mouth of the Little River on a standup paddleboard. She had just a few days left in her first year of high school and we talked about her plans for the summer as we paddled across a bay toward the mouth of the Little River. As usual, it had been a rainy May; we'd had more than five inches of rain in the past thirty days. The reddish brown shore that we'd walked along a few months ago was no longer visible. The lake had risen by a few feet and extended right to the grass. As we paddled over the submerged trees, one reached up from the brown water and caught our paddleboard, holding us for a couple of minutes before we broke free. We passed a small island of tall grasses that hosted egrets and herons. Where it meets the lake, the Little River is a straight channel bordered on each side by high banks covered in green brush and trees. Paddling up the river we navigated several sharp turns, perhaps intended to slow the force of water after heavy rains. The water is thick with sediment here. In the lake light penetrated at least a few feet, but the river was an opaque brown. Tree limbs in the river quickly accumulate trash and other debris, creating small floating islands. This is one of the lake's many mouths, where it swallows everything that washes off the strip malls, farmland, and suburban lawns.

When my family and I began exploring Lake Thunderbird, we soon learned to avoid summer's voracious ticks and visit the lake during the late fall and winter. Initially, our favorite activity was a short hike that begins at the Clear Cove Nature Center on the south side of the lake. My kids were excited when park rangers offered free nature posters in exchange for filling bags with trash. We walked along the orange-brown banks of the lake with the oak forest and tall beige grasses on one side and the sun's reflection off the brown water on the other. We usually had a full bag of trash within five minutes. There is a reason Norman residents call it "Lake Dirty Bird," but for my kids these walks were like treasure hunts. We often found fire rings surrounded by empty cans of light beer and Styrofoam containers of chicken livers. Apparently chicken livers make excellent catfish bait. As the years have passed, we've gotten in the habit of always bringing a few trash bags with us to the lake. Picking up trash is a Sisyphean task. It's impossible to pick it all up and there is constantly more coming. There is a certain satisfaction in the knowledge that trash had been removed from our drinking water, but it does nothing about the roots of the problem.

Stopping pollution at its sources is a much more complex process. Around forty years after Lake Thunderbird's completion, the Central Oklahoma Master Conservancy District (COMCD), the organization that manages the lake, began to address the impacts of Norman's growth on the lake. At the time Duane Winegardner was president of COMCD. Winegardner, a retired hydrologist, invited me to meet him at a Lutheran Church near the University of Oklahoma campus. He began our conversation by spreading a large map on a table and walking me through the boundaries of the Lake Thunderbird watershed. Under Winegardner's leadership, COMCD sued the Oklahoma Department of Environmental Quality (ODEQ) to prevent it from permitting new development that generates runoff into the Lake Thunderbird watershed. COMCD's 2007 suit claimed that ODEQ was allowing discharge into a sensitive water supply.[97]

COMCD agreed to dismiss the suit under the condition that ODEQ would release a Total Maximum Daily Load (TMDL) study by April 1, 2010. A TMDL is a calculation of the maximum amount of a pollutant allowed to enter a particular body of water. The Clean Water Act requires a TMDL for all bodies of water that are classified as impaired. Although the EPA had classified Lake Thunderbird as impaired in 2006, when 2010 rolled around

ODEQ still had not issued the TMDL.[98] ODEQ claimed that it did not have adequate funds to undertake the study. The EPA was placing increased demands on ODEQ and funds from the state legislature were being cut. From Duane Winegardner's perspective, these excuses were legitimate, but it was the COMCD's job to protect the lake and it sued once again in 2011.[99] In 2013 ODEQ finally released the TMDL report for nutrients, turbidity, and dissolved oxygen.

The bureaucracy of governmental regulation seems to increase with acronyms. COMCD sued ODEQ to force it to do its job and release a TMDL. The dull, grinding work of committees to produce lawsuits that create regulations is essential to protecting water quality, but the practical implications of the TMDL are unclear. In 2016 the City of Norman approved a dense 250-page document that outlined plans for complying with the TMDL and reducing the pollutants of concern: nitrogen, phosphorus, and sediment. Some of the plans are based on education, for example teaching watershed residents about the impacts of lawn fertilizers and pet waste on the lake. Others are based on enforcing regulations, like controlling stormwater runoff from construction sites. At the time that Norman's TMDL plan was released the city hired a new stormwater director. In the subsequent years forty to fifty notices of violation were given annually to construction companies that did not follow stormwater runoff regulations. Three years later, however, the number of violations fell to zero. Only one notice of violation was given from 2019 through the end of 2021. It seems that the City of Norman chose to stop enforcing its own regulations. The city government continues to closely monitor water quality in the Lake Thunderbird watershed and engage in education efforts to limit pollution, but like the ODEQ there seems to be a reluctance to enforce regulations. If anything, eutrophication in the lake has become worse in the years since the TMDL was implemented.[100]

With regulating agencies having little impact on Lake Thunderbird, water quality issues have been addressed from another direction. Rather than protecting the lake from eutrophication, the taste of growth was removed. In 2015 the City of Norman began a $35-million project at the water treatment plant, partially intended to address the smell and taste issues.[101] Increased utility fees funded innovations at the plant. Growth creates problems that must be paid for with further growth. Millions of dollars may be effective in removing the taste of urban growth, but this does nothing about growth itself, nothing about the root causes of eutrophication and the damage it does to aquatic life in the lake.[102]

People like me did not even notice the improvements at the water treatment plant. Shortly after we arrived in Norman, my family paid more than $500 to install a reverse osmosis water filter under our kitchen sink. More than the taste of the water, we were concerned with high levels of carcinogenic hexavalent chromium in Norman's tap water. I will come back to the complexities of hexavalent chromium in a later chapter, but my family was not alone in installing a filter or investing in a water delivery service.

The awful taste of Norman's water was a continual reminder of its origins. Drinking tap water is an act of trust in government. Although Norman's water may have been safe, the terrible smell and taste were reminders that in some ways government, at multiple levels, violated residents' trust. Government leaders failed to address the eutrophication that made Lake Thunderbird's water nearly undrinkable. Rather, the City of Norman spent millions at the water treatment plant to remove the taste of growth from its water. On a much smaller scale, families like mine did the same at the household level. With the taste removed, we were free to drink tap water without thinking about the lake and the roots of eutrophication.

This is typical of how relatively wealthy governments and individuals in the United States deal with the destructive consequences of growth. When homes are threatened by forest fires or coastal erosion, the impulse is to invest in fire suppression or sea walls to protect beach front homes. The interventions erase the consequences of growth instead of addressing the problem at its roots. Enacting such solutions is a form of privilege.[103]

Constructing Watershed Communities

Watersheds come in different sizes, but they always create connections. The Mississippi River watershed covers more than one million square miles and drains nearly 40 percent of the continental United States. It stretches from the plains of Southern Saskatchewan to New Orleans, from the Rocky

Mountains in the west to the Appalachian Range in the east. This is the American heartland and if one squints at a map of the watershed, it almost looks like a heart. The tens of millions of humans living in the heartland form communities that are connected by streams and rivers.

Eutrophication highlights the creation of a new kind of watershed community. The people who live in the watershed that drains into Lake Thunderbird and the people who drink the lake's water form a community. They are connected by the lake that was built in the 1960s, when Norman was a sundown town. A racially homogenous enclave built the lake as a key infrastructure of growth that ultimately generated this watershed community. The questions of who pays for growth and who benefits from it were shaped by the watershed community, a community that was itself founded on ideologies of progress and white supremacy.

The people at the center of that community constructed a narrative that connects past, present, and the future. At each stage appeals to common welfare justify the city's actions. The narrative of shared welfare obviously excludes, and yet it persists and wields enormous power. As Dr. George Henderson noted, in many ways white Norman residents embraced his family, and yet they did not want to talk of racism and segregation. To do so would have uncovered the obvious flaws in the notion of common welfare. How could a nearly all-white city pretend to have an interest in common welfare? This is the power of growth and progress—they pushed away thoughts of racial segregation and allowed millions of dollars to be invested in a dam for the sake of the common good. Growth and progress also erased questions about the efficacy of spending billions of dollars on dams in the upper Colorado River basin. The lie of common welfare lubricates the gears of the growth machine and creates Wiindigo infrastructure.

My life and all that I find good about Norman, Oklahoma, are made possible by Lake Thunderbird. I am not suggesting that the dam should not have been built. Rather, we need to be clear about the costs and benefits of water infrastructure. The problem of Lake Thunderbird is the problem of infrastructure more generally. Ideologies of growth and progress are the foundation for constructing communities that exclude as much as they include. The story of a wholesome, progressive community that builds infrastructure to thrive and grow has been told again and again. This story, however, hides the true costs of development. The infrastructure that subsidizes growth is paid for by the public and disproportionately benefits certain groups at the expense of others. The destruction of Absentee Shawnee burial grounds and the trauma of displacement must be included in any true accounting of Lake Thunderbird's costs. To ignore these costs is to both obscure and reproduce the self-devouring consequences of growth.[104] The dam benefited a sundown town, and yet it was supported by the publicly funded Bureau of Reclamation. Like so many cases in U.S. history, Black and Indigenous people provided welfare for urban whites.[105] Each instance of federal support for any of the more than one thousand U.S. sundown towns was a case of welfare for white people. In practice Lake Thunderbird has not served the common good; rather, it has nourished the growth of a community with a highly exclusive conception of citizenship.

A true accounting of the dam is not an argument against its construction. Rather, it is an argument for paying the full cost—providing full compensation for lost land, allowing everyone to enjoy the benefits of Norman's infrastructure, and ensuring that those who benefit the most from infrastructure pay for its costs. When we refuse to nourish growth that only benefits the few, infrastructure becomes more expensive, the cost of growth increases, and self-devouring tendencies of growth are countered.

2 Expanding Citizenship and Debating Growth in the 1970s

WHEN WE MET at a downtown coffeeshop in 2019, Bill Scanlon described himself to me as Norman's posterchild for stormwater. Scanlon lived in The Vineyard, a Cape Cod-themed housing development in Northeast Norman. Nantucket Boulevard runs through the center of the development, and a decorative pond complete with a covered bridge and water wheel greets residents when they return home. Scanlon's house first flooded in 2007. Scanlon told me it rained eight inches in four hours, and he woke up to six inches of water on the ground floor of his house. Seven houses in the neighborhood flooded. The 2015 flood was even worse, and then his house flooded again in 2016. Scanlon did not have flood insurance in 2007, because he did not live in a flood zone. He acquired flood insurance after that, and the premiums were only a little over $400 per year. After he filed insurance claims in 2015, the price of his insurance shot up to more than $2000 per year. The damage from the three floods has cost him more than $40,000 out of pocket and his insurance has paid more than $100,000. When heavy rains come, which is increasingly often in the spring and summer, Scanlon does not sleep at night.[1]

Scanlon participated in the development of Norman's first stormwater utility (SWU) proposal. It was voted down by a margin of more than two to one in 2016. Scanlon was even more involved with the second SWU proposal, which was voted down by a significant margin in 2019. When Scanlon and I first met in 2019 he was representing Ward 6 as a city councilmember and continuing to advocate for a stormwater utility, but city leaders have been reluctant to organize another vote for fear that it will just be voted down once again. Flooding is common in Norman and residents are well aware of the need to invest in stormwater infrastructure. Particularly in Norman's urban core, roads frequently fill with water and driving after even a moderate rain can be dangerous. Eutrophication in Lake Thunderbird is a product of stormwater runoff, and the SWU was intended to address this issue as well. If there is one thing that city leaders, engineers, and water specialists agree on, it is that Norman needs better stormwater infrastructure. City leaders and experts, however, continually told me that most Norman residents do not understand stormwater, which is why voters repeatedly refused to fund an SWU.

Despite the efforts of Scanlon and others, Norman is the only major city in Oklahoma that lacks an SWU. In most cities, not just in Oklahoma but throughout the United States, city engineers and financial staff would simply create a utility. A monthly fee would be collected and invested in stormwater mitigation. This cannot happen in Norman because of a 1975 amendment to the city's charter that requires any increase in utility fees be approved by the city's voters.

Why is Norman one of the few cities in the United States that requires residents, most of whom know little about infrastructure, to vote on increases to utility fees? The answer depends on who you ask. When I began asking this question, former *Norman Transcript* editor and local history enthusiast Andy Rieger suggested that I talk to Harold Heiple, a longtime Norman attorney. Heiple graciously invited me to visit him in his home near Westwood Golf Course. In his mid-eighties when we met, Heiple had the energy, confidence, and humor of a successful attorney. He had spent more than fifty years presenting arguments in courtrooms, often successfully fighting on behalf of commercial interests and real estate developers. Heiple explained that in 1974 a drug bust in Norman led the mayor of Dallas to call Norman the "drug capital of the southwest." Norman's mayor was so angered by this that he used a grant to hire additional police officers. The city then faced the problem of how to pay the officers once the grant money was gone. The city's solution was to raise utility rates by nearly 80 percent. Norman residents reacted by circulating a petition demanding a vote on the utility increase and the right for citizens to vote on future increases. When the vote went forward, residents voted overwhelmingly to amend the city charter to require popular support for any future utility increases.[2]

Heiple told me, "I along with the rest of the business community recognized the real handcuffs that would put on a city council. We were opposing it, but people passed the initiative big time." Heiple represented the City of Norman in an Oklahoma Supreme Court case aimed at blocking the citizens' petition. Heiple's story about the origins of the charter amendment has become a kind of common knowledge among those who follow politics in Norman. When asked about the utility rate increase law, people consistently referenced the 1974 grant for new police hires. Harold Heiple's son, Greg Heiple, served on the city council in 2014; he estimated that the charter amendment had cost the City of Norman nearly a quarter billion dollars due to delaying needed projects.[3] Other Norman city leaders cited this figure and told me that voting on utility rate increases prevents long-term planning as city officials must wait until infrastructure is badly needed before asking citizens for funds. One city council member asked me, "If this is such a great idea, why are we the only community that does this?"

The story about police hiring leading to a massive increase in utility fees seemed an accepted fact around Norman, but then I spoke with John Hancock, the co-chairperson for Norman Citizens for Civic Responsibility (NCCR), the organization behind the petition and charter amendment. I hosted Hancock for a long conversation at my dining room table in the fall of 2019. I had only been interviewing people about water infrastructure for a couple months and knew nothing about NCCR. I imagined that Norman's charter amendment on utility fees would be minor background for more recent conflicts about funding water infrastructure. I was surprised when Hancock explained that the amendment itself emerged out of a battle over who pays for growth and infrastructure. As I gradually dug deeper into archival sources, it became clear that intentionally or not, the story about police funding disconnected the requirement that voters approve utility rate increases from its actual roots in debates over water infrastructure and urban growth.

The 80 percent increase in utility rates was the spark that lit the fire, but opponents of the increase argued that these funds were intended for the construction of water infrastructure to support development. With Richard

Nixon's resignation dominating front-page news and distrust of government extremely high, NCCR transformed the way Norman funds infrastructure and votes for city council representatives. In the process, NCCR ousted the mayor, city council members, city attorney, city manager, and police chief. The new charter amendment was not simply a result of outrage over high utility rates. Rather, it was intended to undermine the power of developers by expanding the formal rights of citizens to participate in governance. Norman became an experiment in direct democracy, in which citizenship included not just the power to prevent public subsidies for growth but also to block new initiatives like the stormwater utility that Bill Scanlon believed would protect his home from flooding.

Subsidizing Growth with Lift Stations

Norman Citizens for Civic Responsibility emerged from a battle over lift stations. At the time, General Motors was planning a manufacturing plant in Midwest City, which borders Norman to the north. Developers were eager to build housing to take advantage of the influx of new families that the General Motors plant would bring to the area. Norman had been a nearly all-white sundown town less than a decade ago, and it was a destination for white flight from Oklahoma City, particularly families trying to avoid Oklahoma City's newly integrated public schools.

To support the expansion of residential housing, the City of Norman planned two lift stations near the Little River, the primary tributary for Lake Thunderbird, which provides more than two thirds of Norman's drinking water. The new lift stations would move sewage over a ridge to where it could flow downhill to Norman's sewage treatment plant and make sewage treatment possible for up to thirty thousand new residents, a huge increase for a town of a little more than fifty thousand. These lift stations were the infrastructure necessary for massive residential development in the Little River watershed. Opponents of the lift stations argued that the city government had increased utility rate fees by 80 percent to pay for lift stations that would support the new development. This was a conspiracy of developers. Public funds were subsidizing growth that profited real estate developers.

In a June 1974 letter to the *Norman Transcript*, published just prior to the city council vote to increase utility rates by 80 percent, Larry Hill wrote,

> In this [anti-growth] climate it is best for them [city leaders] to attempt to keep their proposals [the utility increase] from being identified as involving growth issues . . . Although they sound prosaic, these lift stations are not merely "engineering matters" of only technical interest. The question of whether or not they should be built can be viewed as almost a pure growth issue . . . The building of the stations would constitute a decision to encourage and subsidize the development of a whole new area on "the other side of the ridge" in northeast Norman.[4]

The "other side of the ridge" refers to the Little River watershed. For Hill, a professor of political science at the University of Oklahoma, the lift stations were undesirable because of their environmental impacts, but also because they subsidized development, essentially underwriting the cost of building houses that would be sold for profit. Houses without lift stations have less value because they cannot send their sewage to the treatment plant. In noting that lift stations are not merely matters of "technical interest" and that they are essential to "subsidize" growth, Hill took what at first glance appeared to be a question of engineering and shifted it to an issue of fairness.

Charles Dunn, Norman's mayor from 1972–1975 and owner of several Dairy Queen restaurants, questioned the possibility of limiting growth: "Who do we limit it to and who do we stop? Who do we say can come and who can develop? Do we say it's the scope and authority of the council to tell the university to stop growing? Do we say it's the scope and authority of the council to tell the Chamber of Commerce to stop its efforts for growth?"[5] For Mayor Dunn such decisions were outside the scope of city leaders' mandate. To prevent growth would ultimately involve some level of discrimination and raise questions about why some forms of growth are desirable but others are not. City leaders facilitate growth but do not determine its direction.

In the context of the 1974 utility rate increase debate, Mayor Dunn argued, "We can't build a wall around Norman—as I've stated many times—

and expect people not to come. We live in a vibrant metropolitan, regional area where new industry is locating, where new people are constantly arriving, and so many external forces are at work over which Norman has no control, that to simply say we will stop growth is like sticking our heads in the sand."[6] Dunn constructed growth as an inevitable, almost natural process, that cannot be controlled. He did not acknowledge that Norman was a sundown town less than a decade ago, and that Black people continued to face severe barriers to accessing housing. Instead, he implied that growth cannot be controlled, and it is best to prepare for it, just as one would prepare for severe weather. To naturalize growth, as Dunn did, is also to depoliticize it. It ignores the histories of exclusion and expropriation that supported the construction of Norman's essential infrastructure for growth—Lake Thunderbird. Questions of fairness and the distribution of resources disappear. However, as Hill explained in his letter, in building lift stations, the city does not simply permit growth, it guides and encourages development, in this case toward the Little River watershed.

Larry Hill did not initially believe that the City of Norman could be stopped from developing the Little River watershed. He obtained Norman's environmental impact statement for the new lift stations, a one-page report from the city engineer that there would be no adverse impacts on the land in question. The EPA gets "thousands and thousands of these and they just rubber stamp them," Hill told me. Once it had EPA approval, Hill assumed that the issue was over, but a colleague told him that an appeal was possible. A federal district office had recently opened in Dallas, and the EPA might be convinced to do a full investigation. Hill asked a friend, Larry Canter, a professor in engineering and environmental studies, to do some preliminary research on the potential impacts of development in the watershed. Hill noted that such a study would have been prohibitively expensive without Canter's assistance. Together, they convinced EPA representatives to come to Norman and do a full assessment. The possibility of an EPA environmental impact study led Norman's city council to postpone any further action related to the lift stations.[7] In August 1974 EPA officials visited Norman and determined that the city's assessment was not adequate and that an environmental impact study was necessary before lift stations could be constructed.[8]

The EPA environmental impact study was eventually released in 1977. Based on evidence that urbanization would increase problems with stormwater runoff and eutrophication, the EPA withdrew federal funds and shut down the expansion of Norman's sewage system into the Little River watershed.[9] The EPA study claimed that Norman could accommodate anticipated growth without expanding the sewage system into the Little River watershed, and that such expansion would cause unnecessary urban sprawl. Although Harold Heiple did not mention this when we met, I later learned that he provided legal representation for developers and landowners in the watershed, arguing that residential development could occur in an environmentally friendly manner.[10] Hill told me that a group of city leaders tried to appeal the ruling and wrote a letter to their congressman, Tom Steed, asking him to intervene on their behalf. This, Hill noted, was how things worked in the past—political leaders and wealthy interests collaborated to get around resistance to growth. However, in Hill's words, "there was a new sheriff in town." The EPA had the power to fight back against the conspiracy of developers.

It is unlikely that the EPA would have intervened without the work of two university professors—Hill and Canter. The two knew each other from coaching youth soccer, a sport that often brings people together in Norman. Canter authored a book on environmental impact assessments and possessed an unusual understanding of how the EPA functioned.[11] The workings of privilege and substantive citizenship are clear. Elites—professors, developers, chamber of commerce leaders—used their power to influence government. Although Hill critiqued the conspiracy of developers, he also depended on personal connections to make his voice heard. In this case, elite privilege was used to block growth, but that need not have been the case. The ruling could have easily gone in favor of the developers. The EPA's power was based in expertise and bureaucracy. One had to be well-positioned to influence the EPA. The NCCR reforms were different. NCCR sought to formalize the substantive citizenship possessed by elites so that it is shared by everyone in ways that would undermine the conspiracy of developers and the self-destructive consequences of growth.

Fighting for Control of Utility Rate Increases

NCCR enjoyed broad grassroots support but also depended on the work of experienced political organizers. In the years before John Hancock's return to Norman, he lived in Washington DC observing the Watergate proceedings and worked on an anti-blockbusting campaign in Rochester, New York. Hancock returned to Norman after getting a call from a longtime friend, Larry Wood. Wood told Hancock about the massive utility rate increase and the development of the Little River watershed, and Hancock was sold on the opportunity to work on a meaningful campaign.

A few months after I met Hancock, I called him with a few follow-up questions. My phone call prompted him to remember that he had recently inherited a box of NCCR-related documents after Larry Wood passed away.[12] Hancock dropped a large plastic tub off at my house, filled with newspaper clippings, campaign materials, and photographs. I spent some of the first months of the COVID-19 pandemic sorting through these documents and immersing myself in NCCR's history.

NCCR's work was rooted in a kind of plains populism that was very different from the EPA's more bureaucratic solutions to the problem of growth. Immediately after Norman's city council passed the utility rate increase, NCCR formed and began circulating petitions demanding a repeal of the rate hike and a change in the city's charter to require voter approval for all future increases. Both were clear steps to expand citizenship within Norman to combat the conspiracy of developers and self-devouring growth.

Despite the experienced leadership of Wood and Hancock, NCCR faced an uphill battle in communicating its message to Norman residents. The *Norman Transcript* consistently supported the establishment position of the mayor, city council, and Chamber of Commerce. Andy Rieger, editor of the *Transcript* from 1995–2015, told me that the joke used to be that the *Transcript*'s editors "never met a bond issue they didn't like." During the 1970s Democrats were the dominant party in Oklahoma, and the *Transcript* backed the Democrat establishment position that favored taxes that could be invested to support growth that would generate more revenue.

In a July 1974 *Transcript* editorial, "Our Point of View: Speaking Up for Norman," the editors wrote that "every service, whether public or private, has some kind of price tag attached to it. And, in order to enjoy the service, the citizens have to understand that nothing is free. Too often, of course, those citizens who understand and appreciate this economic fact of life are not motivated to speak up. As a consequence, sometimes a minority of critics appear to have majority support."[13] An NCCR supporter quickly responded that they were hardly a minority, with over three hundred people at their last meeting and thousands of petition signers. The writer closed with, "And you would deny these even the basic privilege of criticizing? Gestapoism!"[14] Like the references to Hitler and Khrushchev regarding the annexation of rural land the previous decade, the reference to Nazi Germany's secret police indicated that some NCCR supporters were in fact well-positioned to debate the distribution of city resources. To compare city leaders to the Gestapo demonstrated that one was not in fact subject to anything like Gestapoism. That said, in the 1970s the *Transcript* was delivered to nearly every doorstep in the city. Multiple parties had voices in determining city policy, but the balance was clearly weighted in favor of the alliance between local media, city politicians, and business leaders. Voting on utility rates was a way to formalize the rights of every Norman resident.

Recall what Larry Hill told me about how towns like Norman are run: "There's an ongoing conspiracy between the bankers, the developers, and the chamber of commerce that really runs all these towns." By its nature a conspiracy is always partially hidden from view. There are hints and allegations. Connections between disparate pieces of evidence are made, but definitive proof is lacking. Conspiracy theories proliferate when generally accepted sources of information are absent. During the final Nixon years paranoia and mistrust were abundant. If the president of the United States supported a break-in at his political opponents' headquarters, then couldn't local officials be conspiring with developers? The belief that one of Norman's primary news sources, the *Norman Transcript*, supported a conspiracy of developers pushed mistrust even further. NCCR's solution to mistrust of city leadership was to decentralize power, so that residents had control over the city's future.

NCCR's petitions easily gathered more than 9,000 signatures, a remarkable amount for a city of Norman's size, and far more than the 1,050 needed. The City of Norman tried to block the petitions by questioning their legality. Representing the municipal government, Harold Heiple argued that requiring a vote on all utility increases "would take the power away from the people . . . If the petition were lawful it would be possible for the people to vote to hold an election each time the city wanted to buy a box of paper clips."[15] The Oklahoma Supreme Court ruled against the NCCR petition seeking to repeal the increase in utility rates, but upheld the petition to allow residents to vote on a change to the city charter that would require voter approval for all future increases in utility rates. To this point, the NCCR had primarily built on popular discontent with the city council's 80 percent increase in utility rates. In Oklahoma it was not difficult to convince people to oppose new taxes and fees. NCCR's next step was to take on the more challenging process of political reform.

City council and mayoral elections were held in March 1975. NCCR endorsed candidates—John Anderhub, John Neal, and Lyntha Wesner—for each of the city council races and invested in campaign posters and advertisements. A free chili dinner with live bluegrass music attracted a crowd to an open discussion of the city council elections. Wesner and Anderhub won in landslides, defeating their closest opponents nearly two votes to one.[16] Neal's race went to a runoff, but he eventually won, meaning that NCCR now had three allies on the six-person council. Charles Dunn did not run for reelection as mayor. William Morgan, who had served as mayor from 1965–69, won the runoff against Sylvia Martin to become mayor. On the day of the city council election the old city council voted to keep the $15 minimum level for utility rates. Once the new council members took their seats, however, they immediately overturned the rate increase, and utility rates were taken back to their June 1974 level of $8.25.

Having stopped the utility rate increase and taken control of the city council, NCCR sought to transform the way the city did business and amend the city's charter to require a vote on utility rate increases. NCCR advocated two additional amendments. One clarified the process for recalling elected officials; the other would change the election of city council members from an at-large system to a ward system. All three amendments passed by wide margins on November 18, 1975, and have had long-lasting impacts on the politics of water in Norman. The debates surrounding the amendments pitted advocates of expertise and established power structures against those who favored more direct democracy and an expansive form of citizenship.

Newly elected mayor William Morgan opposed requiring a vote on utility rate increases. He argued that elected officials should be able to raise funds, make decisions, and govern. The editors of the *Norman Transcript* agreed and claimed that voters do not have the time or the ability to make informed decisions about city governance.[17] Norman's city manager repeatedly warned that without utility rate increases, the city would face significant cuts in staff and would soon lack the capacity to treat water and drill wells needed to keep up with population growth.[18]

Proponents of the change to Norman's charter countered that residents should be trusted to make intelligent decisions about their money and the city. Former mayoral candidate Sylvia Martin paid for advertisements in the *Norman Transcript* that asked, "Who Should Hold the Power to Incur Indebtedness, City Officials or the People?"[19] In an essay titled "Who Pays for Growth," John Hancock directly connected the 1974 increase in utility charges with new lift stations in the Lake Thunderbird Watershed and plans for Norman to be a city of 250,000.[20] New homes are worthless without connection to the infrastructural grid—roads, water, sewage, and electricity. Through their utility fees residents pay for the infrastructure that makes new homes valuable. Although the infrastructure is funded publicly, the profits from the sale of those homes is private. Hancock argued that if the public pays for growth, then the public should make decisions about growth through control of utility rates.

Prior to the November 18, 1975, election, NCCR distributed a four-page newspaper, the *Norman Citizen*, subtitled "A Newspaper of the People, by the People, for the People." Hancock told me that Larry Wood was the author and editor of much of the content in the *Norman Citizen*, which was partially intended as an alternative to the *Norman Transcript*'s continual opposition to NCCR plans. Unlike the social media that would emerge

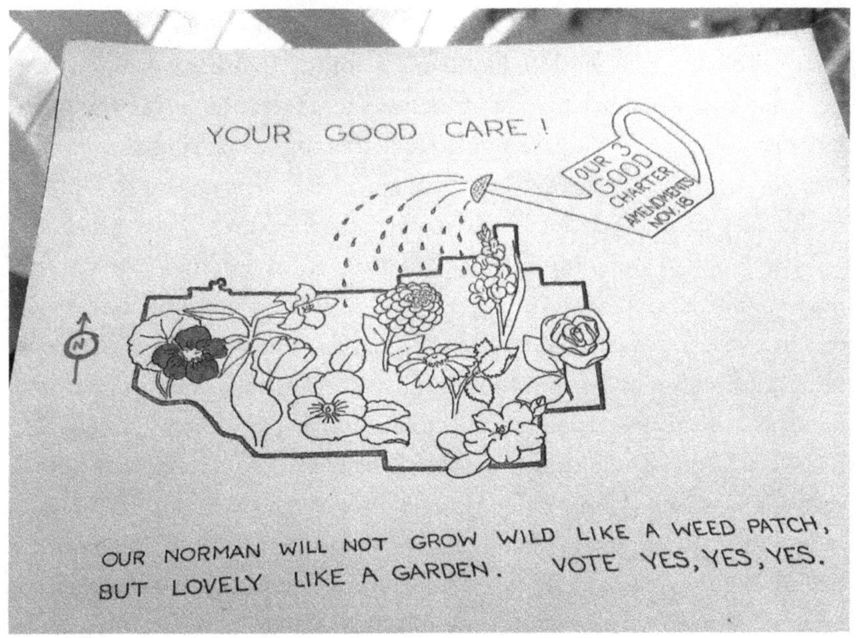

Fig. 1. "Your Good Care." Draft of an image that appeared in the *Norman Citizen*, vol. 1, no. 1, November 1975. From John Hancock's collection, photo by Daniel Mains.

decades later, the *Citizen* was highly centralized, but it did offer a distinctive populist perspective.

The connection between political reform and growth was communicated in a hand-drawn outline of the City of Norman's boundaries filled with blooming flowers that appeared in the *Norman Citizen*. A watering can labeled "Our 3 Good Charter Amendments Nov. 18th" sprinkles water from above. Below the graphic the caption reads, "Our Norman Will Not Grow Wild Like a Weed Patch but Lovely Like a Garden. Vote Yes, Yes, Yes." In other words, giving citizens control over new infrastructure allows them to shape growth to form a "garden," rather than a "weed patch." Controlling the distribution of resources is necessary to realize visions of a future city.

Such explicit references to growth were not new for NCCR. An "Elect John Neal" flier first stated, "Let's roll back the minimum utility charge to

$8.25!!" The straightforward appeal to thrift was followed by "If the builders want Norman to 'develop,' let them pay for it!" In other words, the public should not subsidize private interests. The illustration at the top of the flier depicts a heavyset, cigar smoking man in a top hat driving a steamroller labeled "3 in 1 Construction" over a man in overalls carrying a "Citizens' Rights!" sign and a "Petition." "Tired of it?" the flier reads, "So is John Neal."

The long-term implications of voting on utility rate increases in Norman are not entirely clear. On one hand, a Norman political activist who was involved in NCCR told me that the charter amendment has prevented Norman from sprawling and overbuilding like Austin, Texas. On the other hand, a Norman city council member explained that given how unusual Norman's law is, one would expect the city to be truly unique, but that's not the case. Comparisons with other cities are difficult given all the other factors that shape urban growth. What is clear is that since the charter amendment passed in 1975, Norman residents have incessantly debated infrastructure, often in relation to subsidizing growth. This is a key part of NCCR's legacy—it made infrastructure visible.

The stormwater utility fees that voters rejected in 2016 and 2019 were meant in part to mediate the damage that residential development in the Little River watershed has done to Lake Thunderbird. At first glance it seems ironic that the utility rate charter amendment intended to combat growth in the Little River watershed would eventually stand in the way of solutions to the problem of eutrophication. These, however, are very different types of solutions. The stormwater utility would have supported efforts to prevent phosphorous, sediment, and nitrogen from being washed into Lake Thunderbird. It would have done nothing to address public subsidies for growth that encourage development in the watershed. In contrast, Norman's 1975 charter amendment gave residents a voice in regulating growth, rather than only addressing its consequences.

Slow Growth and Slow Cycling in the Little River Watershed

Voting on utility rate increases has slowed, but not entirely prevented, growth in the Little River watershed. The developments that have emerged in the watershed offer an intriguing mix of bicycle paths and water infrastructure. Bicycling is one of my favorite pastimes in Norman. The flat terrain and smooth roads have made for relaxing pedaling once I found the right routes for avoiding cars. My friend Pete Soppelsa and I started doing regular rides in 2020, with the onset of the COVID-19 pandemic. Cycling was an easy way to socialize with plenty of air circulation. Pete is a historian of technology, and among other things we share an interest in urban infrastructure. Our rides do not involve sweat and Lycra bike shorts. We ride slowly, coasting when possible, so that we can chat and roll. Our destinations often involve some bit of water infrastructure that I have been thinking about.

On a sunny February afternoon, we set out on our longest ride ever—destination Little River. Pete has a garage full of bikes that he has restored, and he arrived at my house on an orange single speed. I have had the same bike for nearly twenty years—a blue single speed road bike that feels like it was made for Norman's flat terrain. We pedaled through the OU campus to connect with the Legacy Trail that we followed along the train tracks north, past Norman's Central Library. When we crossed Robinson Avenue, we entered new territory. Robinson, with its five lanes of traffic, is a mental and physical barrier that I rarely cycle beyond. But we carefully navigated our way to Stubbeman Avenue and continued past Norman North High School. The high school and its sprawling parking lots drain into "Lake Noname," the name given to many retention ponds in Oklahoma.

Past Rock Creek Road, we entered the Trailwoods subdivision. It was near here that we crossed over a ridge that separates the Little River and Canadian River watersheds. On the north side of the ridge, any rain that does not soak into the ground will eventually make its way to the Little River and then flow into Lake Thunderbird. This was our first stop. I wanted to show Pete a stormwater runoff experiment that was built into the neighborhood. I was here a couple months prior with Richard McKown, co-owner of Ideal Homes, the company that developed this neighborhood. On one side of the block, homes had rain gardens and water barrels, on the other side they did not. Rain gardens were placed in the median between the sidewalk and the street, together with signs describing the Little River watershed and explaining how rain gardens are intended to work. McKown told me that because of Norman's clay soils, rain gardens are intended primarily to filter, rather than absorb, stormwater runoff. The rain gardens resembled what I think of as a typical central Oklahoma riparian landscape with a mix of prickly pear cactus, long grasses, and small trees. The gardens between the sidewalk and road create a sense of being enclosed that I find comforting. In contrast, the "control" section of the block had the open feeling that I associate with new housing developments in Oklahoma. There are trees planted in the yards, but this is a new development and particularly in the winter these young saplings do little to disrupt the open flatness. On both sides of the block stormwater was channeled into small canals where it could be tested to assess pollutants that cause eutrophication in the water's eventual destination—Lake Thunderbird. Runoff from rain gardens could be compared with the "control" properties.[21]

The experimental lawns got Pete talking about the frequent failures of geoengineering schemes—using technology to manipulate the environment to cope with climate change, for example, technologies that reflect sunlight back into space to cool Earth. Richard McKown makes a compelling argument that high-density single-family homes can be a form of geoengineering that transforms the environment for the better. Currently much of the Lake Thunderbird watershed is zoned for low density development, often only one residence per ten acres. McKown noted that these are not farms. They are homes with large well-maintained lawns. As a featured speaker at a City of Norman Affordable Housing Town Hall, McKown explained that lawns are one of the most significant sources of pollution in the United States. Not only do they require lawnmowers that spew exhaust, but people also dump excessive amounts of fertilizers on their lawn. Yard grass is the single largest crop in the United States, but fertilizer for lawns is unregulated.[22] McKown argued that rezoning this land for denser housing would help solve the shortage of affordable housing in Norman, reduce space devoted to heavily fertilized lawns, and enable the implementation of living infrastructure like grasses and natural forms of water detention that would filter out pollutants as stormwater travels to Lake Thunderbird—in this vision, better water quality is achieved through development.

The runoff from the experimental lawns eventually makes its way to a series of connected retention ponds. Pete and I pedaled slowly along the

Fig. 2. Retention ponds. Photo by Daniel Mains.

wide sidewalk that parallels the ponds. Like the Legacy Trail near the railroad, paths for biking and walking accompany other forms of infrastructure. Elsewhere in Trailwoods, the bike path follows the greenspace next to powerlines. The grass surrounding the retention ponds is a uniform brown and mowed low, right to the edge of the pond. Brown grass and blue sky are the colors I associate with Oklahoma winter. Pete and I followed the expansive greenspace north along the ponds, crossing over into another Ideal Homes development—Greenleaf Trails. Trailwoods and Greenleaf Trails are directly connected by sidewalks, but not roads. Despite the pleasant weather on a Saturday afternoon, few people were out walking.

In comparison to Norman's historic urban core, where many of the creeks have been confined to concrete channels and can only be accessed on private property, here far more space has been given to stormwater infrastructure. If not for the need for extensive space for stormwater infrastructure, would these trails exist? Following national trends in stormwater management, beginning in the early 1980s the City of Norman required that any new development not increase the rate of stormwater flow.[23] In Norman's historic core, homes are crowded around creeks, but in newer developments ponds that catch stormwater and slow its flow are everywhere. Grasses near the ponds have been allowed to grow in places, creating the appearance of miniature wetlands. Ideal Homes created a series of ponds and a creek that mimicked the natural winding flow of water through the flood plain. A mature deciduous tree is a lone giant next to one of the ponds.

Pete and I left the comfortable trails of Greenleaf and cycled across Tecumseh Road. We found ourselves in an even newer and more expensive development, owned by Aria, Sassan Moghadam's company. Moghadam was the cofounder of Unite Norman. As we moved north home prices had steadily increased from the low $200,000s in Trailwoods, to more than $300,000 in Greenleaf Trails, to now nearly $600,000. We were finally approaching our destination. We again found a bike path that followed the stormwater retention ponds. But just before we reached the Little River, the sidewalk ended at a fence. On the other side of the fence, we could see the dense forest that follows the river, but it could be accessed only by trespassing through a rural backyard. I consulted a map, and it appeared that the neighboring development had river access, but there were no bridges across the detention ponds and streams. We backtracked and entered Little River Trails, another Ideal Homes development. Rather than the usual Oklahoma brick, the houses here were made of wood, many with an urban farmhouse aesthetic. Like the Aria development, there is room for growth in Little River Trails and new homes were under construction.

We gravitated toward stormwater drainage and this led us to a biking trail, this time right on the edge of the Little River. Although the oak tree forest did not extend much more than ten meters on either side of the river, even in the winter it was dense, full of brush and thorny vines. We found what looked like a city easement—a path down to the river paved with cobblestones. Discarded remnants of carpet lined the path. Styrofoam cups, plastic bags, and pieces of fabric were caught in the bushes. We made our way to a ledge overlooking the creek where the water formed a shallow riffle flowing over stones before pooling. The ochre banks on each side of the river were steep, showing signs of erosion.

Upstream the Little River flows through urban neighborhoods that fill the river with runoff when it rains. The Little River is not a place of pristine natural beauty, but it is the primary source for Norman's drinking water and for this reason it has been the site of repeated battles over growth. Protecting this narrow muddy river stands in the way of millions of dollars of profits for Norman's real estate developers. Richard McKown's father, Gene McKown, was involved in many of these battles. The difficulty of accessing capital means that development is often a family business, passed from one generation to the next, and in Norman with few to no exceptions, developers are men. By April 1975 developers like Gene McKown were tired of waiting on the EPA's impact study on the Little River. At a Norman Planning Commission meeting regarding platting an area near what would eventually become Greenwood Trails, Gene McKown told commissioners that he had repeatedly checked on the status of the EPA study and it had not even begun. "There has not been one positive action done. If you are going to attempt to bankrupt people with an action like this, then I plead with you to get EPA . . . to do something." McKown told commissioners as his voice shook, "You are making every attempt to shut down my construction operation. You're establishing a no-growth policy. In effect you are issuing a nonbuilding permit."[24] Many of the commissioners found McKown's plea convincing. Commissioner Landsaw noted, "We're doing the land owners a tremendous injustice. This is their livelihood. Pressure should be put on the EPA rather than creating an economic crisis with the land owners. We're not playing games out there. We can ruin a lot of people awfully quick." By the end of the meeting, the planning commission voted seven to one to approve a preliminary plat for the tract in the watershed. When the EPA finally released their impact study in 1977 and shut down development in the Little River watershed, Gene McKown complained that he had purchased two farms in the area with the intent of developing them for residential housing. "I was a developer; now I'm a farmer, I guess," McKown lamented at a city council meeting.[25]

The case of the McKown family and the Little River watershed complicates the conspiracy of developers narrative. On one hand, two generations of McKown men have profited enormously from real estate developments in the watershed. The McKowns consistently make large donations to Norman politicians. They have the power to hire attorneys to fight for their interests. On the other hand, the McKowns are sincerely concerned with the destructive consequences of growth. They cut into their profit margins to limit eutrophication in Lake Thunderbird. Developers sometimes complain that anti-growth sentiment in Norman prevents affordable housing, but the McKowns stand out for taking steps to address the problem of homelessness. Not only do they build affordable small homes, Gene McKown was given the Norman Human Rights Award in 2017 for leading the way on a $3.2 million project to build thirty-two transitional homes ("McKown Village") for Norman's unhoused population.[26] This is just one of the projects that Gene McKown has collaborated on with Food and Shelter, the primary organization serving the unhoused in Norman.

While addressing city council in yet another debate over lift stations and development in the Little River watershed in the early 2000s, Gene McKown sarcastically introduced himself as "one of those evil developers."[27] Conspiracy theories always oversimplify. Developers do seek to influence governance to their benefit, but people like Richard and Gene McKown can make a compelling argument that their business serves the public interest. NCCR's battle, however, was not simply about what is good for the community: it was about who decides. The model of the wealthy developer donating millions to support the unhoused and working with experts to create environmentally friendly housing is based in paternalism. It assumes that the developer will act in the interest of the public good. Developers maintain a form of substantive citizenship that is only available to a few. NCCR's goal was to formalize this substantive citizenship as a legal right for all Norman residents.

One way the substantive power of developers is expressed is through Planned Unit Developments (PUDs). Like other developments north of Tecumseh Road, Little River Trails is a PUD, meaning that it is not subject to standard zoning requirements. Instead, the City of Norman has approved a specific plan for development. PUDs are a way of getting around zoning regulations but doing so is not easy. It requires expensive assistance from lawyers, engineers, and others. The bicycle trail that Pete and I followed through Little River Trails was written into the PUD, which was approved in 2007. The

PUD states that the trail should eventually connect with the rest of Norman's Legacy Trail system.[28] Such connections are still far from becoming a reality, but for Pete and me, this little section of smooth concrete trail was a welcome reward at the end of a long ride.

Undermining the Conspiracy of Developers with the Ward System

Like voting on utility rate increases, the ward system of electing city council members, adopted in 1975, was intended to create a more expansive form of citizenship that would undermine the conspiracy of developers. Under the at-large system of representation, all voters elected six councilmembers regardless of where they resided in the city. The ward system divided the city geographically into eight wards with roughly equal populations. Residents in each ward elect a representative to the city council, with the requirement that the representative resides in that ward. The mayor continues to be elected by all Norman residents.

The *Norman Transcript* once again supported the establishment position of the at-large system in a series of editorials. *Transcript* editors argued that the at-large system allows council members to advance the interests of the entire city, rather than specific communities.[29] From this perspective, council members maintain a degree of objectivity if they are elected by all residents rather than only the members of their specific ward. A system where ward politics are dominant would reward council members who cater to the specific desires of their constituents and generate unnecessary expenses for the city.

Proponents of the at-large system also noted that residents vote for all six council members and the mayor, whereas under the ward system they vote only for one council member and the mayor, thus significantly decreasing voters' voices. In the words of the *Norman Transcript* editors, "the ward system would permit the individual voter to cast a ballot for only TWO out of NINE who will govern the city . . . Those who believe that we would necessarily have more responsive and more representative government with this system are chasing bubbles."[30]

Ward system advocates countered that the at-large system specifically favored the rich, arguing that the majority of city council members "have come from the moneyed parts of town."[31] NCCR used the *Norman Citizen* to illustrate this claim with a map of the city of Norman showing recent city council members' residences clustered within a few blocks of each other. I enjoy riding my bicycle on Smoking Oaks Road and checking out sprawling houses constructed in the 1960s where many council members lived. It is easy to imagine well-to-do city council members discussing city politics at neighborhood cocktail parties. Many council members also lived near Imhoff Creek. In Norman, creek-side living allows for expansive properties, greater privacy, and frequent visits from birds and other wildlife. The ward system would break apart this geographic concentration of power and force council members to reside throughout the city.

Advocates of the at-large system pointed out that if it was biased, one would expect to see more benefits accruing in the neighborhoods where council members live, but instead one finds streets that are notorious for flooding.[32] NCCR, however, was critical of a particular perspective on development that councilmembers shared. This was not a case of the wealthy using city funds to improve the neighborhoods where they lived. Critiques of the "moneyed parts of town" were directly related to growth. Real estate was one of the most lucrative businesses in Norman during the 1970s. Developers could invest money in the campaigns of city council members, making it very difficult for critics of publicly subsidized development to win city-wide elections. A candidate running in an individual ward can do more door-to-door campaigning and meet with individual constituents. This is impossible for a citywide election, making it necessary to purchase expensive newspaper advertisements to reach voters. In this sense, an attack on the at-large system was also an attack on publicly subsidized growth. The ward system broke apart the connections between wealth, development, and elections. Rather than relying on developers and wealthy individuals for campaign funds, the *Norman Citizen* described donations to NCCR from over six hundred people, most of whom gave less than five dollars.

For NCCR the at-large system was directly connected to elitism. A *Transcript* editorial claimed that under the ward system, "the best candidates may not be elected because only a limited number of council seats are available for each ward and selection can be due to geographical accident as well as to a candidate's merit."[33] A letter draft in Wood's collection called this claim "intellectual snobbery of the highest order" and argued that "a University professor or a wealthy business man is no more 'qualified' to be a council member than is a truck driver or a University employee, or a student."[34]

Over forty years after the introduction of the ward system, connections between geography and representation are clear. Norman's Ward 5 encompasses much of the rural area that was annexed by the city during Lake Thunderbird's construction. In terms of area, it covers nearly as much space as all the other wards combined. Ward 5 is home to a rural population that leans politically conservative and libertarian. In an at-large system, the specific interests of rural residents would be outweighed by the far larger urban population. Under the ward system, Ward 5 elects its own councilmember.

That does not mean that there is a typical Ward 5 councilmember. Sereta Wilson beat incumbent James Chappel in 2017 to represent Ward 5 until 2020. Chappel was Norman's first, and to this point only, African American councilmember, and was appointed to replace Lynn Miller after she became mayor.[35] My first meeting with Wilson was at Yellow Dog Coffee, a coffeeshop in Norman's urban core that she owns with her husband. Wilson is a vivacious extrovert with tattoos of a dog and sunflowers on her arms. Wilson's outspokenness was partially what got her elected, but it also made her the target of misogynistic attacks. Since the 2010s a great deal of debate has occurred on public Facebook pages devoted to each of Norman's wards. Wilson was masterful at navigating social media. She told me, "I would confess that I participated in, and maybe even cultivated some of that toxicity. When it was in my favor it was fun . . . They [Ward 5 residents] almost hero-worshipped me for a little bit."

Together with other council members, Wilson came under attack from Unite Norman in the summer of 2020, ostensibly for her vote to not grant the Norman police the full amount of their request for an increased budget. At that time Norman's mayor and the majority of city councilmembers were women. The matriarchy of hate, clucking lesbo hens—these were some of the names being thrown at the women who led Norman. Wilson turned it into a joke on the Ward 5 Facebook page, writing that these would be great band names. Someone even made a flyer for a Matriarchy of Hate and Clucking

Lesbo Hens concert. But, in this case the wave of toxicity directed at Wilson could not be countered with humor. Some attackers claimed that Wilson's use of profanity was unprofessional. The same qualities that had made her a relatable human rather than a typical politician were now weaknesses.

Wilson suspected that recall efforts and personal attacks were motivated by her strong opposition to development outside of Norman's urban core. When I spoke with her in 2021 she described something like the conspiracy of developers. "Moneyed interests" buy cheap property beyond the city's urban development plan that is not currently zoned for residential housing. Developers hire a lawyer and convince a sympathetic city council to approve a change in zoning. Once the development is approved, the city builds infrastructure out to the new neighborhood. The developers then return to the city council, explain that the infrastructure is already built, and request approval to build more housing. As a councilmember Wilson opposed any new development beyond East 48th Street in order to preserve Norman's rural areas and protect the Lake Thunderbird watershed. Wilson noted that in one of the cases that she successfully opposed, the developer would have replaced 27 houses on 10 acre lots with 270 houses on single acre lots. She estimated a profit of $40,000 for each house, meaning she cost the developer $10 million. Developers told her, "You won't be here forever." They were fighting the long fight, and they had the resources to wait for a new council member.

Of Unite Norman's recall efforts directed at the mayor and city councilmembers in 2020, only Ward 5 gathered enough signatures to initiate a recall vote. Wilson, however, resigned from her position before the recall could move forward as she was moving to Ward 4 in Norman's urban core. A temporary replacement for Wilson was named until the next scheduled election was held early in 2021, when Unite Norman backed candidate, Rarchar Tortorello, won the Ward 5 seat. Tortorello's campaign focused almost entirely on backing the police, but in response to direct questions he was clear that he supported growth and development in Ward 5. Although the ward system does make it easier to compete against well-funded candidates, Tortorello had the advantage of receiving more than seven times the campaign donations of his nearest competitor. Many of those donations came from business owners located outside of Ward 5.[36] Tortorello posted photos of himself on Facebook traveling to the January 6, 2021, "Stop the Steal" rally in support of Donald Trump, and he opposed COVID-19 vaccines and masking. Perhaps because of this, he beat out three opposing candidates to win the Ward 5 seat without a runoff. As a councilmember Tortorello often voted to support development, a move that drew some backlash from his constituents, and he was not reelected.

Despite the intentions of NCCR, the ward system has not always countered the power of developers, but it did change the dynamics of representation in Norman. The interests of wards are highly complex, encompassing, for example, the balance between policing, urban growth, and COVID-19 policy. The ward system made councilmembers more directly accountable to specific communities. It is unlikely that Tortorello could have won a seat on the city council in an at-large election. The same is true of many councilmembers across the political spectrum. Distribution of resources through infrastructure is one dimension of the relationship between ward residents and their representatives. It is often overshadowed by other values, including appeals to national politics, but the ward system has supported a closer connection between policy decisions and geographically specific visions for the city.

In opening the city council to people like Tortorello, the ward system has created a complex relationship with expertise. City councilmembers can no longer be depended on to advance the establishment position. I attended a meeting in August 2021 that Tortorello organized at the Little Axe Community Center, on the eastern edge of Norman's city limits, intended to inform Ward 5 residents about the implications of city water wells for their private household wells. Tortorello greeted me at the entrance with a firm handshake. He had close-cropped hair and the build of someone who spends a lot of time lifting weights. He wore a tight-fitting t-shirt that said "Freedom" on the back above an image of the American flag. The meeting featured presentations from engineers who explained that city wells are very deep and therefore do not impact the shallower household wells. The audience did not seem to be entirely convinced, and Tortorello intervened to repeat the engineer's points.

When the discussion of wells and aquifers wrapped up, Tortorello made a quick announcement. Mayor Breea Clark had recently proposed using federal funds to incentivize COVID-19 vaccines.[37] Tortorello made clear that he opposed any incentives for vaccines. "I am not vaccinated, and I do not wear a mask, but I am perfectly healthy," he announced, "masks don't work." "This is horseshit!" an audience member shouted. "No, it's not!" shouted back a white-haired man with a neatly trimmed moustache. A couple of people walked out of the meeting. Tortorello calmly shifted topics, made a few comments about public transportation, and the meeting closed.

As I drove home on Highway 9, which runs alongside the south side of Lake Thunderbird, I could not stop thinking about those last few minutes of the meeting. In many ways the entire meeting was based on the importance of expertise. Tortorello encouraged residents to listen to engineers who are experts on aquifers, even if common sense tells them that huge city wells pull water from nearby household wells. Tortorello, however, also made it clear that he did not believe expert advice on the topic of COVID-19, and he directly opposed many City of Norman policies related to the virus. In other words, experts should be trusted in some cases, but not others.

Police Scandals, Race, and the Limits of Expanding Citizenship

In late July 1975, as Norman residents were debating changes to the city's charter, the Norman Police Department launched a raid on local saloons and confiscated more than fifteen hundred bottles of liquor.[38] Until 1984 the sale of liquor by the drink was illegal in Oklahoma, although saloons typically operated as "private clubs" that allowed members to keep personal bottles at the club. In the aftermath of the raid, authorities learned that some police officers were receiving free drinks at the Holiday Inn's Normandy Club. Multiple officers were asked to resign, and others were demoted.[39]

Shortly after, citing health problems, Police Chief Bill Henslee stepped down, but requested another position, which City Manager Dick Gray granted. Henslee took a $6500 cut to his annual salary but was still paid $15,500 a year.[40] Norman residents were outraged. "Let's get rid of Dick Gray! He's the fly in the ointment," suggested a letter to the *Norman Transcript*.[41] The NCCR steering committee released a letter critiquing City Manager Gray and demanding a thorough investigation into his conduct in awarding Police Chief Henslee a new position.[42] Councilmember John Neal led the demand to investigate police misconduct and encountered heated opposition from City Attorney Fielding Haas.[43] Norman residents argued that Haas's conduct during city council meetings was arrogant.[44] In the face of mounting public pressure, Fielding Haas resigned in early September and Dick Gray resigned in October. Both Gray and Haas had held their positions well before NCCR emerged as a political force in Norman and had actively opposed NCCR's reforms. Upon resigning Haas said, "I quit because . . . we've had a lot of turmoil here—a councilman who's mixed up with this bunch of activists—and it got to the point where this lawyer didn't wish to represent his client anymore."[45]

Prior to resigning, Gray criticized Councilmember John Neal, claiming that Neal had participated in radical activities as a student at the University of Oklahoma in the early 1970s.[46] Neal responded that although he was present for some of these activities, he was not in fact a student radical. Rather, he was working undercover for the Federal Bureau of Investigation. Neal claimed he prevented violence on campus and helped thwart a planned bombing of the ROTC Armory.[47] The FBI released a statement confirming Neal's account. Neal explained that his recent work with NCCR was not connected with the FBI and came from an honest desire to reform governance in Norman. Neal wrote,

> A small group evidently believes that it is radical to protect our citizens from outrageous utility rates, that it is radical to require Central State Hospital, the University and other large users to pay their fair share for water and other utilities. Some even evidently believe it is radical to require city employees to conduct themselves with courtesy and respect toward the people of Norman. I do not believe those achievements are radical. Our efforts to eliminate special interest control and create a city government that is truly responsive to the will of the people is in the best tradition of the American democracy.[48]

NCCR forced a rethinking of citizenship in Norman, asking if city leaders could be trusted to represent the interests of residents. City Manager

Gray responded by trying to undermine trust in NCCR's leaders. What is real and who can be trusted? John Neal was a fake radical and an FBI informant, but he claimed to be genuinely concerned about governance and fairness in Norman. Sometimes Neal was an imposter, sometimes he was real. Neal argued that city staff like Dick Gray and Fielding Haas were imposters, representing the interests of developers rather than most Norman residents. In this atmosphere of distrust, turmoil, and debates over citizenship, it is perhaps no surprise that policing became central to the discussion. Police have a sort of super citizenship, possessing rights that extend beyond other residents. In Norman, residents were questioning precisely how far these rights should extend.

Free drinks for police officers was not the only scandal that Norman's police department faced in the summer of 1975. Equestrian polo also contributed to Police Chief Henslee's fall. Clark Hetherington's mother told him at age five that polo would be his passport to the world, and in many ways she was correct. Hetherington went on to be vice president of Polo and Equestrian Operations at Palm Beach Polo and Country Club, where he became good friends with celebrities like Sylvester Stallone and Tommy Lee Jones.[49] Hetherington was born and raised in Norman, where he was a successful real estate developer who "ended up developing a third of Norman over the years."[50] Hetherington hosted polo matches on his rural Norman ranch. Chief Henslee was accused of colluding with Hetherington to not arrest undocumented migrants who cared for horses on Hetherington's ranch.[51] In June, two officers were watching a match at the polo grounds on a day that Chief Henslee happened to be out of town. The officers noticed "three suspicious looking men," whom they arrested after discovering they were undocumented migrants.[52] Although Hetherington denied the men worked for him, one of the officers making the arrest claimed that Heatherington told him that Chief Henslee had assured him that migrants would not be arrested on the ranch and that he should call Chief Henslee to straighten things out.[53]

Internal conflict within the Norman Police Department may have led to the arrests. Some officers were upset that Chief Henslee prevented them from going to the polo ranch to interrogate suspects after a robbery at a Norman grocery store.[54] I find it unlikely that it was a coincidence that Chief Henslee was out of town when the arrests at the ranch were made. My reading of the situation is that there was a conflict within the Norman Police Department over the limits of racial profiling. Some officers appeared to oppose the police chief's demands that racial profiling not extend to the undocumented employees of powerful developers.

Critiques of special treatment are at the heart of both scandals. NCCR and other Norman residents were outraged that police officers were receiving free drinks, the employees of a wealthy polo club owner were immune to prosecution, and the police chief was rewarded for apparent incompetence with a cushy new position. People like Hetherington, Police Chief Henslee, and City Manager Dick Gray appeared to possess a kind of super citizenship that gave them personal control over public institutions like the Norman Police Department. They used these institutions to advance their own interests, rather than those of the public. This flew in the face of NCCR's goal of empowering all residents with expanded formal citizenship.

The police scandals, however, also demonstrate the limits of NCCR's attempts to expand citizenship for Norman residents. Police critics did not argue that racial profiling itself was problematic; rather, they were upset by the inconsistent application of profiling. Critics of the Norman Police Department did not question what made the three arrested migrants look "suspicious." Rather, they questioned the power of a wealthy real estate developer to protect his employees from racial profiling.

As I worked my way through the *Norman Transcript*'s coverage of NCCR, another headline caught my eye—"Police Chief Ordering End to Stopping Young Blacks."[55] In September 1974 Police Chief Henslee ordered officers to stop indiscriminately stopping young Black men. The end to a policy of racial profiling came only after complaints from the Norman Human Rights Commission and the American Civil Liberties Union. The Norman Human Rights Commission was founded in 1973 by Barbara Henderson, who moved to Norman in 1967 with her husband Dr. George Henderson. I asked George Henderson if he remembered NCCR, and he did not, instead noting the activism of the Norman Human Rights Commission.

NCCR was concerned with uncovering a conspiracy of developers. They pulled back the veil on previously hidden relationships between city leaders, developers, and local media. They instituted changes to Norman's city charter that undermined the power of this conspiracy. Despite NCCR's clear mission to formalize for all the substantive power already possessed by elites, it seems to have turned a blind eye to issues of race. Racial profiling was not a hidden conspiracy. It could be carried out openly because in the mid-1970s people of color lacked substantive citizenship in the city of Norman. NCCR did nothing to address this fundamental source of inequality.

NCCR's Legacy of Expanded Citizenship

In the aftermath of the November 18, 1975, election in which voters approved all three amendments to the city charter, the *Norman Transcript* proclaimed that "probably the most significant aspect of Tuesday's city election . . . is the visible shift of power from the so-called establishment, to a people-and-issue-oriented organization . . . By and large, the power structure of the city, business, retailers and the newspaper, joined by some university elements, were solidly against the ward system, the utility rate amendment, and the recall proposition."[56] NCCR claimed a victory for a more responsive form of government, in which voters can make decisions on the issues that impact their lives.[57]

NCCR was never simply an anti-tax movement; rather, it sought to transform the nature of citizenship in Norman, Oklahoma. The "establishment" referenced in the *Transcript* editorial possessed a form of substantive citizenship that allowed it to determine policy and direct resources. NCCR sought to formalize these rights for all residents. Fighting high utility rates was a key part of NCCR's campaign, but it was always linked to the demand that Norman residents should control utility spending. The ward system also reformed citizenship. It brought a more responsive mode of government by connecting voters and councilmembers through shared neighborhoods. For many NCCR supporters, shifts in the nature of governance and citizenship were inextricable from questions of redistribution and who pays for growth. Allowing all residents to shape growth was intended to undermine the power of developers to influence city government.

NCCR did more than give Norman residents the power to make decisions about infrastructure. In making the relationship between infrastructure and growth visible, NCCR created constant debates about growth. NCCR's work allowed Norman residents to see abstract relationships between lift stations and the redistribution of wealth. Decisions about infrastructure were no longer exclusively controlled by city experts. Each time the city requests additional utility funds for a new project, Norman residents have another conversation about who pays for growth and who benefits from it. This is a systemic solution to the problem of self-devouring growth. Rather than erasing the problems of growth from public consciousness, like the water treatment plant removing the taste of Lake Thunderbird's eutrophic waters, NCCR's reforms gave residents the power to stop subsidizing new development.

Norman's leaders continually lament the challenges of preparing for the future without a stable stream of funding for water infrastructure. In August 2022 Norman residents voted on nine proposed changes to the city's charter, one of which would have allowed the city council to increase utility rates by 3 percent annually. Residents approved six of the proposed changes, but the proposal to enable council to increase utility rates was voted down by a margin of more than two to one.[58] Norman residents refuse to give up their direct control over utility rates.

Expanded citizenship is a partial solution to the conspiracy of developers and eutrophication. Newly empowered citizens, however, cannot act to address shared problems when they lack a unified sense of community. Cases of police racial profiling revealed the limits of a reformed citizenship. Norman residents were excluded from public safety because of race. Such instances of exclusion fracture the unified community that is necessary to oppose the self-destructive consequences of growth.

Mistrust compounds this tension. In the United State, a decade of war, assassinations, and youthful rebellion followed the completion of Lake Thunderbird. Norman would never return to a time when residents could unite around a shared vision of a "progressive, wholesome city." The ward system and voting on utility increases were solutions to problems of trust. Norman residents demanded more control over local governance precisely because they believed the government was conspiring with developers. Without trust in experts to guide future plans, however, enacting a vision of the future city is challenging. In the following chapters I explore struggles to build infrastructure and plan for the future in an atmosphere of extreme distrust and fractured community.

3 Urban Creeks and the Tragedy of a Commons without Community

ONE OF MY FAVORITE things about Oklahoma is the storms. The sky darkens, the wind howls, and then it hits, blasts of thunder that shake the house and torrential rain that can last for hours. There are stretches when it seems like the sky has forgotten how to rain. A month or two of sun and then it comes, sometimes just a single storm and sometimes day after day of rain. I moved to Norman during the horrendous drought of 2011, but two years later it rained so much that my kids went wading in our backyard.

Asphalt, concrete, and roofing shingles transform rain into stormwater runoff. An inch of rain on my twenty-three-hundred square foot home will produce more than fourteen hundred gallons of runoff. All that water must go somewhere. Some of it will be absorbed by my lawn, but much will flow downhill into a creek. Humans have long depended on creeks, but only recently with urbanization have creeks become so important for getting rid of stormwater. As cities grow and impervious surfaces increase, the power and volume of stormwater intensifies, creeks are paved over and transformed to drainage channels, and their names are forgotten.

On a mild December day my friend Aaron and I walked Norman's Merkle Creek upstream, north from Normandy Shopping Center. The creek is paved in places and littered with trash, and yet the presence of water and plants attracts more wildlife than seemingly any other place in the city. We see swallows' nests under a bridge, small fish swarming any place where there is standing water, frogs, a turtle, butterflies, and a beaver dam. It has been a warm December, and the wildlife seems to be thriving.

Each time I walk one of Norman's creeks my geography of the city is disrupted and recreated. Merkle Creek's existence is easily forgotten. Unlike Imhoff Creek, which is spanned with multiple pedestrian bridges, or Bishop Creek with its expansive Eastwood Park, there are few places to engage with Merkle Creek. I had visited Normandy Shopping Center many times without realizing that a creek flowed just beyond the asphalt and buildings. In contrast, Aaron grew up in Norman during the 1980s and he has many childhood memories of exploring Merkle Creek.

Aaron is an artist and often paints creeks. Walking with Aaron my eyes are tuned to details. He turns over a rock and catches a small crawfish—it is entirely brown except for the bright red tips of its claws. He points out the long grass that has been matted by wind and water and collects leaves. Aaron notes that this is the sort of thing he likes to sketch, but it is difficult, partially because our eyes are not used to this type of image. He compares this small bit of the landscape to a part of a word, meaningless on its own, and only understood in a broader context. He helps me see beauty in the details of the streambed, like the networks of roots that have been exposed by erosion. Some of these things can only be seen after hours and hours of sketching. The act of concentration focuses the brain. Just as Aaron helped me to see the creek differently, spending time in creeks opened my eyes to new connections and changed my perceptions of the city.

Walking upstream from Main Street, Merkle Creek takes us past the backyards of large houses, built in the 1970s. A few months earlier I visited Harold Heiple in this neighborhood. Heiple had lived in Norman since 1962 and served on numerous city committees. In some ways his career began with Merkle Creek. He had only been practicing law for a few years when he learned of city plans to purchase the Southeast Corner of 24th and Main and turn it into a public park that would encompass a significant stretch of Merkle Creek. At the time, the area was an active farm. Heiple immediately objected that this was some of the best potential commercial real estate in the city. "You got no business putting a park there and losing the sales tax dollars that will be generated at that location," he told me.[1] Heiple led a successful campaign to oppose the park and devote the land to commercial development. He told me this story within the first few minutes of our meeting to demonstrate his relationship to the city. Perhaps opposing the park was foundational to him becoming an attorney for so many of Norman's developers. That proposed park eventually became the Normandy Shopping Center that drains into Merkle Creek. This was before Norman instituted regulations on stormwater runoff generated by new development. A parking lot produces more than fifteen times the amount of runoff as a meadow.[2] Soon after the shopping center's construction, downstream residents complained that their backyards were being washed away by stormwater runoff.[3]

Today Normandy Shopping Center shows its age. Some businesses are thriving, but other retail spaces are empty as shoppers have gravitated toward newer big box stores. Regardless, the asphalt remains as impervious as ever, collecting water that pours into Merkle Creek. I brought a trash bag with me on my walk with Aaron, but it was quickly clear that picking the trash from Merkle Creek would require a dumpster rather than a bag. Full bags of trash were scattered around the channel that runs from the parking lot into the creek. The plants that edge the creek were wrapped in layers of shredded plastic shopping bags.

Heiple served on the Stormwater Citizen's Committee that developed the failed 2019 stormwater bond and utility proposal. After telling me that a successful stormwater utility must accommodate the business community, Heiple offered what for him was a foundational principle in managing a city: "Rule number one in municipal finance: Money to a city is like blood to your body. If the blood doesn't circulate in the body, the body dies. If the money doesn't circulate in your city, the city dies." In other words, a healthy city that is livable for everyone depends on taxes, and those taxes come from businesses. Without large businesses, there would be no tax revenue to pay for needed services like police and fire.

The relationship between impervious surfaces and stormwater is a variation on eutrophication and self-devouring growth.[4] Growth generates tax revenues, but the more the city grows, the more land is covered by impervious surfaces that create stormwater.[5] Growth means more water flowing through the city's stormwater system of gutters, pipes, and creeks; more water flooding streets and washing away backyards. To examine growth in isolation from creeks obscures its destructive consequences. Harold Heiple told me a city depends on the circulation of money, but it also depends on controlling the circulation of water.[6] Getting into creeks, literally and figuratively, illuminates the self-devouring consequences of growth.

Creeks and the Tragedy of the Commons

Urban creeks are a tragedy of the commons, but not in the sense that many people would assume. Garrett Hardin, an ecologist, famously illustrated the tragedy of the commons with the example of sheep herders and a pasture that is open to all. The sheep herders will be guided by rational self-interest to fill the pasture with as many sheep as possible. The pasture, therefore, will be overgrazed and ruined for future use. Hardin concludes, "Freedom in a commons brings ruin to all."[7]

Urban creeks are like the pasture in the sense that they are open to all. Anyone can let water flow from their property into the creeks. There is little incentive not to release as much water as possible into the creek. As the volume of water in urban creeks increases, the creek and the commons are destroyed. The creek erodes its banks, damages bridges and channels, and washes away trees and backyards. Through urban growth and the expansion of impervious surfaces, the users of the commons destroy the shared infrastructure they rely on to remove stormwater.

Hardin's story of the tragedy of the commons is often interpreted as an argument in favor of private property.[8] If shepherds owned their pastures, they would have an incentive not to overgraze. Matthew MacLellan, however, offers a useful reinterpretation of Hardin's parable by focusing on the notion of "freedom in a commons."[9] Historically, true freedom in a commons has rarely existed. Commons are governed by complex regulations that determine their use.[10] For example, communities regulate logging in shared forests or fishing in shared waters. Tragedy occurs not in the absence of private land ownership but when self-interest encounters a resource with no publicly imposed limits.[11]

In a car-dependent society, impervious surfaces are essential for operating a business, and the maintenance of those surfaces relies on shared creeks. Asphalt would continually flood if water did not run off into creeks. The freedom to channel runoff into urban creeks supports economic growth, but this freedom is highly destructive. There is limited public regulation of stormwater in Norman. Owners of parking lots and big box stores do not directly experience the consequences of the stormwater they generate. It is the downstream ecosystems and backyards that are destroyed by the runoff from the parking lots.

Limitless growth is directly opposed to the maintenance of the commons. When I interviewed Harold Heiple, he argued that economic growth is necessary for maintaining a healthy city. The city nourishes growth and increases its tax revenues by protecting business owners from paying for the consequences of their impervious surfaces. There is no end to this logic of growth. Economic growth creates impervious surfaces, which generate struggles with stormwater. The money to solve these problems must come from more growth, which in turn creates more destruction. Borrowing from the future creates debts that will be paid with more borrowing. It becomes necessary to continually nourish growth to pay for the consequences of past destruction.

Urban creeks are tragic when they are a commons without a community to protect them from cycles of endless growth. The community necessary to govern the commons is fractured by a failure to hold owners of impervious surfaces responsible for the stormwater runoff they generate. The City of Norman has tried and failed to fund solutions to stormwater problems. Without shared regulations to govern the commons, individuals battle to protect their private property from creeks and other forms of stormwater runoff. Freedom in the commons means that everyone must protect their property, but only select individuals are able to shield themselves from the dangers of an unregulated commons. Such individual solutions to problems of growth further fracture the community needed to regulate the commons. Exploring creeks—their ecology, history, and sensory dimensions—helps us see the relationship between impervious surfaces and self-devouring growth.

Creeks and Growth One: Imhoff Creek

In late July 2021 Norman city engineers were preparing to resurface a bridge that extends over Imhoff Creek, when they noticed that the bridge was severely damaged. It was shut down immediately, closing one of the primary roads to the University of Oklahoma. In the context of climate change and shifting weather patterns, heavy summer rains have become the new normal. They repeatedly turned the creek into a raging river and eventually damaged the bridge to the point that it could no longer support traffic. This was no surprise to many of Norman's water engineers, who had told me that Imhoff Bridge would be the first casualty if money was not invested in stormwater infrastructure. The failed 2019 stormwater bond proposal included $17.5 million for projects on Imhoff Creek, nearly one third of the total bond.

Imhoff Creek flows through the center of urban Norman, and its watershed has the highest percentage of impervious surfaces of any of Norman's creeks. In 2019 many of the city's proposed stormwater projects were designed to alleviate damage to private property just downstream of Imhoff Bridge, near where the creek leaves the city. Every year homeowners on this section of the creek lose more and more of their backyard. Trees and fences are gradually being swept away and houses are threatened.

David Dary moved to Norman from Kansas in 1989 to lead the University of Oklahoma's School of Journalism. Dary lived in a house near Imhoff Creek, downstream from the damaged bridge. After moving to Norman, David Dary signed the forewords to his books, "On the banks of Imhoff Creek."[12] Dary deeply loved living on the creek, but he feared its increasingly destructive powers.

The creek was a source of beauty and connection with nature—Dary counted more than ninety-five species of birds in his backyard—but it was also a threat. Dary's backyard was slowly crumbling away and there was nothing he could do about it. As a journalist and author of more than twenty books, Dary kept files on many things, and among them were a small stack of papers relating to Imhoff Creek. Dary's files contain documents with titles like "How to Control Streambank Erosion," "Cost Effective Gully Treatment," and articles on specific erosion prevention tools like gabion baskets—rectangular mesh baskets that are filled with small rocks. There are copies of email exchanges with city councilmembers and engineers. A fifty-two-page document titled "A Comparative Look at Public Liability for Flood Hazard Mitigation" and printouts from a website called Erosion Law indicate that Dary was considering suing the city. I imagine Dary up late at night, reviewing his photos of the rising waters and the storm damage, searching the internet for erosion control techniques, emailing city employees, printing documents, creating files, all attempts to manage a situation that was clearly not only beyond his control but beyond that of the City of Norman. One of the documents in Dary's files is titled simply "Options to Try." These included writing letters to city officials, contacting a local attorney, getting an estimate from an engineer for the cost of protecting the property, contacting local television stations, and writing letters to the *Norman Transcript*. Dary tried all of these, but they led nowhere. Dary was experiencing the creeping terror of climate change. Could he wait this out and hope for help from the city or a change in weather, or should he pull up stakes, sell his house at a loss, and leave?

A "Time Line" written by Dary traces twenty-five years of change on his property between 1989 and 2013. Heavy rains occurred every few years, bringing piles of trees, branches, and other debris rushing down Imhoff Creek. In 2011 the high water even brought a fifteen-foot sailboat that lodged in the debris pile. Heavy flows of water hit the debris piles, forcing water into the banks and causing more erosion with each storm. As the banks crumbled, large trees lost their base and tumbled into the creek. The erosion expanded. The Darys tried to fight the erosion, planting vegetation between their retaining wall and the creek, installing a French drain, and dealing with damaged trees. City employees cleared debris from the creek but did nothing to prevent the underlying structural problems that were causing the damage. A real fix to the Darys' problem would cost millions of dollars. In a 2011 email exchange, Norman's stormwater engineer suggested to David Dary that the only way to fix his problem was to convince his neighbors to vote to fund stormwater infrastructure.

Dary saved newspaper clippings documenting the struggles of neighbors with similar problems. One property owner estimated a loss of twenty to thirty feet to the backyard. Three times he had rebuilt his fence, only to have it wash into the creek again.[13] A 2007 letter to the editor of the *Norman Transcript* noted that recent rains had washed away seven trees. "Does anyone care? This summer's rain has finally taken a huge bite out of Imhoff Creek, one of Norman's oldest green spaces."[14] City officials certainly did care. An expensive stormwater study served as the basis for the Stormwater Master Plan, which ranked the Imhoff Creek project fifth highest in priority among nearly fifty other projects around the city. In the winter of 2015, prior to the heavy rains of May, David Dary served on a committee to evaluate proposals from engineering companies to address the Imhoff Creek issues. Despite city officials voicing support for the Imhoff Creek project, after more than twenty years of discussion the city is still searching for funds to support creek restoration.[15]

Although such funds are scarce, Norman residents have repeatedly approved new bonds for road maintenance. City of Norman staff told me that solving the problem of "Lake McGee" was one of their signature accomplishments. For many years, moderate rains consistently flooded the busy intersection of McGee Drive and Lindsey Street, forcing traffic to be rerouted. In Norman, stormwater projects are often combined with work on roads. During the process of renovating Lindsey Street, the City of Norman installed a massive pipe to carry water from the McGee/Lindsey intersection to the Canadian River. The pipe was large enough that a car could be driven through it, and for the most part it solved the Lake McGee problem. Projects like this are part of adapting to climate change and reproducing lifestyles that are based in growth. In the years I have lived in Norman I have noticed far less flooding of roads. Investing millions in renovating roads keeps people driving. Instead of limiting stormwater runoff, city government mediates the impacts of impervious surfaces by channeling water elsewhere. Like removing the taste of eutrophication, the consequences of growth are hidden but the fundamental problems are not addressed.

Many Norman residents took to social media to question the city's proposal to invest millions of dollars to save private property along Imhoff Creek.[16] One longtime observer of Norman politics explained to me that if people build their house on a beach, they should expect hurricane damage. The same is true of people who live on creeks, he suggested. If someone's backyard is falling into a creek, they should handle the problem on their own.

These arguments, however, overlook the basic dynamics of impervious surfaces and stormwater infrastructure, which are fundamentally technologies of community. David Dary's property did not generate the stormwater that was washing away his backyard. All the upstream impervious surfaces in the Imhoff Creek watershed funneled water past his property. The destruction of private property along Imhoff Creek is not an inevitable result of creek-side living. Longtime residents on Imhoff Creek remember when it was possible to plant gardens on either side of a small stream they could easily step over. Today, that stream is a deep half-pipe of concrete. To understand how Imhoff Creek became stormwater infrastructure that destroys backyards, we need to go for a walk.

My son, Gus, stayed home from school complaining of an upset stomach and a headache, but when the afternoon rolled around, he was feeling fine. We both needed to get out of the house, so we set out on a walk down Imhoff Creek. It was a warm, blustery Wednesday in November. The low sun was at a perfect angle to illuminate the trees overhanging the creek. There were still many green leaves, but also patches of red, yellow, and orange. I had slept poorly, tossing and turning with disappointment about the election day results, particularly the win for a far-Right state superintendent of education who promised to ban critical race theory and set up a voucher program to support private schools. The walk in the fresh air and sunlight was exactly what I needed.

As usual, we entered the creek at the bridge near our house, about a mile and a half downstream from Imhoff Creek's headwaters. There had been rain during the past week, but it was quickly absorbed and only a trickle of water ran along the narrow concrete creek bed. In 1936 workers lined the upstream portion of Imhoff Creek with stone and concrete as part of a WPA project intended to create jobs and ease the movement of water out of the city. Paving the creek nearly one hundred years ago was the first step in what has become a long-term struggle to confine the creek to as small a space as possible. Creeks like to meander, and the WPA project pinched Imhoff Creek into a narrow channel that disconnected it from a flood plain where the occasional overflow might be absorbed. The WPA paving placed the long-term management of Imhoff Creek on a trajectory that has been very difficult to change. With the paving, it began to shift from a creek to a nameless drainage channel. Imhoff Creek is a place with a history and an ecosystem to be protected, but a drainage channel can be ignored. To return to the meandering creek of the past could mean removing the paving and the houses built along the narrow channel. Instead, the WPA paving has necessitated more interventions as areas downstream are paved and straightened. The environmental interventions of the past limit the options of the present.[17]

Imhoff Creek was paved to accommodate growth. Creeks are a commons, but paving prioritized some uses of Imhoff Creek over others. A smaller, straighter creek opened more land for development, one factor that increased impervious surfaces in the Imhoff Creek watershed. In 2017 more than 43 percent of the land in the Imhoff Creek watershed was covered by impervious surfaces.[18] Most of these are upstream, meaning large amounts of water are directed into the WPA channel, where it is then forced downstream at increasing speeds. The WPA did not pave the entirety of Imhoff Creek. When increasingly large volumes of water traveling at high velocity reach the end of the paving, erosion occurs. Today when the rain pours in Norman, Imhoff Creek is transformed from a slow trickle into a rushing river, easily twenty feet across and ten feet deep at the bridge near my home, a mile upstream from the damaged Imhoff Road Bridge. Rushing water slams into the sides of the channel, digging ever deeper and pulling soil from the banks. Sediment is eventually washed into the Canadian River rather than spilling out onto the flood plain where it can regenerate the soil.

Gus and I walked downstream, using the creek to pass under Lindsey Street to where the creek widens and flattens. Here, sediment accumulates in the center of the concrete creek bed and provides a base for long grasses and brush to grow. Gus told me that together with his friends he named this patch of growth "Corpse Island," because they once found three opossum carcasses caught in the grasses here. Gus assured me that City of Norman bulldozers clear Corpse Island every spring. He is learning the rhythms of the creek. It serves as a refuge for children who are seeking to escape adult supervision. Particularly in the early days of the COVID-19 pandemic, my kids were daily creek walkers. Many people who grew up in Norman have stories of using Imhoff Creek to navigate the city. The creek offers a kind of

Fig. 3. (*top*) Imhoff Creek after a heavy rain. Photo by Daniel Mains.

Fig. 4. (*bottom*) Imhoff Creek normal flow. Photo by Daniel Mains.

Fig. 5. "Hobo Cave." Photo by Daniel Mains.

pedestrian byway that connects elementary schools and parks and avoids the noise and danger of cars.[19]

We continued under a wooden pedestrian bridge and reached a tunnel high and wide enough to invite exploration. The tunnel is covered in graffiti and if one follows it back maybe one hundred yards under the roads and strip mall parking lots, one side of the tunnel is painted with the words "Dead Boyz Den." On the other side of the tunnel is a painting of a twentieth-century style television, complete with antennae. Gus pointed out changes in the graffiti above the tunnel's entrance. It was once labeled "Ratz Nest," then "Hobo Cave," and now it simply said "Peeps." It was here that Gus and a dozen neighborhood kids once pulled hundreds of large brown carp from the creek. A neighboring housing development had released the carp from their koi fish pond, but there was not enough water in the creek for the fish to swim downstream and the fish were dying on the creekbanks.

Beyond the tunnel the creek channel deepens, and intersecting pavers replace the concrete. Sometimes rubber boots are needed to navigate this section of the creek, but we easily walked alongside the trickle of water. We peeked out from the channel into the expansive backyards of the houses that back up to the creek. The houses along this stretch of Imhoff Creek are generally large and desirable, with the creek providing a bit of extra privacy. Further downstream the creek became a smooth half pipe of concrete, built after the 2015 storms. Here the channel is so deep and the sides so vertical that small staircases are built into the sides so that workers can enter and exit the creek. The channel ends in a bed of rip rap—large chunks of concrete and stone. As we approached, we saw a young red fox making its way toward us, hopping from stone to stone. When it saw us, it exited the creek into a backyard.

The volume and velocity of water that comes out of the WPA channel is simply too much for earth and stone to handle, so the only real option was to continue paving downstream. A channel covered with a filter fabric liner and blocks was constructed in 1999. In May 2015 massive rains produced more than twenty-three inches of rain, more rain than the entire year of 2014.[20] More than four and a half inches of rain fell in a single day. This was the sort of storm that has become increasingly common due to climate change. During these rains, stormwater got under the filter fabric, which then rolled up the blocks into a ball in the middle of the channel. City engineers evaluated more than a dozen possible replacement blocks before determining that concrete was the most effective and low-cost solution to the problem. The new concrete channel cost more than $650,000, which was initially paid for with emergency funds. Once the May 2015 rains were declared as a natural disaster, the city was able to request federal reimbursement for the project. However, with so many weather-related disasters nationally, reimbursement is becoming increasingly time-consuming and difficult.

After the fox sighting, Gus and I turned around and retraced our steps, but it is possible to continue downstream, using the rip rap to stay out of the water. Soon the rip rap ends, and the creek bed becomes a mix of sandy dirt and stone. Small trees and brush grow alongside the creek, catching trash that stormwater washes down the channel. This section of the creek is owned by a homeowner's association and the City of Norman lacks an easement for maintenance. The homeowner's association has opposed interventions like paving or rip rap. A concrete pedestrian bridge spans the creek, built by the construction contractor who once lived here. Now unused, it seems a ruin from the recent past. The creek passes under the Imhoff Street bridge that was closed for many months in 2021 for repairs. Beyond the bridge the creek deepens and collects in large pools. The banks here are too steep for walking. Looking up from the creek to the backyards of David Dary's neighbors, at least twenty feet above, the erosion damage is clear. There are large plastic tubes dangling down from the yards, perhaps intended to deliver runoff directly to the creek so that it will not wash away more of the property.

From here Imhoff Creek twists and turns until it reaches the Canadian River, which begins in Colorado and travels more than one thousand miles before it feeds into the Arkansas River in eastern Oklahoma. The Canadian River is a wild changing river, appearing and disappearing as it throws up little hills of sand along its banks. In Norman it is a popular place for homeless camps, teenage parties, and shooting guns. On a walk along the Canadian River, I learned that large spirals of thin wire are what remains after burning tires.

Impervious surfaces connect everyday urban life with Imhoff Creek, the Canadian River, and all the other rivers they eventually feed into. As water moves over these surfaces connections are continually created. Rainwater flows from a strip mall on Main Street into the WPA-built creek channel and then joins water from other roads, roofs, and parking lots to eventually create so much velocity and volume that the creek rips away the soil from its banks. The solution to erosion is more paving, which ultimately creates a larger and more powerful force of water after heavy rains. Paving creeks is a kind of enclosure of the commons in the sense that it transforms the creek so that it is primarily suitable for only one use—channeling stormwater runoff away from impervious surfaces. Throughout the United States, however, urban communities are experimenting with forms of stream restoration designed to prevent erosion and flooding by allowing streams to take up more space and spill over into flood plains.[21]

To the extent that people depend on impervious surfaces, shouldn't they also be responsible for the damage they cause? But who is the "they" in this question? Should the business owners who profit from impervious surfaces pay the bulk of the costs? It was easy to argue that a $17 million investment in stormwater infrastructure was too much to pay to save the backyards of a few homeowners, but what if that money preserves a major road that tens of thousands of football fans use to access the university's stadium every fall? Imhoff Creek connects the asphalt parking lots and the damaged bridge, but these connections are only visible when we learn to see creeks.

Creeks and Growth Two: Bishop Creek and the Eagle Cliff Development

I am always eager for a new perspective on Norman's creeks, so I was excited when Ruth Borum Loveland agreed to show me one of her favorite spots on Bishop Creek. Ruth is an artist. She began making what she calls soil studies in 2019. She collects soil, often near bodies of water, processes it with mortar and pestle, and paints with the powdered pigment. Ruth's Bishop Creek soil studies are often grids of varying shades of red and brown painted on a white surface.

Ruth picked me up from my house on a beautiful Friday morning in late April. Her car was filled with stuff connected with her numerous creative projects. A three-foot diameter circular mirror sat in the backseat. The stack of books between the driver's and passenger's seats included *Charlotte's Web* and Cormac McCarthy's recent book, *The Passenger*. The morning air was unusually clear. A storm had dropped three inches of rain on Norman two days prior and pushed out the heat and humidity. Tornadoes had ripped through a small town just fifteen miles away, causing significant damage. We've had our roof replaced twice in twelve years after golf ball–sized hail, but this storm only brought dime-sized pellets. In Norman, the clickety-clack of hammers putting new shingles on roofs is a year-round soundtrack.

I've known Ruth more or less since I moved to Norman. I was happy when she bought a house just a couple blocks from my family. When my friends in Portland, Oregon, look down their noses at Oklahoma, I remind them that in Norman artists can afford to buy wonderful houses in walkable neighborhoods. Our sons are the same age and we used to run into each other at playgrounds and Imhoff Creek. Ruth once told me about a hot day in August, when together with her son she sat in the rain on the concrete banks of Imhoff Creek. It was the first rain in weeks and the creek was filled with a thick earthy sludge. Ruth and her son sat in the cooling rain watching the creek slowly fill with water and break apart the earth, sending it flowing downstream.

Ruth drives us to a sprawling apartment complex that I had never noticed before. At the back of the complex she parks under massive oak trees that border the creek. We pull on our rubber boots and descend a steep bank to Bishop Creek. On the far side of the creek the banks rise straight up, maybe thirty feet or more of red stone and dirt. Tree roots dangle down from the clifftop. Closer to the ground, small ledges jut from the cliff. The ledges look like they are formed from stacks of thin layers of stone, like the pastry of an apple strudel if it was made from red dirt. When Ruth was here last summer this cliff was crawling with spiders that seemed to emerge from little holes in the rock. Just upstream the creek pools, but here it flattens out into a wide ankle-deep riffle flowing over red clay. This is an ideal base for Ruth's soil studies. There is the usual scattering of trash, but that's not where her attention is focused. She picks up clumps of earth and uses them to mark the back of her hand. One is sandy and grainy leaving light red marks. The other is clay and leaves a deeper brick red streak. The lump of clay is somehow both soft and firm, and its smoothness feels good in my hands. Ruth tells me that her soil studies are relics of the creek. The soil studies remove a basic element of the creek from its context in a way that distills and intensifies color and texture. The abstract grid of soil captures the strange beauty of this place within our city that is so often unseen. The small art gallery that Ruth runs in downtown Norman is called Magic Sad. There is magic in urban creeks, but also something sad.

Ruth points out white streaks in the red earth and explains that they are likely fossils of tree roots. She picks up a stone that has split in two. Many of the stones break easily here, blurring the line between rock and soil. These found objects are incorporated into her art. We explore a narrow tributary that merges here with Bishop Creek, pausing to pore over small stones and

Fig. 6. Bishop Creek. Photo by Ruth Borum Loveland.

agates. Ruth points to what at first looks like a bluish green stone. On closer examination it is a cow's molar, washed smooth by the water and sand. Ruth places this in her bag to save for later. She explains that in other places one might be drawn to the expansive landscape of the ocean, but here in Norman we have creeks. In the creek one's attention is continually drawn to smaller and smaller details—the soil, rocks, and sediment.

Jimmy Austin Golf Club is just upstream from the towering red cliff. The forest of mature oaks ends abruptly and the creek cuts through a field of neatly mowed grass. Men wearing slacks and pastel polo shirts navigate a sand trap. Ruth tells me about a series of photographs—"balls in the woods"—that she shares on Instagram. She describes it as a study of decomposing recreational objects lost in the woods. In the dense brush near the golf course, we see a desiccated tennis ball half buried in thick spring growth, another ball in the woods. Like in the creek, Ruth draws my attention deeper into the details of the dense forest landscape.

Fig. 7. Golf balls in Bishop Creek. Photo by Ruth Borum Loveland.

Like my walks with Aaron, spending time with Ruth helped me see Bishop Creek differently. Whatever I think the creek is, it is inevitably something more. Continually encountering creeks through art, walks, or my monthly chemical testing remakes my vision of the city. Bishop Creek is a wildlife habitat, a pleasant place to escape the heat, and a source of artistic inspiration, but it is also a stormwater drainage channel. In 2016 more than 35 percent of the Bishop Creek watershed was covered with impervious surfaces, an amount that has certainly increased. Just downstream from the cliff where Ruth gathers red clay, Bishop Creek passes under Highway 9 and continues downstream for another mile or two, past the Eagle Cliff Housing development and through the Potts Family Farm before emptying into the Canadian River. In 2021 the intersection between the Bishop Creek watershed and Eagle Cliff development became a site for yet another battle over stormwater and development.

Norman's City Council meets every other Tuesday. Meetings begin at 6 p.m. and often last past midnight. For those who can't attend in-person, meetings can be streamed live or watched later. For me, watching city council meetings holds the same fascination as reality television. There are winners and losers, colorful characters, and angry outbursts. I love watching people passionately debate zoning policies. I am not the only one who gets sucked into the drama. Videos of city council meetings accumulate hundreds of views. Sometimes clips of particularly contentious exchanges are circulated on social media.

In mid-October 2021, as the Delta variant of COVID-19 passed through Oklahoma, many of the seats in the council chambers were taped off to enforce distancing among the residents who came to speak. Most of the crowd was intensely interested in the council's vote regarding a proposal to expand the Eagle Cliff housing development near Bishop Creek where it empties into the Canadian River.

It is unusual for developers to attend city council meetings; they are usually represented by their attorney. During the period of my research that attorney has nearly always been Sean Rieger. This Tuesday Attorney Rieger provided introductory remarks but then turned the microphone over to co-owner of Shaz Investments and Home Creations, Jalal Farzaneh. Farzaneh's statement began, "Forty-three years ago in October my brother and I came to the United States. We came with the promise of rule of law in this country." "Frankly, my family is living the American dream," said Farzaneh, explaining that after coming to the United States from Iran he worked at Church's Fried Chicken to put himself through school, and that Home Creations has constructed more than fifteen thousand new homes. Farzaneh then gave a $15,000 check to the Eagle Cliff Homeowner's Association to help deal with problems caused by stormwater runoff and closed his presentation by asking God to bless the United States of America.

In comparison to the Farzaneh family's other charitable activities, $15,000 is quite small. The family has given more than $8 million in gifts to the University of Oklahoma, and OU's College of International Studies is housed in Farzaneh Hall. Many of the Farzaneh family's gifts support Persian studies at OU, including a seven-foot statue of Persian mathematician and poet Omar Khayyam.

Attorney Rieger's presentation emphasized that the proposed expansion of the Eagle Cliff development meets the city's engineering criteria. When called upon, city staff and engineers stated that the project met all city standards. Rieger also noted that the city has repeatedly granted permission to expand the Eagle Cliff development and that Norman's existing infrastructure has the capacity to serve additional homes. Rieger continually noted that the City of Norman's 2025 Land Use and Transportation Plan requires urban development densities in areas where substantial investment in urban infrastructure has been made. The Eagle Cliff development's streets, water, and electricity are all ready for expansion.

At the time of this meeting, Dr. Derek Rosendahl was president of the Eagle Cliff Homeowner's Association. He holds a PhD in meteorology and specializes in assessing uncertainties in future climate projections. Typically, residents are each given three minutes to speak before council, but Rosendahl was given fifteen minutes to speak on behalf of the Eagle Cliff residents. Rosendahl emphasized that Norman's 2025 plan for growth does not match current environmental conditions. The 2025 plan was released in 2004. The city's stormwater masterplan was released in 2009 and based on rainfall data from 1996. According to Rosendahl, the rest of the country is using future projections to make decisions about planning, while Norman is making decisions based on twenty-five-year-old data. Rosendahl's slides included graphs demonstrating major increases in the frequency and intensity of extreme rainfall events during the past hundred years. The weather has changed, and conditions from the past cannot be used to make decisions about the present. Areas that were expected to flood once in a hundred years are now covered with standing water for months every year, evidence that the flood plain has moved.

Development has also increased upstream along Bishop Creek. Rosendahl claimed that a fifty-acre plot of land just upstream from Eagle Cliff, also owned by Home Creations, was cleared of forest and brush in 2020. Rainfall on the plot washes trees and sediment downstream, causing increased flooding. Rosendahl showed photo after photo of washed-out ditches where stormwater from the Eagle Cliff neighborhood has carved up backyards as it flows down into Bishop Creek. Ten-to-twenty-foot drops are common where stormwater drains off roads at the edge of the development. Homes are being constructed below the level of the street. Rainwater drains from the street into yards and carries away more soil and plant life. "I am sorry, but $15,000 isn't going to deal with this, it's going to take millions of dollars to deal with this," Rosendahl explained. "Every homeowner is left with buying a home, thinking it's good, and all of a sudden their backyard drops off." Like Imhoff Creek, property was being washed away by stormwater, and restoration was well beyond what any individual family could afford. Rosendahl closed his presentation by telling the council that as a climate scientist, he is certain that the flood plain has moved, and if the council does not stop this development, the city will be stuck buying up flooded homes.

Attorney Rieger responded to Rosendahl's presentation, "If your [City of Norman's] regulations are out of date and inapplicable, then you have to change the regulations . . . You can't take his [Farzaneh's] land because you think the regulations are no longer any good, you have to change the regulation . . . He has a right to develop his property." The city council was in a difficult situation. On the one hand, Rosendahl presented convincing evidence that the city's regulations concerning zoning and flood plains were no longer applicable in the context of a changing climate. On the other hand, Rieger was correct that those regulations must be changed. Changing regulations is a time-consuming process. Until it concludes, how can builders operate? Can they be expected to plan based on imagined future regulations?

City councilmember Steven Tyler Holman represented Ward 7, where the Eagle Cliff development is located. He directed challenging questions to Norman's director of public works, Shawn O'Leary, asking, "Have we ever approved developments that meet these standards, have gotten our approval from staff, but then after they're built, we found out that there are significant problems that the city has had to address?" Holman listed neighborhoods—Cambridge, The Vineyard, and Summit Lakes—in which the city approved new development, only to be called in later to deal with property destruction caused by stormwater.

The city council voted seven to two not to approve the zoning changes necessary for the expansion of Eagle Cliff. It appeared that the council shared Holman's concerns that the project would necessitate long-term financial support from the city. A history of development-induced stormwater problems was compounded by Rosendahl's analysis of climate change. Rosendahl suggested that the city's flood plain maps did not fit with the realities of a changing climate. Until the city's laws and regulations are updated to account for new rainfall patterns, development must proceed with extreme caution.

Councilmembers Kelly Lynn and Rarchar Tortorello voted in favor of the zoning change. Both men were elected with support from Unite Norman in 2021. They were visibly distinct as the only council members not wearing face masks at the meeting. Masks were not only about preventing the spread of illness: for both sides, they had become complex symbols of one's politics, relationship to expertise, and at least in this case, position on zoning changes. In explaining his support for the project, Councilmember Lynn noted, "All I know is it is their land. I believe in freedom, I believe in liberty, I also believe in the rule of law . . . It is his land. This is America. This is freedom. This is what we should be doing." Unite Norman cofounder and real estate developer Sassan Moghadam wrote on the Unite Norman Media Outreach Facebook page regarding the Eagle Cliff decision, "Last Tuesday, our city council sent a very clear message: 'We are closed for business. We don't want progress and development to happen in Norman. If you are wanting to invest in this community, we will go against our own rules and regulations to run you off.'"[22] Moghadam went on to contrast development with what he perceived as the city's openness to homeless camps.

Zoning is fundamentally about shaping the future. Moghadam articulated a distinct vision for a future community in which "progress and development" are contrasted with what for him were signs of decay—homeless camps and public food pantries. In rejecting requested zoning changes the city council sought to shape the future in very pragmatic ways. Councilmember Holman's comments indicated an opposition to zoning changes that would eventually force the City of Norman to bail out homeowners with public funds. Decisions made many years ago to permit development along the banks of Imhoff Creek left landowners and the city in an impossible situation. Landowners cannot afford to protect their land from rising stormwaters, and the city has struggled to fund a solution. Holman and the city council signaled they would not let this happen again by permitting development that will generate more destruction from stormwater. This was a small step towards preserving the commons, but it did not last long.

In the days after the council's decision, Sean Rieger filed a lawsuit against the City of Norman on behalf of Jalal Farzaneh's company, Shaz Investments. In the lawsuit Rieger claimed that the city council did not provide clear guidance based on city ordinances or codes to deny the request for rezoning.[23] In 2023 a judge ruled in Shaz's favor and ordered the City of Norman to let Shaz move forward with its plans to build 140 new homes in Eagle Cliff.[24] The request for rezoning was returned to the city council. Stephen Tyler Holman argued against it, going head-to-head with Rieger, even quoting from other legal cases in an extended debate, but the rezoning was approved by a five to four vote at the June 27, 2023, meeting.[25]

Creeks, Growth, and the Illusion of Community

At the time of the Eagle Cliff debate Steven Tyler Holman was the longest-serving member of Norman's city council. When I met with Holman in 2023, he told me that he had served longer than all other current city council members combined. He attributed his ability to avoid burnout to truly caring about Norman because he was born and raised here. Holman is particularly knowledgeable about infrastructure and urban planning. His fascination with infrastructure emerged during his childhood in Norman when he navigated the city by bus. Holman's day job is managing the Friendly Market—a medical cannabis dispensary. His blurb on the City of Norman website notes he still works the door once a week at The Deli, Norman's oldest live music venue.[26] With his long dark hair pulled back into a ponytail, thick-rimmed black glasses, and well-trimmed goatee, Holman is a recognizable figure in Norman. Prior to the legalization of medical cannabis in Oklahoma, the Friendly Market was targeted by the Norman Police Department for the sale of pipes that could be used for the consumption of cannabis. The Norman police confiscated the Friendly Market's cash and merchandise, a move that had forced other similar shops out of business. Holman and the owners of the Friendly Market fought back, and charges against the Friendly Market were eventually dismissed. Holman was only able to fight the two-year legal battle because the Friendly Market had financial support from the DKT Liberty Project.[27] In 2020 Unite Norman targeted Holman with a recall petition but failed to gather the signatures necessary for a recall vote. Holman told me that Unite Norman's goal was to elect a city council that would rubberstamp anything that developers put forward.

In the case of Eagle Cliff, Holman fought to prevent development that could eventually force the city to deal with stormwater damage to private property. Perhaps not coincidentally, just months earlier the city council included more than $100,000 in the annual budget to pair with a FEMA grant to address stormwater flooding issues in The Vineyard development. It was not an easy decision. Flooding in The Vineyard appeared to be a result of poor engineering that did not fully consider the possibility of upstream development. Some councilmembers questioned why public money should be spent to protect private property. They argued that the developer should be held accountable. Residents asked why money was being spent in The Vineyard but not in the numerous other neighborhoods that were struggling with stormwater. However, Holman and others countered that the Vineyard project was part of the city's stormwater masterplan and would improve the entire stormwater system. After hours of debate, the budget passed, but The Vineyard was a reminder that permitting new development could create future expenses for the city if stormwater problems emerged.

In explaining at a city council meeting why Norman residents should contribute money to save private property Holman said, "I don't want us to have that attitude in Norman where we say, well, it's not my problem, and I shouldn't have to deal with it, because as a city we all are paying taxes and we're spending money to address problems all over the city. That's what living in a city is kind of all about, is that we use our collective resources to address the collective problems that we're all having."[28] Holman argued that people are willing to help when they feel a sense of community. The water that floods houses in the Vineyard, or that causes erosion to backyards on Imhoff Creek or in Eagle Cliff, does not come from the impacted properties. It flows from elsewhere in the city. In this sense stormwater is a community problem. This is how cities work. Asphalt, concrete, and roofing bind people into a community that is connected by flows of water.

Members of the Stormwater Citizens Committee, which was tasked with developing the 2019 Stormwater Utility proposal, often responded to my questions about the distribution of the benefits of stormwater infrastructure with appeals to community. One member told me that questions about "what does this do for me" took her by surprise. This was a very common question as they held community meetings to educate people about the SWU, and it led to the decision to include projects in every ward for the 2019 bond. She explained, "This is my community. The community has issues. My neighbor three miles away floods . . . If they need help, I want to help them . . . Having clean water is a community wide issue." An engineer who was a member of the Stormwater Citizens Committee expressed a similar perspective:

> Community is important. Community is how you build a great place to live like Norman . . . One of the things we ran into in all these hearings is that the community is limited to these small groups: 'We're East Norman and this is our concern, We're West Norman and this is our concern . . .' Nobody's looking out for the whole community and saying . . . how can we work together and make this better for everybody.

Councilmember Holman and others argued that Norman residents have a responsibility to solve shared problems because they are a community. Listening to Holman's speech for the first time I felt a rush of emotion. The idea of people coming together to help each other is appealing. People like David Dary face problems with erosion or flooding due to no fault of their own. The problem is too great for individuals to handle without help. The idea that we would do nothing as others' homes are destroyed by stormwater is abhorrent.

Discourses of community, however, hide the essential issue of who is responsible for stormwater runoff. It is true that David Dary did not generate the stormwater that washed away his backyard, but it is also true that not everyone in his watershed community is equally responsible for the stormwater. Abstract conceptions of community obscure the role of developers and commercial interests in generating the stormwater that flooded The Vineyard, damaged the bridge over Imhoff Creek, and eroded backyards in Eagle Cliff. Councilmember Holman invoked the importance of community, but it is not the community that caused flooding and erosion. Creeks connect downstream damage with upstream impervious surfaces. Discourses of community appeal to a powerful desire to help one's neighbors, but they hide corporate welfare in the sense that community assumes that the public will pay for the damage caused by private property.

The community is asked to pay to protect and restore private property from stormwater damage. This same community, however, is unable to regulate the commons of urban creeks and stormwater flows that threaten property throughout the city. In the absence of regulation, owners of expansive impervious surfaces are free to channel water into the commons, and residents must appeal to community to save their property. The FEMA grant that ultimately improved The Vineyard's stormwater detention pond was an individualized, rather than systemic, solution. The same is true of FEMA grants being sought to restore Imhoff Creek. Even successfully blocking development in Eagle Cliff would only have slowed a cycle of growth and destruction. A systemic solution that regulates the commons would have required Eagle Cliff's developers to invest more money in stormwater infrastructure at the time of construction. Increasing the cost of development acts as a soft barrier to growth. Rather than a token $15,000 check, the developers would have been required to invest hundreds of thousands, if not millions, of dollars in infrastructure to absorb stormwater runoff as it makes its way to Bishop Creek. Perhaps the cost would have discouraged Shaz Investments from building a new residential neighborhood. More likely, the cost would cut into Shaz's profits, or would have been passed on to homebuyers. In any case, rather than relying on a sense of shared community to pay for solutions, protecting the commons by paying the true cost of development at the time of construction would have disincentivized certain types of growth, perhaps limiting the creation of new impervious surfaces. Developers often push against this possibility. Rather than investing in infrastructure, it is more cost effective to hire an attorney who will lobby the city council to permit new construction. If that fails, a lawsuit is one more option to continue nourishing the growth that is necessary for profits.

Community, Nimbyism, and the Commons

The relationship between community, responsibility, and the commons is not unique to stormwater and creeks. Forests and aquifers, for example, are often shared commons that some profit from far more than others. To claim that it is the community's responsibility to maintain the commons ignores vast differences in use. Attention to creeks helps assess responsibility and the relationship between use of the commons and its depletion. The same is true for other commons—the more we use multiple methods to explore forests and aquifers, the better we understand how all community members do not have an equal responsibility for the commons' preservation. Those who profit from the commons have a particular responsibility for its maintenance. References to an abstract community obscure this responsibility and the regulations needed to preserve the commons.

In the absence of regulating the commons, community members are left to fight to preserve their own backyards, a process that is rooted in privilege. David Dary spent years engaging in a particular form of nimbyism to save his backyard from Imhoff Creek.[29] Dary was saying "Not in my backyard" to the stormwater that runs off impervious surfaces to erode backyards and flood houses. There were perhaps two ways to save David Dary's backyard. One was to address the system causing the problem, in this case excessive stormwater runoff from the city's ever-expanding impervious surfaces. The second was to build infrastructure around the yard to protect it from increased stormwater flows. The latter option is a classic form of nimbyism—protecting property without addressing underlying factors behind environmental degradation. The systemic approach differs because it protects everyone's backyard. Nimbyism and the power to protect one's property are inseparable from citizenship. Those who possess an expansive form of substantive citizenship have a greater likelihood of saving their backyards.

There are many reasons why the City of Norman applied for a FEMA grant to complete the Vineyard project, but it is highly unlikely that this project would have been completed without the tireless efforts of a former city council member who lived in the neighborhood.[30] It's unlikely the city council would have voted to prevent the Eagle Cliff development without expert presentations like Dr. Derek Rosendahl's. Even with David Dary, the former head of OU's School of Journalism, working on the case, little was done about the erosion in backyards along Imhoff Creek. Dary was, however, appointed to a committee that evaluated engineering proposals for creek restoration, and in 2021 the City of Norman began the process of applying for millions of dollars in grants to prevent the backyards of Dary's neighbors from suffering further damage. In practice, certain people, often relatively affluent white men like me, repeatedly exercise their power to save their homes and backyards. They exercise this privilege in the face of the even greater power of developers who can invest millions in hiring attorneys to fight not just a battle, but the long war to open land for development. The Eagle Cliff case was a lesson in different levels of substantive citizenship. Rosendahl and the Eagle Cliff Home Owners Association won a battle, but ultimately lost the war against developers and their attorneys.

Developers often cry out that nimbyism stands in the way of growth. Norman mayor Larry Heikkila (2022–2025) called the opposition to the Eagle Cliff development a case of "mob rule." Heikkila told me that the loudest and most emotional voices convinced the city council to ignore the expertise of city staff and reject plans to expand the development. The problem of nimbyism, however, is not that it sometimes slows growth, but rather that it depends on the expansive substantive citizenship of the few. I firmly believe that those impacted by a project should have a voice in its planning, but at the same time nimbyism often facilitates growth's self-destructive consequences. Nimbyism means carving out isolated spaces of protection from climate change and growth that do little to address broader processes of destruction, like eutrophication. A false ideology of community facilitates rather than slows this process. Just as the City of Norman spent millions of dollars removing the taste of economic growth from its drinking water while doing little to prevent the destruction of Lake Thunderbird, appeals to community mask self-destructive growth. Neighborhoods come together when they have a common threat, but that communal desire to improve the city evaporates when the threat disappears. If my backyard can be saved, the drinking water tastes fine, and the roads don't flood, I can look the other way and ignore what is happening around me.

Together with appeals to an abstract sense of community, nimbyism obscures responsibility for the destruction of the commons. Those who own greater amounts of impervious surfaces have greater responsibility for the destructive consequences of stormwater. To claim that it is the community's responsibility to address stormwater problems hides this fact and implicitly subsidizes further growth. Using the privilege of expansive substantive citizenship to protect one's property does the same. Spending time with urban creeks helps reverse this process by helping to see the city differently. Creeks are a shared resource, but not everyone uses them equally. Creeks highlight connections between asphalt parking lots and backyards located miles downstream. When we see creeks, we also see that some people have greater responsibility for self-devouring growth than others. It is only by recognizing this dynamic and regulating creeks accordingly that an equitable community can be formed, and the tragedy of the commons avoided.

4 Facebook, Stormwater, and Digital Eutrophication

"BAN THE WORD IMPERVIOUS."[1] "I have learned to hate the word impervious."[2] Comments like these were common in Facebook discussions of Norman's stormwater infrastructure policy in 2016. Impervious surfaces were the basis for fees intended to fund a stormwater utility (SWU). The 2016 SWU plan developed under Mayor Cindy Rosenthal (2009–2016) would have charged property owners a monthly fee of $1.25 per one thousand feet of impervious surfaces plus a $1 management fee. More than 80 percent of property owners would have paid less than $9 per month.[3] Fees would have funded street sweepers, increased monitoring of construction sites, and maintenance of stormwater pipelines, creeks, and channels.[4] This was not a nimbyist proposal. Rather, it would have regulated the commons to help everyone's backyard. The 2016 SWU would not have covered major projects like the restoration of Imhoff Creek, but it would have addressed some of the fundamental causes of flooding and erosion. It would have created systemic financial incentives to limit impervious surfaces, reduced the damage from stormwater runoff, and been a step toward undoing the self-destructive tendencies of growth.

Norman is the largest city in Oklahoma without a dedicated utility to fund the maintenance of stormwater infrastructure. In most cities, city staff would simply design and implement a stormwater utility, but as the preceding chapter made clear, because of Norman's law to vote on any increases in utility fees, the seemingly mundane issues of stormwater runoff and impervious surfaces have been topics of intense debate. The 2016 SWU proposal faced immediate resistance from the conspiracy of developers. Car lots, big box stores, and storage rental units are made almost entirely of impervious surfaces. SWU fees would have been quite low for residents, but not so for the businesses that are nothing but parking lots and roofs. They would have paid hundreds or even thousands of dollars per month. Car dealers complained that they had already spent hundreds of thousands of dollars to build detention ponds that slow the rate of stormwater runoff.[5] Owners of car lots and storage unit rentals invested in a major campaign, filling mailboxes with fliers urging a "no" vote.[6] The Norman Chamber of Commerce opposed the SWU, the first time the chamber had opposed a City of Norman ballot measure proposal in five years.[7] The editorial board of the *Norman Transcript* also opposed the SWU, arguing that the plan was rushed, citing a number of flaws in relation to the crediting process for mitigating stormwater runoff, and urging the city council to provide caps on payments for businesses.[8] The "no" votes won by a margin of nearly seventy to thirty.

When I asked city leaders why the 2016 SWU plan failed, many blamed Facebook. In many ways the 2016 SWU was another battle over growth and infrastructure, but this time was different. Although both sides published editorials in the *Norman Transcript*, the real battles were fought on public Facebook pages devoted to each of Norman's eight wards. City leaders' remarks about the role of Facebook in local politics were consistently derisive. "Ward pages are tearing the city apart," claimed Amanda Nairn, cochair of the Stormwater Citizens Committee (SCC). A different Stormwater Citizens Committee member told me, "I don't use Facebook, I despise it." Another committee member simply stated that social media is the devil. Mayor Lynn Miller (2016–2019) argued that the Facebook ward pages are full of misinformation, people can say whatever they want, and it "doesn't matter how many martinis you've had that night, or what you've smoked." Mayor Breea Clark (2019–2022) noted that "discourse online has gotten incredibly negative, and it's not productive," and this was before the summer of 2020 when Mayor Clark was the target of death threats on Facebook. These critiques come from across the political spectrum. Harold Heiple told me, "I've never been on Facebook . . . Never will be. You've got no control over the truth. What can you do when someone gets on there and just slanders the hell out of you?" Still, disdain for Facebook does not mean that city councilmembers did not use it to engage with Norman residents. Particularly in 2016 many engaged extensively, often debating each other on Facebook. Each of Norman's ward pages had at least two thousand members, making them excellent sites for connecting with Norman residents.

Where rhetorical battles over water infrastructure in the 1970s largely took place in the editorial section of the *Norman Transcript*, Facebook was the battleground for the stormwater utility votes in 2016 and 2019. Andy Rieger, editor of the *Norman Transcript* from 1995–2015, told me that in 2020 the staff at the newspaper was down to about half of the twenty-two employees who were on hand when he started as editor. Despite a growing population, subscribers decreased from around twenty thousand in 1995 to six thousand in 2022. Like many local papers, the *Transcript* is now owned by a national media company. The paper is no longer printed on Monday and Tuesday, and in 2022 the entire staff that wrote and produced the paper comprised only nine people.[9] Rieger told me that the key difference between social media and "legacy media," like daily newspapers, is that people who post on social media are not trained as journalists. They do not fact check their information and they do not tell both sides of a story. This creates an overwhelming atmosphere of mistrust. People trust little of what they read on Facebook, and yet they continue to rely on Facebook for information. Truth becomes a battle.

In researching the debates over water utilities in the 1970s, I turned primarily to the *Norman Transcript*. In a given week, the paper carried perhaps five articles and two or three letters to the editor on the topic. Although the readership declined, the *Transcript* offered a similar mix of articles and letters to the editor in relation to the stormwater debates of 2016 and 2019. This discussion was dwarfed by the debates on Facebook ward pages. Each ward page contains hundreds of posts on the topic. A single post could generate thousands of words in responses and comments, making ward pages ideal spaces to explore the complex intersection between trust in government and water infrastructure.

In the United States, media consumption has not only shifted from local newspapers to social media. As local newspapers have withered and disappeared, Americans have increasingly consumed their news from national sources like Fox News, CNN, and the *New York Times*, which, like social media companies, are owned by massive corporate entities.[10] As someone who probably gets far too much of his news from the *New York Times*, I have observed patterns in how writers on the center-left think about social media and truth. First, they describe the collapse of journalism to demonstrate that in the absence of shared sources of trusted information people embrace misinformation. For example, in a 2022 *New York Times* opinion piece, Richard Hasen, a professor of law and political science, called social media "cheap speech." He argued that even with high levels of political polarization, the January 6, 2021, insurrection would not have happened with the information technology of the 1950s. Local newspapers would have mediated and critiqued the more than four hundred tweets Donald Trump used to spread misinformation in the weeks following the 2020 presidential election.[11] Second, commentators discuss social media algorithms and the creation of information bubbles that support political polarization. Algorithms that prioritize conflict create another kind of self-devouring growth. Social media companies profit from conflict, and in the process produce a divided society.[12]

Third, they note the rise of social isolation in the United States. Polarization and social isolation create a desire for consistent political narratives, in which one's side is always right. One of my favorite *New York Times* opinion writers, Michelle Goldberg, has written about the relationship between social isolation and engagement with mass movements. Like many *Times* writers, Goldberg quoted extensively from Hannah Arendt's *The Origins of Totalitarianism*. She cited research showing that 17 percent of Americans do not have a single person they talk with about important issues and concerns, and these people were significantly more likely to support Donald Trump and buy into QAnon type conspiracy theories.[13] The *New York Times* has extended its reach to cover news in small towns that are far from New York City. A lengthy 2021 article on Enid, Oklahoma (population fifty thousand), noted social science research on isolation and loneliness in relation to the Enid Freedom Fighters movement that fought mask mandates and recalled city councilors.[14] Yuval Noah Harari, historian and author of the best-selling *Sapiens*, wrote in the *Times* that conspiracy theories can be a source of comfort in an increasingly chaotic world. They provide the illusion that one can easily understand and explain the complex events unfolding around them.[15] Finally, these kinds of articles discuss how these dynamics create a cycle in which people are increasingly likely to consume and share disinformation on social media to gain approval from their likeminded friends and followers.[16]

At first glance this narrative appears to describe the case of the 2016 stormwater proposal. Opposition to the 2016 SWU was strongest in Norman's mostly rural Ward 5, which is also one of the most politically conservative areas of the city. "It's a group of people who votes against their better interests often," a former councilmember told me about Ward 5. Others who participated in the 2016 stormwater debates were dismissive of rural residents' concerns. They argued that Ward 5 residents' worries about high SWU fees were trivial and that they had been influenced by social media misinformation and ad campaigns financed by car dealers and big box stores. From this perspective, rural residents were pawns in the developers' conspiracy to avoid paying for the costs of their impervious surfaces.

This line of thinking, however, is precisely why rural residents were alienated from city governance. Why trust a system that assumes you are easily manipulated and cannot act in your own interests? When the system is failing you, and you are told that your concerns are meaningless, it makes sense to look for leadership from political outsiders. "Lecturing us like children did not help their [SWU advocates] case much," a Ward 5 Facebook participant commented after the 2016 SWU proposal was voted down.[17] In many ways Ward 5's relationship with Norman's historic urban core mirrors the urban/rural political divide in the United States.

A deep dive into Norman's Facebook ward pages demonstrates that social media is not always "cheap speech." There was misinformation, to be sure, but there were also highly complex debates over stormwater infrastructure. There were talented communicators from across the political spectrum who used extensive research to support their arguments. In many ways Facebook was a site where Norman residents struggled to attain a more expansive form of citizenship by shaping policy and influencing the votes of others.

Ward pages were neither social bubbles nor digital information utopias in which the free exchange of ideas somehow allowed truth to emerge. The popularity of social media demonstrates a deep hunger for communication and connection, but social media platforms like Facebook are structured by their owners' desires for ever increasing profits. Facebook and X are owned by some of the wealthiest and most powerful people in the world. They are highly problematic, but at the time of my research Americans had few other options for mass communication. As an information ecosystem, Facebook was something like a channelized creek that confines high volumes of water to a narrow space to create a fast moving and destructive stream. Facebook channeled huge amounts of discourse into a constrictive digital environment. But just as surprising forms of life emerge from the cracks of concrete lined creeks, Facebook ward pages also produced new and unexpected interactions.

Well-funded opposition from the business and development community was not the only factor behind the 2016 SWU's failure. Debates on Facebook ward pages reveal that the 2016 SWU failed in part because it marginalized the perspectives of Norman's rural residents. A seemingly systemic solution to the problems of growth and stormwater created its own opposition by denying rural perspectives. At the same time, social media induced a kind of information overload in which distinguishing truth from falsehood was increasingly difficult. Like most people in the United States, Norman residents were left wading through a sea of information that ultimately produced mistrust in expertise and governance. This was a form of digital eutrophication. Facebook nourished an explosive growth of discourse that eventually suffocated itself, leaving most Norman residents with a simple response to new ideas and policies—"No."

"Don't Tell Me like U Know What I Have Been through or Have Bc U Dont!!!"

In 2016 Ted Cruz and Bernie Sanders were the winners of the U.S. president primaries in Oklahoma, but in Norman political discussions were centered on local issues, particularly the proposal for a stormwater utility. Norman's ward pages were filled with lively debates about how best to fund this new utility. At that time, it was common for the mayor and city councilmembers to engage in Facebook arguments, often debating each other. The first Facebook ward page was created in 2012 for Norman's Ward 4 by its city councilmember. Initially it was common for a ward's city councilmember to administer its Facebook page and approve or deny posts. This practice more or less ended after a councilmember was sued in 2019 for allegedly censoring political commentary on a Facebook ward page.[18]

Mistrust of government is perhaps most acute in Ward 5. Geographically, Ward 5 encompasses nearly all of the east half of Norman. It is predominantly rural and stretches from new housing developments just a couple miles east of downtown all the way past Lake Thunderbird. Ward 5 encompasses much of the area that the city annexed more than fifty years ago as administrators sought to gain control over the Lake Thunderbird watershed. When its residents are not talking politics on Facebook, they're often posting that someone's dogs, hogs, goats, or cattle are loose.

Although the 2016 stormwater utility plan had a certain elegance in connecting fees with impervious surfaces and responsibility for stormwater runoff, it drew immediate backlash. Yes, water runs off impervious surfaces, but what about packed dirt versus a grassy lawn? Surely runoff levels will be different. My roof is impervious to water, but what if I surround my house with rain barrels and water gardens? What about rural Norman where houses are surrounded by acres of forest and pasture? There are impervious surfaces in rural Norman, but their runoff is likely to be absorbed locally. It seemed that particularly for rural residents, measuring impervious surfaces was too simplistic. In their view, the 2016 SWU was a solution created by those who did not understand the lifestyles of their neighbors. Although the city promised to provide credits for rural landowners and landscaping that absorbs stormwater, the specific method of offering credits was never articulated. Don't worry, city officials said, trust us, we'll find a solution. We can measure impervious surfaces and account for all these variations. We have good engineers; we can solve this problem through better measurements. But why should rural Norman residents trust the same people who clearly discounted their needs in developing this plan?

Opposition from Ward 5 was a key reason the 2016 SWU was voted down. At that time, Ward 5 did not typically have high participation in municipal elections. In the 2016 SWU vote, however, Ward 5 residents made up more than 3,300 of a total 16,181 voters, and they voted "no" on the SWU by a margin of 86 to 14. The total number of voters was twice the amount of those who had participated in recent municipal elections.[19] Ward 5 residents complained that although they may own large amounts of impervious surfaces, they also own woodlands and pasture that absorb runoff. Their runoff does not stress the system in the same way as that of urban residents. Rural residents often have barns, gravel roads, and other structures that under the 2016 proposal would have led to SWU bills of over $20 per month, far more than the $6–7 per month estimated for the typical Norman household.

Debates over impervious surfaces repeatedly played out on Norman's Facebook Ward pages. The exchange below is excerpted from a Ward 5 Facebook discussion that involved around a dozen participants.[20] There were hundreds of similar discussions in the lead up to the 2016 SWU vote. I have identified the two participants in this exchange based on their Facebook profile pic. Black Cat's profile pic is the black cat ("Sabo-Tabby") with claws bared associated with the Industrial Workers of the World. Red Stater's pic is an election map of the central United States centered on Oklahoma, with all counties that voted Republican shaded red. Every county in Oklahoma is red. Most users of Facebook ward pages use their real names and in many cases their accounts are public, making it possible for other users to investigate who they are engaging with. During heated debates, participants sometimes dig through their adversary's Facebook page for information to be used in personal attacks.

> Red Stater: The amount of impervious surface amounts to 8% of my rural acreage, while the same land area in the high-density city core has five to six times that much impervious surface, at least, yet I will pay more than twice what city residents pay on average. Rationalize that as being land-rich, dismiss it as dilution credit, or what-have-you, but I don't see that as equitable, especially considering how my area will enjoy precious little benefit from the new utility.
>
> Black Cat: Red Stater—how are you counting?! Everyone pays the same rate for impervious surface . . . city or country. A city area with 5–6

times the impervious area would pay 5–6 times the fee . . . that is how constant rates work. Calling what you want a dilution credit isn't dismissive—it is DESCRIPTIVE. You want a lower fee not b/c you are creating less runoff; you are claiming to contain your own runoff w/ undeveloped land. That just IS a dilution credit. You are free to argue for that, but don't deny what it is.

Black Cat: Red Stater—you pay more because you have more impervious surface. Why is this hard? If you have a surface—w/ concrete, asphalt, or even most gravel then water runs off it. That's impervious . . .

Red Stater: My rural property has a much higher ratio (12:1) of permeable to impervious surface than high-density urban property (1:1), with a much higher capacity to absorb runoff before it leaves my property and enters the watershed. Why is this so hard to grasp, Black Cat?

After the election of Donald Trump as U.S. president in 2016, there was a great deal of chatter about social media and "bubbles," based on the idea that Facebook algorithms filtered content so that users were likely to see posts that fit with their worldviews. This was decidedly not the case with Norman's ward pages. Although particular ward pages were often more friendly towards one end of the political spectrum than the other, a wide range of viewpoints were present. On Facebook ward pages opposing views collided in ways that were unlikely to happen outside of social media.

The conflict between rural and urban residents was fundamentally about fairness. Urban residents like Black Cat claimed it was unfair for rural landowners to avoid paying for their impervious surfaces, while rural Ward 5 residents claimed it was unfair to be charged for runoff that is mitigated by their land. They were debating the absorption of impervious surfaces in relation to lawns, forests, and fields. These detailed policy-based Facebook discussions defy stereotypes of social media as bubbles. Participants explored relative rates of impervious surface coverage and asked if one part of the city would subsidize the other through stormwater payment rates. The discussion was decidedly nonpartisan.

But perhaps because of the discussion's complexity, the conversation quickly broke down. The dispute over the technical dynamics surrounding the relationship between pervious and impervious surfaces continued, but both parties became frustrated with their inability to convince the other, and the conversation shifted. Red Stater accused Black Cat of wanting to "outlaw private property" and made a tangential, but interesting, claim that "Lake Thundermud" was destined to run into problems based on the nature of its primary tributary, the Little River. Black Cat attributed an "it-is-mine-so-I-can-degrade-it-if-I-want position" position to Red Stater. The debate had been centered on relative rates of impervious and pervious surfaces, but Black Cat and Red Stater moved from technical questions to ideology.

For fans of personal attacks, this is where the conversation gets fun. Red Stater offered a mild dig, which Black Cat turned to his advantage by claiming it was evidence that Red Stater had no argument beyond personal insults. Red Stater offered a similar rhetorical flourish, accusing Black Cat of putting words in his opponents' mouths. Both Black Cat and Red Stater are confident posters who are skilled in using their opponent's words against them. The conversation finally shifted to Thomas Aquinas, socialism, and property rights—topics only abstractly related to the SWU issue.

Like much of Facebook discourse, the exchanges were highly performative. Interesting ideas were exchanged regarding impervious surfaces and runoff, but they were mixed with insults and references to political ideology, which ensured that the murky truth regarding rural runoff remained secondary to affective positioning. Among other things, Black Cat and Red Stater were producing a valuable product for Facebook. It is unlikely that Facebook would have attracted so many users without such entertaining performances. Although Norman's ward pages each usually had more than two thousand members, most members offered only an occasional comment or silently observed. A few prolific and skilled posters like Black Cat and Red Stater engaged others and attracted an audience. Around 2016 Facebook would award these posters with a coffee cup badge that signified their status as "conversation starters." They were nourishing the discourse that Facebook depended on for growth.

"Conversation starter" posters did more than generate profits for Facebook. They engaged in a kind of play; there is pleasure in debating political opponents.[21] There is also a certain joy in consuming the back-and-forth. The thousands of Norman residents who followed the Facebook ward pages came to know these prolific participants. Depending on one's political persuasion some were heroes and others were villains, public personalities who lived in close proximity but were best known digitally by their profile names and pics. The conversation between Red Stater and Black Cat may not have changed minds about the SWU, but it offered a uniquely local form of entertainment. At least briefly, Facebook functioned as a digital political salon that corresponded with geography.

Facebook debates connected local issues with national politics and broader ideologies. Most readers of Facebook ward pages did not have strong opinions about the implications of the balance between pervious and impervious surfaces for rainwater absorption. They did, however, have entrenched opinions about socialism and the rights of property owners. Truth claims produced through Facebook were based on creating a consistent and coherent alignment of beliefs. Debates like the one between Red Stater and Black Cat not only entertained, they allowed readers to sort policies based on political affiliation. The better policy was the one that the reader's team supported. Even when bubbles were broken down, the nature of Facebook discourse continually sorted people into opposing camps. Once debates on Facebook moved from impervious surfaces to political ideology it was nearly impossible to reverse the direction. The wave of information was too much. In 2020 COVID-19 took these divisions to another level. Whether to vaccinate, wear a mask, open schools, or close bars became questions of political affiliation, and Facebook allowed participants to know exactly which set of policies are consistent with their political ideology.[22]

I am one of those people with a perhaps irrational dislike for Facebook and other forms of social media. I have never had a Facebook account or participated in any other form of social media, aside from group texts. I am far too insecure to expose my thoughts and experiences on social media to unknown audiences. I knew that Facebook was a crucial site for political discourse in Norman, and I initially hired an undergraduate student to help me sort through the ward pages. To be honest, I was a little afraid to wade into what I assumed was an extremely toxic environment. My research assistant got me started, but soon it was necessary for me to dive in and explore on my own. I still do not have a Facebook account, but Norman's ward pages are open to the public so I was able to conduct this research without any barriers.

Facebook is a powerful affective experience. I found myself repeatedly returning to the ward pages in search of something new. It's amazing how fast the time passed as I read, searching for passionate bickering or one more clever takedown. The posts were occasionally logical but often chaotic; tone is as important as content. Ideas and good information coexist with lies and rants. My eyes dry out, the screen and mind lock. When I finally force myself to pull away, I feel unwell. Particularly during the summer of 2020, reading debates over COVID-19 and race and policing was physically exhausting. Yet, like a drug, Facebook pulled me back despite the hangovers.

Truth is constructed through engagement with Facebook, not just in connecting policies with political ideologies but through rhetorical style. The excerpt below also comes from the Ward 5 Facebook page.[23] Black Cat was once again advancing claims that high levels of pervious surfaces do not reduce the damage done by impervious surfaces. In this case he was debating the owner of a small cattle ranch.

> Black Cat: Cattle Rancher—The bill isn't for a service to *you*—it is to pay for the public damage your property does to others. The silt from your gulley ended up in everyone's water. You *should* care about damage to the Lake, but you don't get to do damage to a common resource just b/c you don't. Right now, the citizens of Norman are subsidizing your cattle operation by allowing you to discharge your stormwater for free.
>
> Cattle Rancher: Damed [*sic*] if I don't work to keep it from containing the storm water runoff that's all I do!!!! Don't tell me what I have

> or haven't done ur not here sweating ur ass off working 15 hour days on a tractor or bulldozer . . . don't tell me what I have bleed and cried over as I desperately held onto my land from falling into the ravine . . . so don't tell me like u know what I have been through or have bc u dont!!!

Once again, Facebook was producing truth, but not through the exchange of ideas. In this case truth was produced through affect. Cattle Rancher connected her experiences working the land with the repeated phrase, "don't tell me . . ." that directly rejects expertise. Personal experience brought knowledge and the right to speak, and Black Cat had no right to tell Cattle Rancher how to manage her land.

In contrast to Red Stater and Black Cat, Cattle Rancher writes in a voice that would have been out of place in the editorial pages of the *Norman Transcript*. This is a rhetorical style that is specifically suited for Facebook's informational ecosystem. It is not a language of expertise. Cattle Rancher emphasizes her experience and work on the land as truth—tears, blood, and sweat that have been spilled on the land are directly opposed to Black Cat's truth claims. Black Cat advances claims based on abstract logic that applies regardless of the actual conditions on the ground. Black Cat told Red Stater, "Your remaining pervious surface is worse off b/c of your impervious surface—that is just the science of the matter." Black Cat implied that he knew what is happening on the rancher's land based on a universally applicable relationship between impervious and pervious surfaces. Science tells us that impervious surfaces always damage pervious surfaces, but the cattle rancher's experiences tell her something else.[24]

Readers of the Ward 5 Facebook page were confronted with a conflict that reaffirmed a popular sentiment among rural Normanites that those in the urban core use city government to impose their beliefs, despite having little understanding of rural lifestyles.[25] Truth in this case depends on stylistic preferences. Those who prefer appeals to generalizable science will accept Black Cat's truth regarding stormwater runoff. Those who trust in personal experience will side with Cattle Rancher on stormwater policy. For Ward 5 residents who embrace a rural lifestyle, the choice is easy. Cattle Rancher's investment of blood, sweat, and tears in the land is evidence of shared understandings of rural life and an ability to generate true knowledge about the relationship between earth and water. To oppose Black Cat and the 2016 SWU was to reject the elite expertise that Ward 5 residents often associated with the city government. Facebook debates reproduced a deep distrust of institutions, and in this case, institutions were closely connected with water infrastructure.

Only Ward 4, Mayor Rosenthal's home ward, voted in support of the 2016 SWU. Ward 4 is also where I live. It is located near the University of Oklahoma where Rosenthal was a professor, and it is one of the most politically liberal of Norman's wards. Perhaps this was the one neighborhood that was primed to trust Rosenthal's leadership. Indeed, I voted "yes" on the 2016 SWU without thoroughly investigating the issue. This is where Facebook has the power to surprise. I did not follow the Facebook SWU debates in 2016. Perhaps if I had, narratives like Cattle Rancher's would have opened new perspectives and helped me see beyond the position of my political team.

This is the central challenge of governance in an era of distrust and social media. Basing a stormwater fee on ownership of impervious surfaces is a logical method for directly confronting the self-destructive qualities of growth. To ignore the impacts of impervious surfaces is to effectively provide public subsidies for the big box stores that send runoff from their massive parking lots and roofs into the city's creeks. For voters in rural Norman, however, appeals to fairness and equity did not ring true. Rural voters were not advocating payment caps for businesses. They wanted a plan that reflected the realities of a rural environment. In Facebook discussions, Ward 5 residents made it clear that they know their environment. They were not going to be told what is best for them by city administrators and university professors. Arguments about fairness and responsibility for stormwater runoff lost their legitimacy when the plan was clearly unfair to rural residents. A systemic solution to the problems of growth failed in part because it was biased against rural lifestyles. Rather than connecting urban growth with stormwater damage, through Facebook discussions *impervious surfaces* came to signify a technocratic elitism that ignores local experience.

Taking a Drive in Ward 5

I do not feel at home in rural Norman. I have walked or biked nearly every block of Norman's central urban core. I have stories about so many places in urban Norman, but very little connection to rural Norman. Outside of Lake Thunderbird State Park, there is almost no public space in rural Norman. A proposal to develop a public trail along the Little River was shot down by neighbors who were concerned that hikers would face many unexpected dangers—everything from ticks to sex offenders.[26] Over the years I've visited a few friends who live in rural Norman, but aside from this, I have encountered rural Norman largely within the confines of my car. For me, a car limits my connection with a place. The speed is too fast, I am distracted by driving, my mind is somewhere else, and I miss all the details that make a place special. I don't feel like I know a place unless I have walked or biked it. But sometimes I will drive just for the sake of driving, without a destination in mind, to soak up a bit of rural Norman.

On a hot May afternoon, I did my best to find roads that would allow me to follow the Little River as it flows east to Lake Thunderbird. I started near the Hollywood Corners Bar and Grill, a historic live music venue that was owned by the late country music star Toby Keith. From there I drove east occasionally catching glimpses of the river, a brown muddy stream bordered by red banks and lush green trees. May is the wettest month of the year in Norman. With all the rain and sunshine, you can almost watch the plants grow. Few residences are visible along the road, it's mostly pasture and clusters of forest near the river. Eventually, as I made my way south and east again, gradually driving toward the lake, I found myself at an old cemetery. The sign near the gate said Falls Cemetery, 1900. My map told me that if I were to push through the brushy forest behind the cemetery for a few minutes I would reach the inlet where the Little River empties into Lake Thunderbird. I was excited to find a public space where I could get out and walk around. The patchy grass was mowed to ankle height and a few mature cedars and oaks offered shade from the blazing sun. There were maybe 150 graves. In some cases, multiple generations of the same family are buried side by side. Most passed away in the early twentieth century, but some died more recently. There are even headstones for people who are still alive. These planners already have a plot and headstone ready, making certain that Falls Cemetery will be their resting place. Later, a bit of internet research revealed that there was once a Falls School across from the cemetery.

The cemetery was a reminder that there are people who have a connection to rural Norman that I cannot fully comprehend: not just the families who have been here for generations, but those who have chosen to make this place their home in more recent years. For the most part my encounters with the residents of Ward 5 and rural Norman are limited to the narrow digital window that is Facebook. A Ward 5 resident posts a photo of a spectacular sunset captioned, "for all the crap Ward 5 goes through you don't get this in the city."[27] Around a dozen others quickly share similar photos. The post communicates a sense of grievance and connection to place. It's not clear specifically what crap Ward 5 goes through, but there is a strong feeling among its residents that they have been slighted or mistreated by city government. The rewards of living in rural Norman are based in qualities like a sunset that is not hidden by neighboring buildings, ample space for domestic animals, and a sense of privacy.

I grew up in a rural area like this, also outside of a college town, and near a large reservoir. Unlike Norman, the rural area where I was raised was not incorporated into the city—Eugene, Oregon. My family relied on well water and a septic tank, and for many years we hauled our trash to the dump. As children, my friends and I spent our days wandering through fields and forests. I rode the school bus into Eugene and I always felt different from the kids who could walk home from school on sidewalks. Although much of my extended family lived in this rural area, there was a certain loneliness in the distance from other kids. But that loneliness was balanced with pleasures like an unobstructed view of the sky. My parents still live in my childhood home, and when I visit, I never miss the opportunity to watch the sun disappear behind the hills in the west.

These subtle feelings of place and home divide Norman. Differences such as these are very difficult to communicate through a medium like Facebook. The lack of a shared environment and sense of home is one more factor that generates mistrust.

Conspiracy, Mistrust, and the 2019 SWU Proposal

Days before the 2016 SWU vote Cindy Rosenthal, who had just completed her second full term as mayor, published a letter in the *Norman Transcript*: "Let's be honest: the opponents want caps and lower rates for businesses that profit from large amounts of impervious surfaces and fewer regulatory requirements on land development practices. If these businesses get caps as the *Transcript* suggests, who will make up for subsidizing large businesses? The answer is clear—homeowners and small businesses . . . If this plan fails, you can be certain that the next proposal will not be as fair as this one."[28] Rosenthal had been mayor for seven years, but she was articulating something like the conspiracy of developers—large businesses were working to oppose the 2016 SWU and the common good, and they were aided in this effort by the *Norman Transcript*. This was a view held by many 2016 SWU proponents.

Mayor Rosenthal's predictions were in many ways correct. Rosenthal's term ended a few weeks before the 2016 SWU vote, and she was replaced by Ward 5's councilmember, Lynne Miller. Mayor Miller supported the 2016 SWU but also felt that it was important to involve the business community in formulating a new stormwater plan. She appointed a stormwater citizens committee (SCC), to be cochaired by Andy Shearer, who was a former president of the Norman Chamber of Commerce, and Amanda Nairn, an advocate of the 2016 SWU and longtime volunteer for different local water related initiatives. Some Norman residents expressed dismay that the SCC included several real estate developers, engineers, and attorneys. Based on the SCC's recommendations, Norman's City Council ultimately developed a 2019 plan for a tiered system with rates increasing in relation to impervious surfaces, but with caps for businesses and residences and a reduction in fees for rural properties with acreage. Although the Norman Chamber of Commerce did support the 2019 plan, it did not actively campaign for it. Many Norman residents who supported the 2016 plan opposed the 2019 version. They argued that the 2019 plan was unfair because it did not adequately charge owners of large houses and businesses for their contributions to the city's stormwater problems and did not incentivize limiting impervious surfaces.

Discussions on Facebook ward pages played a key role in building mistrust and shaping truth in this case as well. Black Cat and others advanced the idea that the 2019 SWU privileged commercial interests. A former city councilmember, Ed Crocker, was active on Facebook and published multiple *Norman Transcript* editorials claiming that SWU funds would be secretly used to support commercial development in Norman.[29] Members of the SCC told me that vocal opposition from Crocker and others was a key reason the 2019 SWU failed. Opposition from rural residents was another factor. Under the 2019 proposal, rural residents would pay a maximum of only $6 per month, but many were still not convinced. A bad taste lingered from the 2016 proposal, and the 2019 plan was defeated 60 to 40. Turnout in Ward 5 was lower than in 2016, but there the proposal was voted down by the same overwhelming 85 to 15 margin. Mistrust generated by perceptions of inequity, financial mismanagement, and a history of exclusion from policymaking doomed the popular support that was needed to create an SWU.

Facebook was still a place for Norman residents to engage directly with those at the center of local policy making and build more expansive forms of citizenship. By 2019, however, the tenor of Facebook discussions had shifted. City councilmembers still occasionally weighed in but rarely engaged extensively. The joy and creativity found in many of the 2016 debates had faded. Rather, in 2019 we see the beginning of digital eutrophication. Cycles of discourse that produce more and more debate consumed the oxygen within the Facebook ecosystem and left participants exhausted, treading water in a digital dead zone filled with conspiracy, doubt, and the simple statement of "No."

Perhaps the most frequent and vocal critic of the 2019 SWU was a Facebook participant who I call "MAGA Hat" based on his profile pic.[30] In April 2019 MAGA Hat posted on the Ward 5 Facebook page:

> In 2016, the CON [City of Norman] sent out flyers telling us all our municipal water at Lake Thunderbird was being polluted by stormwater runoff.
>
> LIES . . .

In 2017, the CON paid a consultant to build an "education" narrative and "advertising" (i.e., propaganda) campaign to convince Norman voters our drinking water quality is being affected by stormwater runoff.

LIES . . .

The CON is trying to convince citizens that current ODEQ & EPA fines are going to bamkrupt [*sic*] the city if "we don't act now." Yet, they provide ZERO scientic data to justify their scare tactics.

LIES . . .

Chlorophyll a is not a drinking water pollutant.

LIES . . .

The CON is promoting creek "liners" (i.e., concrete waterways) as being the solution. In fact, this practice is an environmental disaster for riparian areas.

LIES . . .[31]

MAGA Hat was a middle-aged professional male, a former U.S. marine, and someone with a passion for stormwater. I occasionally saw him post about other issues, but he was particularly active in the 2019 stormwater debates. He usually posted on the Ward 5 page, but his comments were everywhere. He continually attacked the City of Norman for spreading what he characterized as lies, and he called the stormwater utility a hoax intended to provide the city with a slush fund that could be spent according to the city council's whims. The volume and frequency of his attacks led to responses from multiple city council members, the mayor, and members of the SCC. Although it is difficult to gauge the influence of Facebook posts, Norman residents often responded positively to MAGA Hat, thanking him for sharing valuable information, for example, "I came to the ward 5 page specifically looking for concise information about the fine that is being threatened, and you more than provided that and more. Good on you!"[32] Perhaps twenty years ago people would have searched for reliable information in the local newspaper, but in 2019 they turned to Facebook ward pages.

MAGA Hat also attracted criticism. His attack of "LIES," quoted above, was a response to critiques from Ward 5's council member and one of Ward

5's representatives on the SCC. Amanda Nairn, cochair of the SCC, joined the discussion in response to further attacks on the committee. Nairn began, "While I usually would not participate in such a destructive conversation because it is not productive, there are many of your comments that are simply false." She then went on to provide a point-by-point refutation of MAGA Hat. Nairn got into the weeds of stormwater infrastructure, pollution, and mitigation strategies. She explained that Lake Thunderbird is impacted by "NON point source discharge"—water that moves through streams and creeks and picks up contaminants on the way to the lake. Nairn clarified that Chlorophyll A is a problem caused by contaminants, rather than a contaminant itself. Contaminants like phosphorous and nitrogen lead to overproduction of Chlorophyll A. The City of Norman did not advocate channelizing creek beds and lining them with concrete, this is no longer considered a best practice for preserving riparian zones. Nairn noted that all SCC meetings were open to the public, meeting minutes are publicly available, and the process was as transparent as possible.

MAGA Hat responded that the bulk of pollutants from rainwater runoff come from Norman's urban core that mostly drains into the Canadian River, not Lake Thunderbird. He also repeated his claim that Chlorophyll A is good for aquatic environments and raised new arguments about city funds, EPA regulations, the shared responsibility of other municipalities, recreational activities at Lake Thunderbird, and the selection of SCC members. MAGA Hat closed his eight-hundred-word response to Nairn:

> I would ask that you step out of your politically motivated echo chamber and go knock on some doors and explain to the hard working tax payers why we need to pay for rain falling from the sky and running over the ground. I suspect you'll never do that, but maybe it'll spark something within you to question this incredibly bad logic and ever worse legislation.
>
> And, until I can be convinced, I will be on here every day posting real information and asking real questions. And . . . I don't know the definition of "quit."
>
> Have a great evening!

Facebook provided an outlet for people like MAGA Hat who are passionate about policy and truth. MAGA Hat must have put hours every day into researching, writing, and responding to others about stormwater policy. MAGA Hat's energy and intensity are inspiring, but there is also something tragic about investing so much time in a social media platform like Facebook that is so limiting. Like many Americans, MAGA Hat desperately wanted to engage with his community and influence policy, and in much of the United States at the time Facebook was the primary place where this could happen.

Nairn responded briefly to clarify that she was not an employee of the city and had volunteered for more than ten years on boards and committees related to water in Norman. MAGA Hat responded with more critique, to which Nairn did not respond. Engaging with MAGA Hat was exhausting. At one point city council member Stephen Tyler Holman responded with sarcasm and frustration: "The entire 9 member City Council, entire 15 member Citizens Committee, entire City legal department, and the entire outside legal Bond Counsel for the City are all wrong and one guy [MAGA Hat] has all the answers and his word is to be taken as gold . . . got it."[33]

MAGA Hat's critique of the SWU was effective because he created doubts about the City of Norman's narrative regarding stormwater. After the 2016 SWU proposal, rural residents were primed not to trust the city government. Although I do not agree that city representatives were telling "LIES," MAGA Hat did shine light on misleading claims. He was correct that threats of fines from ODEQ and the EPA for violating Lake Thunderbird's TMDL were unlikely to be enforced. Norman could be fined, but ODEQ did not have a history of enforcing penalties for violations. MAGA Hat was also correct that most of Norman's urban core drains into the Canadian River. The vast majority of funds from the 2019 stormwater utility and bond were intended for stormwater infrastructure and maintenance in the Canadian River watershed, rather than Lake Thunderbird. In contrast, the City of Norman's messaging regarding the 2019 proposal often focused on the quality of drinking water and the potential fines associated with the total maximum daily load restrictions in Lake Thunderbird. MAGA Hat was not alone in recognizing that this was misleading. One piece of misleading information causes people to question everything else. If the city was not entirely honest on one issue, trust eroded and it was easy for some to assume the entire project was a hoax.

This is a key element of conspiratorial thinking. Conspiracy is about connections and hidden plans. Raising doubts about narratives advanced by those in power, in this case the City of Norman, allows other alternative explanations to be advanced. If stormwater proposals are not in fact about improving the quality of water in Lake Thunderbird, then what is their true purpose? What is the city trying to sneak past the residents? MAGA Hat did not offer a clear alternative narrative aside from suggesting that the city seeks to accumulate funds that council members can deploy according to their whims. For the sake of the proposal, however, simply creating doubt was enough to convince people to vote "no."

Like many Facebook participants, MAGA Hat rarely conceded an argument, but even if he did, he raised so many other critiques that it was very difficult to engage all his claims. Nairn was correct that the City of Norman did not intend to invest in concrete liners for waterways, but MAGA Hat simply moved on to new arguments. In high school debate this strategy is called "spread," throwing out so many arguments that your opponent is spread thin and unable to respond to everything. If one of those arguments still stands, the debate is won.

Explaining science is difficult, while producing doubt is easy. Advocates of the 2019 stormwater bond and utility, like Nairn, consistently told me about the complexity of stormwater and the difficulty of conceptually connecting rainfall runoff in one part of the city with flooding elsewhere. Eutrophication is a complex, multistage process, and it is not easily explained in a Facebook post, particularly when responding to so many other claims and arguments. A few readers might be inspired to undertake the hours of research necessary to assess the respective claims, but the vast majority are left with the sense of doubt and uncertainty that proliferates in Facebook's virtual world of debate in which everyone is an expert.

The strong belief that those with economic and political capital conspire to advance their interests creates an overwhelming sense of doubt and mistrust, particularly regarding the advice of institutional experts. In this environment of uncertainty, it is extremely difficult to reach the consensus needed to address dire problems like global climate change. Indeed, in Oklahoma powerful political leaders have worked hard to sow doubts about climate change. In 2012, U.S. Senator James Inhofe, who represented Oklahoma from 1994–2022, published the book *The Greatest Hoax: How the Global Warming Conspiracy Threatens Your Future*. To label something as a conspiracy implies that it is a plot that cannot be fully uncovered. Inhofe's arguments follow the form of classic conspiracy theory—the same parties that claim global warming is real stand to benefit from its existence. Like MAGA Hat, Inhofe claimed that the hoax is designed to give more power to government. Whether it is the U.S. federal government or the Norman City Council, they claimed that panics over eutrophication and climate change are intended to place power and resources in the hands of government leaders.

Although I clearly disagree with Inhofe and MAGA Hat, Norman residents had ample reason not to trust local government: for example, the institutional racism that shaped Lake Thunderbird's construction and the power of real estate developers to influence policy. MAGA Hat's endless critique simply added to this distrust. It is easy to give in to cynicism and uncertainty. If the truth cannot be known, it is perhaps better to simply disbelieve rather than be duped.

In this final example from the Ward 5 Facebook page, voters refused to believe the assurances of their councilmember, Sereta Wilson.[34] City councilmembers were less active in Facebook discussions in 2019 than in 2016, but some like Wilson still directly engaged with their constituents. In contrast to MAGA Hat, these Norman residents do not offer counterarguments, they express personal appreciation for Councilmember Wilson, but they are not convinced.

Small Business Owner: This is just the beginning, this charge will only go up and up with no end in sight , it's a forever taxing charge that can be raised whenever they want ! It's a NO vote for me !

Sereta Wilson: Small Business Owner—not true! Any changes to a utility has to be voted on by the residents . . . per charter.

Small Business Owner: Sereta Wilson—OK so your saying this will never go up without a vote of the people, it's a fee a special fee just like the CIC on the water bill , I love you to death but I DO NOT believe you on this one. Again it's a fee not a utility bill it's just Piggie backed on the utility bill just like the CIC add on. It's a forever $$$$$$ and no way to go but up and up.

Sereta Wilson: Small Business Owner—if we can raise it willy nilly then why are we asking everyone to vote on it now 🤷‍♀️?

Small Business Owner: Sereta Wilson—That's why I'm voting No , ! Not convinced and grateful along with disappointed with you voting for it

Sereta Wilson: Small Business Owner—I understand you voting NO . . . but I want to make sure others understand that it only goes up if it's voted by the people to go up.

I am sorry that I let people down by voting for it. But I know our city needs it, and I know it will help our community, including ward 5.

Councilmember Wilson stated clearly, and accurately, that the SWU fee cannot be raised without a vote. Other residents joined the discussion to support Wilson on this point, but it did nothing to convince Small Business Owner. It did not matter what evidence Councilmember Wilson provided to support her claims. Despite a personal affection for Wilson, Small Business Owner refused to believe. Governance, in this context, is extremely difficult. The requirement that residents approve all utility rate increases was born of mistrust in government. Voters believed the government was conspiring with developers to waste their money. In 2019 there was no clear narrative explaining mistrust, but doubt was overpowering. It was like a conspiracy without a theory. Many residents seemed to believe that city government was practicing deception for the sake of deception. Even councilmembers like Wilson, who were well known and liked, were not trusted.[35]

Digital Eutrophication and the Construction of Mistrust

By the end of 2021, many of the prolific and entertaining contributors to Facebook ward pages were gone. Instead, the ward pages were devoted primarily to announcements for local events. When debate erupted the exchange usually died quickly. If digital eutrophication had already begun in 2019, the events of 2020 rapidly accelerated the process. COVID-19, the 2020 elections, and race and policing brought Norman residents back to Facebook for a few more cycles of intense discursive growth. With everyone stuck at home staring at their screens, discourse built and built until the oxygen was extinguished. Facebook nourished conflict until the digital ecosystem collapsed. Some moved on to Twitter (now X), others took breaks from social media, and the Facebook ward pages became something like the aquatic dead zones that result from nourishing too much growth.

In 2020, one year after the stormwater debates, my friends and I laughed about what had seemed like intense arguments over stormwater policy. In the context of the COVID-19 pandemic and vitriol filled arguments over masking, social distancing, and vaccines, we longed for a return to discussions of stormwater policy. During the pandemic, political ideology on all sides was often more important than scientific evidence. The wave of information that had felt overwhelming during stormwater discussions became a tsunami of social media, journalism, and political rhetoric. Expressing the wrong opinion on social media could end friendships. Seemingly every week brought a new decision that required extensive research—When should I wear a mask? Do I send my kids to school in-person, online, or some hybrid? What's the best vaccine? Do I need to get boosted? Can I trust medical advice from a government led by Donald Trump? How can I trust pharmaceutical companies that are so clearly motivated by profits? Not only did I lack the expertise to answer these questions with confidence but I also knew that accurately or not my decisions would signal my politics and values to others.

This is the world of information in which decisions about water infrastructure and policy are made. We are operating in a media-saturated environment that Norman Citizens for Civic Responsibility could not have predicted in the 1970s. Anthropologist Adam Hodges argued in 2020 that we were living not in a post-truth era, but a post-trust era, and misinformation must be countered by rebuilding trust in public institutions.[36] A return to the authoritative voices of twentieth-century legacy media, however, is not possible or desirable. Recall that the *Norman Transcript* sometimes served to advance alliances between government leaders and developers. There was good reason for the mistrust of government and legacy media that led many Americans to access much of their news via social media. Rebuilding trust is impossible without addressing inequalities in substantive citizenship—different abilities to make demands on public institutions.

A strong desire to communicate and exchange ideas brought people together on Norman's Facebook ward pages who otherwise would not have met, online or offline. The ward pages were not social bubbles, but neither were they places where new ideas were formed, and minds changed. Facebook profits from the sale of conflict, and perhaps the primary result of ward page discussions was the production of mistrust.[37] As I detail in the following chapter, a lack of trust makes planning for the future extremely difficult. The 1975 change to the city's charter that required a vote for utility rate increases democratized decision-making and expertise. It empowered all Norman residents and undermined alliances between developers and city leaders. It did not, however, offer an alternative source of expertise and truth. Rather, the rise of social media brought numerous competing truths, many of them based in uncovering plots and conspiracies. When people use social media to attack the economic self-interest of the Chamber of Commerce or the city government's desire for a slush fund, the goal is to uncover and reveal. Mistrust and conspiracy are the dominant discourses on social media. Sometimes real plots are revealed, but few alternatives are offered. In the end, "No" is the only consensus that can be reached. At times, "No" is the most effective way of halting self-devouring growth, but "No" is not enough. It is too late for that. In a world of eutrophication, we cannot simply say no to nourishing growth, we must find ways to deal with the damage that has already been done. The struggle is how to reach consensus for shared solutions amid so much justified mistrust, particularly when our communication tools are owned by billionaires who seek ever-increasing profits.

5 Planning for Future Water in a Time of Mistrust

DRINKING TAP WATER is a continual act of trust. Taste, smell, and appearance do not tell me if the water will make me sick. Instead, I must put my trust in the experts who treat and test the water I drink. Regardless of how I feel about local elected officials, if I am in the United States, I do not hesitate to pour a glass of water from the tap and drink it down. There are of course cases like in Flint, Michigan, in the 2010s when high levels of lead in water made people sick and the local government initially ignored residents' complaints. I trust, however, that these cases are the exception rather than the rule.

When my family and I moved to Norman in 2011 my relationship with tap water changed. Even before I tasted the water, I had heard that there were high levels of carcinogenic hexavalent chromium in Norman's tap water. To be honest, that meant nothing to me at the time, but I read a reference to "Erin Brockovich chromium." While I hadn't seen the movie starring Julia Roberts, I knew the basic storyline about one of those cases where private corporations and the government worked together to cover up a massive public health disaster. I did not need to hear much more than that. I had a story to frame my understanding of Norman's water and knew I did not want my family drinking it. The Erin Brockovich story tapped into a key narrative of mistrust that resonates with the conspiracy of developers—government leaders not acting in my interests because they are financially dependent on private corporations.

"What are you doing for water?" was a common conversation starter among new faculty that fall at the University of Oklahoma. New arrivals to

Norman were often told not to drink the tap water. If people weren't familiar with chromium, *Erin Brockovich* was referenced, and they were quickly convinced. My wife did the research and learned the only way to remove chromium from tap water is with a reverse osmosis filter. "Sure," I said, "let's do that," and we dropped around $500 on a filter for the tap in our kitchen. I have a reputation for thrift, and I do not spend $500 easily, but the filter seemed like a necessity. I did not trust the water or local governance, so my family invested in an individualized solution to protect ourselves. I distrusted tap water in Norman because I embraced a narrative about industrial pollution and government cover ups. With time, cracks began to emerge in the application of that narrative to Norman, and my distrust faded. My family and I eventually discarded our filter and today we feel relatively confident drinking straight tap water.

Trust is a relationship to the future, a form of hope based on positive experiences in the past.[1] I trust tap water because I have not had problems with it in the past, but trust depends on more than my personal experiences. Trust emerges not only from the calculation of the likelihood of a future event but also from stories and narratives. Building trust requires constructing a hopeful narrative that connects the past to the future. My trust in the quality of tap water is based on beliefs about the power of the state to harness science and expertise to produce safe drinking water. Mistrust is also constructed, but from a different type of narrative. It is a form of pessimism based in doubt. Mistrust of government proliferates in a world saturated with stories like Erin Brockovich's battle with PG&E in Hinkley, California.

As I write in the early 2020s, it is nearly sixty years since Lake Thunderbird was completed, and once again Norman is facing questions about its future water supply. The productive lifespan of the reservoir was estimated at one hundred years when it was created. As silt builds up in the lake, its capacity for holding water decreases. Norman's population is three times what it was when the lake was built, and the city continues to grow. The 2060 Strategic Water Supply Plan outlines how Norman can gradually expand its water supply to accommodate growth and meet the needs of nearly two hundred thousand people by augmenting Lake Thunderbird with treated sewage.[2]

Norman can only access the funds to carry out the 2060 plan with a vote of the people, and this requires trust.

Trust is based in a shared vision of the good, a common desired future.[3] In contrast to the time of Lake Thunderbird's construction, in the early 2020s appeals to a singular "progressive, wholesome" city were impossible. National political partisanship, social media, COVID-19, debates over policing and race, Donald Trump, and social isolation divided Norman. Mistrust was actively constructed as groups differentiated themselves from others based on conflicting values that undermined shared interests. Debates over who pays for water infrastructure, sewage reuse, and chromium filtration were inseparable from the stories that Norman residents told themselves about their city. In 2022 Norman residents voted down a water rate increase that would have funded improvements in the water system. Although they had very different reasons for opposing the increase, Norman residents shared a strong distrust for city leaders.

Subsidizing Growth and Undermining Trust

Sitting around a backyard fire on the first Tuesday of April 2022, talking about the night's local election results, a friend pulled his long hair back from his face, sipped from a can of ale, and explained why, like most voters, he voted "no" on the first proposed water rate increase since 2015. The rate increase would have generated nearly $4.7 million annually to fund automatic meter readers, a groundwater blending facility to improve chlorination levels, and water line replacements, but my friend was not concerned with the specifics of how the money would be used.[4] Instead, he explained that voting on utility increases is the only form of leverage we have on city policies. He would not support a water rate increase unless connection fees for new homes were also increased. Low connection fees mean developers are not paying the full cost of their reliance on public infrastructure, my friend explained. It is a complicated argument, but one that many people in Norman were making during the run up to the vote. Norman residents did not trust their city's leaders, and voting "no" on the water rate increase was one way to hold these leaders accountable.

Public meetings are one of the tools that city governments use to build trust. Around two months before the water rate increase vote, the City of Norman hosted a meeting on the water connection fees that new home builders pay.[5] Outside of city staff, only around a dozen people were present at the meeting. A consulting group the city had hired to determine appropriate connection fees for drinking water and wastewater delivered a slide presentation remotely. As I watched a video recording of the meeting on my laptop, I continually paused the video and listened again, trying to understand the formula for calculating connection fees. The man giving the presentation, visible in a small box within the slides, explained that connection fees represent costs to reserve capacity within facilities that serve all. Specific fee levels are based on the value of existing capacity, demand, and plans for future capacity. I wrote down "unit cost capacity" in my notes, but I am not sure what that means. I was lost. I watched again but still did not understand how connection fees are calculated.

The formula for calculating connection fees is extremely dense, but their importance is clear. New houses use existing infrastructures that residents have already purchased, like water pipes, wells, and the water treatment center. New houses also increase the need for new projects, like Norman's plan to augment Lake Thunderbird with treated wastewater from the Water Reclamation Facility. Connection fees are intended to cover these costs. Without connection fees, new construction essentially gets infrastructure for free, and everyone's utility fees subsidize real estate developers and new home buyers. Experts are hired because it is so difficult to determine how much developers should pay for each new house they build to compensate for existing infrastructure and future needs.

A highly technical slideshow for a dozen people in a dimly lit city conference room does little to inform Norman residents about connection fees. The public meeting was a performance of transparency that allowed city leaders to claim they had updated the public on the status of connection fees. The meeting, however, took on a life of its own. Following the presentation, the audience was given a chance to ask questions. Even in the grainy video of the dimly lit conference room, I recognized the distinctive bright blue Kansas Jayhawks sweatshirt worn by the first speaker, Dr. Stephen Ellis, a professor of philosophy and former debate coach at the University of Oklahoma. Ellis, who sometimes combines his Jayhawks sweatshirt with blue denim overalls, is a frequent speaker at city meetings. He noted that the city plans to use wastewater augmentation to increase long-term water capacity. Why then, he asked, are we looking at different scenarios for calculating connection fees? The next comment came from Sean Rieger, attorney to many of Norman's developers. I do not know if developers had paid Rieger to be present at the meeting, or if he was there for his own reasons. Rieger, wearing his usual dark suit, directly disputed Ellis's question, arguing that much of the connection fee is for existing infrastructure rather than building new capacity. Along with Ellis and Rieger, Dr. Cynthia Rogers, a professor of economics at OU and an expert on tax increment financing (TIF), offered the bulk of questions and comments as the discussion continued for a full hour after the presentation. Rogers is also a frequent participant at city meetings, where she delivers clear evidence-based arguments. Rieger repeatedly sought to reshape the discussion in ways that undermined Ellis's and Rogers's push for higher connection fees. All three directed their comments toward the presenters, but it felt like they were debating each other.

As a closing comment, Ellis noted that the situation was like the 1970s in the sense that utility rate increases, rather than connection fees, were funding new development. He promised to advocate for a "no" vote on the water rate increase if connection fees were not raised. At a city council conference the following day, council members agreed that connection fees should be raised by 25 percent to match the proposed 25 percent raise in residential water rates. This was an informal agreement; the actual policy would be voted on at a later city council meeting.

When I started conducting interviews related to stormwater policy, nearly all city officials suggested I speak with "Rogers and Ellis," referring to Dr. Cynthia Rogers and Dr. Stephen Ellis. City council members come and go, often grabbing residents' attention for a year and then fading from public discussions, but people like Ellis, Rogers, and Rieger persist. They have been debating city policy for years. Rogers and Ellis do not just share similar views on city policy, they are also married. City officials were frustrated that although Rogers and Ellis supported the 2016 stormwater utility, they strongly opposed the 2019 proposals for reasons of equity. I interviewed Ellis and Rogers individually early in my research, but I really got to know them through reading their prolific Facebook posts. Rogers and Ellis run their own public Facebook group, Neighbors 4 Norman, which had twenty-nine hundred members in February 2022 and was up to thirty-seven hundred members a year later. Rogers told me Facebook is "a game changer. Good and bad, but I think it's mostly good." Like Norman's neighborhood Facebook ward pages, discussion on Neighbors 4 Norman is not as lively as in years past, but the page has many readers who treat it as a source of local news, filling the gaps in the coverage provided by the increasingly thin *Norman Transcript*.

Water infrastructure is just one of the couple's interests. Rogers and Ellis engage in public discussions related to education policy, homelessness, and policing among other issues. In their Facebook discussions, the focus is firmly on Norman, and they rarely directly engage with national politics. They often take unconventional positions; for example, in 2023 they advocated against a bond that would fund projects for Norman Public Schools. Like many people I spoke with, I voted "yes" on the school bond, but I appreciated Rogers's and Ellis's critiques. Rogers and Ellis do not limit themselves to Facebook. They frequently write letters to the editor of the *Norman Transcript*, speak at city council and school board meetings, and attend public events and meetings that are connected to city policies. They are well known among the many Norman residents who use Facebook to follow local news. In a Facebook post Sassan Moghadam, real estate developer and cofounder of Unite Norman, called Rogers and Ellis "two of the most despised individuals in Norman" and "the true Cancer of Norman."[6] Others have repeatedly encouraged Cynthia Rogers to run for mayor.

A few days after the public meeting on connection fees and subsequent city council conference, Ellis posted on the Neighbors 4 Norman Facebook page, arguing that a $250 increase in connection fees was not enough. Without a more significant increase, he would advocate a "no" vote on the water rate increase. His post concluded, "Remember—our Norman elders fought for the right to vote on utility rates precisely so we could keep the Council from using utility money as a slush fund for other projects (e.g., so-called 'economic development'). Please join me in pledging to *vote NO on any utility rate increase* until the water connection fees cover the costs of new development."[7]

A month later and just two weeks before the public vote on water rates, it was time for the city council to vote on the $250 increase in connection fees. Councilmember Elizabeth Foreman (Ward 6, 2020–2024) introduced an amendment that would add an additional incremental raise in connection fees in fall 2022 on top of the $250 increase. The amendment passed with multiple councilmembers noting that voters were telling them they would vote "no" on the water rate increase if connection fees were not increased. Councilmember Foreman announced, "Your council has done their part, now please do yours, and go vote yes on April 5th" on the water rate increase.[8] Stephen Ellis, however, never got behind the rate increase.[9] He continued to argue that connection fees were not high enough and that increased water rates were a slush fund that the city could use to subsidize development. Did Ellis convince six hundred of the nearly three thousand members of the Neighbors 4 Norman Facebook page to vote "no"? If so, he played a major role in voting the water rate increase down.

To the extent that capitalism is based in collusion and plotting—the conspiracy of developers—it is a highly productive environment for mistrust. In his Facebook post calling for people to vote "no" on the water rate increase, Stephen Ellis referenced "Norman elders" and subsidized development. In doing so he drew on a well-established narrative of mistrust—the power of developers to influence city policy. It is a narrative that separates the interests of Norman's leaders from its residents. It was precisely the "elders" from NCCR who worked to make the politics of infrastructure visible and ensure that debates over infrastructure would continue for generations to come. Arguments against subsidizing development led residents to take direct control over utility rates. Empowering voters is a means of combatting mistrust, but taking power away from bureaucrats and experts destabilizes long-term plans. Utilities Director Chris Mattingly pleaded for unity to get the water rate increase he needed, but it seemed that Norman residents agreed only that they did not trust their leaders. Coming together to construct a shared vision of the future was far more difficult.

Ellis and others were essentially arguing that equity in who pays for growth was more important than upgrading the city's water infrastructure. In comparison to residential utility fees, connection fees make up a small amount of the city's water budget, but low connection fees carry great symbolic weight in representing public subsidies for real estate developers. Adding an additional five hundred dollars to connection fees will not slow growth in Norman or generate enough funds to significantly impact Norman's water budget. Rather, pushing to increase connection fees is a statement of one's values and vision for a future community. It is an argument that equity in distributing the costs of growth combats mistrust and achieves the unity needed for long-term planning.

Water Rates, Policing, and Trust

A survey conducted after the 2022 water rate increase vote confirmed that mistrust in government was one of the primary reasons Norman residents voted "no."[10] There are, however, many reasons to mistrust government. To recall from an earlier chapter, Norman's mayor Larry Heikkila (2022–2025) told me that Norman residents voted down the water rate increase because they did not trust city council after the June 16, 2020, meeting when council "defunded the police."[11] Politically, Heikkila was very far to the right of Stephen Ellis, and yet both opposed the water rate increase in part because they mistrusted local governance.

The water rate increase was not the only item on the ballot that Tuesday. There was also a runoff in the election of Norman's mayor. Incumbent mayor Breea Clark (2019–2022) had led the city through the COVID-19 pandemic and supported the controversial June 2020 move to direct funds from the Norman Police Department's requested budget increase toward creating a mobile mental health crisis unit. Mayor Clark's opponent, Larry Heikkila, was a self-proclaimed conservative who promised to return funding to the police. Heikkila won the election by seven points, a slightly closer margin than the failed water rate increase.

I met with Mayor Heikkila at his city hall office in late November 2022, around five months after he took office. While waiting for Heikkila I learned the password for the Norman city hall WiFi—April1889, the month and year of the land run that opened Oklahoma to settlement. Heikkila retired from twenty-six years of service in the U.S. Navy in 2010. His city website states that he is pro-business and pro-growth.[12] Heikkila wore a white button-down shirt, slacks, and cowboy boots to our meeting. He answered my questions with great confidence, speaking without hesitation. Heikkila was planning to again ask voters for a water rate increase in 2023. "Why do I think it will work this time? Last Tuesday we authorized the money, 1.3 million dollars, for the police department to buy gear, we gave [the police] a good raise. We did the things that the people told us to do." The money for gear was a reference to the Lenco BearCat, an armored vehicle. Norman's Police Department had been asking for funds to purchase a BearCat for years, and after extensive debate the city council had approved the funds in the days before my meeting with Heikkila. He told me that he was well aware of Norman's need for increased funding for water infrastructure, but he voted against the spring 2022 rate increase because he felt it was too high for residents on a fixed income. Now that he was mayor and the city was headed in a different direction, he would advocate a water rate increase in 2023.

My conversation with Mayor Heikkila led me to watch the full video of the more than ten-hour June 16, 2020, meeting in which the city council voted to allocate a portion of the police department's requested budget increase to a mobile mental health crisis team. More than 12,500 people have streamed the video of this epic city council meeting.[13] I viewed it in the days after Tyre Nichols was beaten to death by Memphis police officers, events that necessarily shaped my interpretations of the meeting. Around three and a half hours into the meeting, public comments began. Person after person approached the city council to describe their experiences with the police and demand change. Comments, limited to three minutes for each person, went on for more than four hours. Audience members snapped their fingers to show approval for speakers who supported defunding the police. The speakers were primarily young, some of them high school students. Most were women and many were people of color. This was not the older white crowd that shows up to city meetings on water policy.

Speakers shared the names of friends and family who had died at the hands of the police in Norman during the past decade. A young woman began her comments, "I would like to say a name today, Martin Sanchez-Juarez, also known to his family members and loved ones by Isaac. On December 14, 2014, his wife called 911 because Isaac had lost his memory and was having a mental illness episode . . . [an officer called to the scene] shot Isaac three times . . . killing him when he was twenty-five feet away from her."[14] The speaker explained that the officer who killed Isaac was working as a School Resource Officer (SRO) at Norman High School, the same high school that Isaac's daughter currently attended. "I am here today not only to call for the defunding of the police department as a whole and the reallocation of those funds . . . I am calling for [the officer] to be fired . . . I am calling for the end of the SRO program." Each speaker was unique, but there were recurring themes. Mothers gave impassioned speeches about the awful experiences their children had with police at schools. Others, mostly women of color, described their experiences of mistreatment at the hands of police. Young white men explained that their privilege protects them from these abuses, but the problems are real, and the solution is to defund a broken system.

The few supporters of the police who spoke did not question the negative experiences that others had with the police. Rather, they argued that bad cops are individuals who do not reflect the system. They encouraged the audience to go on a ride-along with the police and attend listening sessions. An African American police officer waited until one in the morning to speak in support of Norman's Police Department. A live text chat was recorded with the video stream. With few exceptions, the chatters were critical of police reform. Each instance of police violence was rationalized: Isaac was wielding a hammer when he was killed; the kindergartner who the police pulled out of school was probably doing more than throwing a tantrum; the speakers advocating defunding the police are not from Norman, they are activists from Oklahoma City. One speaker at the meeting closed his comments in support of Norman's police by stating, "All lives matter."

The June 2020 meeting led some Norman residents to mistrust city council in part because they believed it had undermined public safety. Although Norman's city council did not defund the police, many who spoke at the June 2020 meeting advocated defunding, and some Norman residents saw this as a direct threat to their security. Divisions, however, were deeper than that.

Policing and race were such potent sources of tension because of their implications for identity politics and conceptions of community. On one hand, if a valorized institution like the police department is racist, then substantive differences in citizenship are real. This means that white privilege is also real. As Arlie Hochschild argued in her influential ethnography of conservative Americans, *Strangers in Their Own Land*, white men often struggle to find where they belong when community is defined in these terms.[15] On the other hand, to defend the police by rationalizing instances of violence or arguing that they are isolated cases was to claim that substantive differences in citizenship do not exist. This perspective denies the lived experiences of the many people who spoke at the June 16, 2020, city council meeting. The two perspectives are based in fundamental, perhaps irreconcilable, differences in conceptions of community.

Ward 3's councilmember, Kelly Lynn, was a major supporter of Heikkila's mayoral campaign and in many ways is emblematic of battles over identity and community. Lynn was elected in 2021 with support of Unite Norman, the group founded largely in backlash to the June 16, 2020, meeting. Lynn has served in the Army National Guard since 2007, is a practicing attorney, and has an interest in religious leadership. In January 2023 he announced plans to complete a masters of divinity and form a church for members of the military and first responders.[16] He wears his hair shaved on the sides with perhaps half an inch left on the top and an equally well trimmed beard. Kelly Lynn appears to take pleasure in making his opponents angry, or in the parlance of the times, "owning the libs." After winning a runoff for the Ward 3 council seat, Lynn's response to the *Norman Transcript*'s request for comment was simply, "Scoreboard!"[17] During his two years on city council, Lynn was a highly polarizing figure. He lost his bid for reelection in 2023, and it is unclear if he will remain active in city politics or move on to other pursuits.

At the March 2022 city council meeting regarding increasing connection fees, Kelly Lynn offered the final comment from council before the vote. Lynn speaks with a distinctive Oklahoma accent and his voice conveyed great passion as he explained,

I'll vote for the water increase on April 5th myself, I know these are different pots of money, but when we have our priorities so out of whack, we don't have contracts with our police and fire, we're about to spend millions of dollars on homeless people, but we're asking you to spend more on water and increase connection fees. We just don't have things right, now, and it's hard for me to get behind this and champion either one of them when we can't do the basic functions of government. Water is one of those. Another one, you can look back to the old west, what was the only government position that they had, it was law and order. That is the most important thing of government.[18]

Despite claiming he would vote for the water rate increase, Lynn seemed to encourage voters to do the opposite, noting that more money would come out of their pockets and public safety needs were not being met. Lynn used homelessness and public safety as symbols to construct a particular vision for the future and implied that voters should withhold support for new water infrastructure until the city council enacted that vision.

Following the failed water rate increase, Lynn continued to connect water rates with homeless issues and claimed that Norman residents would not be happy with the city spending money on low-income housing that he characterized as a homeless shelter. In a heated exchange with Ward 1 councilmember Brandi Studley (2021–2023), Lynn shouted, "I'm just telling you that you're messing up our ability to do regular business, so when you're begging people to pass a water rate again, because we couldn't get it done because they don't trust you in the first place, remember this moment when you said 'push this through' and they're gonna say, 'oh hell no, we're not going to give you any more money.'"

Studley had experienced homelessness and was a longtime homeless advocate prior to taking a seat on the council in 2021. She was not one to back down from a fight and fiercely responded to Lynn, "We all will remember this moment when certain council members gaslit the public and lied about what this actually is . . . It's time to help people who cannot help themselves. We are a city that helps everyone, not just people with money."[19] "Gaslighting" was Merriam-Webster's word of the year for 2022, and Studley put this overused term to good use in relation Lynn's claims.[20] Lynn repeatedly referred to single-room occupancy affordable housing as a "homeless shelter" that would attract more homeless people to Norman.[21] Affordable housing is intended to help people get off the streets or protect them from becoming homeless in the first place. I became so frustrated with Lynn characterizing affordable housing as a shelter that I emailed him a complaint. He responded promptly, stating simply, "This is absolutely a homeless initiative. It will be a homeless shelter."

In arguing with Kelly Lynn about the distinction between affordable housing and a homeless shelter, or quibbling about whether Norman "defunded" the police, I was missing a broader point. Homelessness and policing were not only about policy, but they also symbolized a particular vision for the future. Before water could be addressed, trust must be established, and that requires a foundation of shared values. References to defunding the police evoked a complex web of identity politics. For many Norman residents a city council that defunded the police was necessarily opposed to their interests and values. Heikkila and Lynn used these symbolically charged terms to build mistrust. The failed 2022 water rate increase became further evidence that trust could only be regained by purchasing a $1.3-million armored vehicle for the police and opposing affordable housing. Leaders like Mayor Heikkila and Councilmember Lynn prioritized a particular form of identity politics over nourishing growth. From their perspective, the trust needed for future planning could only be achieved by enacting a shared vision of membership and belonging. In some cases, like the rise of Unite Norman in 2020, conservative identity politics are used to advance the interests of developers, but the 2022 water rate vote was different. The failed 2022 water rate increase prevented the nourishing of growth that supports capitalist accumulation. By the end of 2022 connection fees for new houses had increased by $500, and residential water rates remained unchanged. In other words, developers faced increased costs, but very little new money was available for expanding Norman's water infrastructure in ways that would support growth. For Heikkila and Lynn, it was more important to signal an allegiance to the police and antipathy toward homeless people than to support a water rate increase that was needed for growth. The relationship between trust and planning meant that at least in this case, identity politics trumped the economic interests of developers.

2022 was a year of debate about water rates, policing, and homelessness. It was also a year of tragic deaths. In January gun violence erupted outside of a homeless shelter in downtown Norman. An unhoused Black woman shot and killed an unhoused white man and shot and wounded another man. Norman Police responded and shot the perpetrator multiple times but did not kill her.[22] The unhoused man who was killed had family in Norman and had battled mental health issues for many years. Councilmember Lynn used the incident to bolster his argument against city-funded homeless shelters in Norman.[23]

Just a few days after the 2022 water rate increase vote in April, on a beautiful Saturday morning during the University of Oklahoma's parents' weekend, Shed Euwins was jogging through the university's campus. When Euwins confronted the driver of a car about reckless driving, the driver shot and killed him. District Attorney Greg Mashburn declined to press charges, arguing that the shooter acted in self-defense and was protected by Oklahoma's stand your ground statute.[24] Shed Euwins was a Black man with dreadlocks; the identity of the driver was not released. District Attorney Mashburn claimed that Euwins was dealing with mental health issues when he approached the driver but did not question the mental health of the man who killed Euwins.[25]

Four weeks after Euwins's death, my family and I joined around forty others at a Justice for Shed rally at the site where Euwins was killed, perhaps one hundred yards from my office.[26] At the rally, Euwins's family and the Oklahoma Coalition against People Abuse pushed for charges to be brought against the shooter, but nothing happened, and a year later much of Norman seemed to have forgotten about the incident.

In December 2022 Shannon Hanchett died in the county jail after being held for twelve days. Hanchett, known as the "Cookie Queen," was the owner of the Cookie Cottage, a small downtown business in a historic building. She was a white woman in her late thirties, a mother of two, and a local mental health advocate. The arresting police officer claimed that Hanchett was "exhibiting behavior consistent with some type of mental health disorder."[27] Hanchett was arrested for dialing 911 during her interaction with the police officer. The officer also accused Hanchett of resisting arrest.[28] Hanchett was experiencing a mental health crisis, she inappropriately called 911, and for this she was arrested and held in jail until she died. In the weeks after Hanchett's death another woman who was struggling with mental health issues also died at the county jail.[29]

In a city like Norman with a population of a little over one hundred thousand, these deaths are personal. All three of the deceased were parents. Most Norman residents are no more than a couple degrees of separation from the people who died. Even if they do not know them personally, it's likely they know one of their family members, or their kids go to school together. Each death is a reminder of the violence that lurks beneath the veneer of a pleasant college town. Violence will often find those who are not protected by layers of privilege. Debates about connection fees and water rates may seem quite distant from violent deaths, but they are about establishing foundations for a safer community.

When city council met on the Tuesday following Hanchett's death, Councilmember Studley argued that the arresting officer should have contacted a mental health professional to deescalate the situation. She called for the city to follow through on the decision made in June 2020 to create a mobile mental health crisis unit. Kelly Lynn responded, "I find it repulsive to bring TV cameras in here and use this terrible tragedy as a political moment to try to lay this at the feet of our policemen."[30]

Each of these deaths was complex and cannot be attributed to a single cause or policy decision. But each of the deaths is in some ways an act of violent exclusion. In being jailed because of a mental health crisis, Hanchett was excluded from the community. When his killer was not prosecuted, Euwins was excluded from expectations of justice. The unhoused man who was murdered outside of a homeless shelter was excluded from public safety. Investing city resources in affordable housing and a mobile mental health crisis unit was specifically intended to create a more expansive community and counter violent exclusion. I do not know exactly why these three people died in 2022, but I do know that for those who were already marginalized Norman was a place where such violence was not only possible, but likely. Each incidence of violence shatters trust in a local government that should be ensuring our safety.[31]

Reclaiming Wastewater to Support Future Growth

Is there anything that demands more trust than asking residents to drink their treated sewage?[32] The City of Norman wants residents to trust it with channeling treated sewage into its primary supply of drinking water, a practice that is increasingly common in the United States.[33] Such reuse is a direct acknowledgement of the consequences of growth.[34] Without incurring great expenses, the city cannot draw water from elsewhere. If it is to continue growing Norman has few options beyond recycling its wastewater. The same is true of many cities in the arid west that are attracted to wastewater recycling by its low cost and limited environmental impact relative to options like desalinizing seawater.[35]

The City of Norman's Water Reclamation Facility (WRF) has gone through many name changes. It was once the Sewage Treatment Plant, then it became the Wastewater Treatment Plant, then the Pollution Control Facility. "Water Reclamation Facility" is partially aspirational. The facility does reclaim water in the sense that it cleans wastewater and channels it into the Canadian River, but to fully reclaim this water would mean putting it to use beyond the city's few small irrigation projects. That's what the City of Norman hopes to accomplish by channeling treated wastewater into Lake Thunderbird to meet Norman's growing need for water during dry months.

I called the WRF early in my research, thinking there might be a tour I could join. Instead, the facility manager, Steve Hardeman, invited me for a one-on-one visit. Norman's WRF is located on the edge of town, south of Highway 9 and north of the Canadian River. It's a little sliver of the city that is often forgotten. Near the WRF the city's composting facility gives off a pungent smell of rot. Dogs bark from the outdoor kennels at the City of Norman's Animal Welfare Center. The police firing range is also down here, but it has always been vacant when I have passed by. The area hosts a variety of energy infrastructure: a field of solar panels, an electric power station, oil derricks, a rusting metal silo that appears to have once been connected to an oil and gas operation. It is a part of the city rarely visited by anyone aside from avid birders. A neighbor took my family and me on a birding tour of Norman that included the road that dead ends past the WRF, near the Canadian River. I was surprised to see dozens of people walking up and down the road, peering into the dense forest with high powered binoculars, and listening carefully for the calls of migrating songbirds. Most Norman residents will never have reason to visit this edge of the city, and we can easily avoid thinking about what happens to our waste after we flush the toilet.

When we met, Steve Hardeman had been at the WRF for more than thirty years, and he communicated a clear sense of pride in his work. Given the size of the facility, there was a striking lack of workers. Only fifteen employees are present during the day, mostly running tests to make sure everything is working properly. It was just Hardeman and me walking around the pools and machines that transform sewage to water. There was a faint odor in the air, but not as bad as I expected. Hardeman explained that the City of Norman invested millions to reduce the smell, partially to avoid disturbing employees at the nearby National Weather Center. Erasing the smell of sewage helps us forget its existence.

It takes about twenty-four hours for sewage that enters the plant to exit and flow into the Canadian River. Machines first separate the biodegradable solids, which will be treated and used as fertilizer on a local hay farm. The only thing that is not reused is sediment and what Hardeman called "rags." These are removed and then directly conveyed into dumpsters that are emptied in a landfill. No chemicals are added during the water treatment process, which relies entirely on air and bacteria. The brown wastewater is moved through a series of pools, each roughly the size of a backyard swimming pool. Different levels of air are introduced to encourage harmful bacteria to be eaten by other bacteria, which then die when their food source is exhausted. Finally, the wastewater is exposed to ultraviolet light that damages the membranes of bacteria so they cannot reproduce. Oxygen is added back into the water when it leaves the plant to bring the water up to a level that can support fish life. At the end of the tour Hardeman drove me in a golf cart to where the reclaimed water is dumped into a tributary that flows into the Canadian River. We passed through a former landfill that is now covered with tall grasses and sunflowers, excellent habitat for Oklahoma's state bird, the scissortailed flycatcher. The site where the effluent enters the creek is a peaceful pool shaded by large trees. Hardeman told me that in the spring so many gar fish come here to spawn that you can almost walk across them. It is this reclaimed water that the City of Norman hopes to channel into Lake Thunderbird.

The plan to augment Lake Thunderbird with water reclaimed from the city's sewage emerged from years of discussion and planning. I spoke with Chris Mattingly in his city hall office in May 2021, not long after he took over for Ken Komiske as director of Utilities. Like all the city employees I contacted, Mattingly was quick to respond to my initial email and set up an in-person meeting. Mattingly worked for the city on water and sewer issues for more than twenty years before becoming director of Utilities. Elected officials, like the mayor, are Norman's public face, but long-term city staff like Mattingly keep the city running. Mattingly is a skilled communicator who conveyed a high level of enthusiasm for all things water-related. Over the course of an hour, he gave me a brief history of water planning in Norman to explain why Norman plans to route reclaimed water to Lake Thunderbird.

Serious updates to Norman's long-term plans for its water supply began in 2006 when drought, new restrictions on arsenic levels in drinking water, and heavy water use combined to bring Lake Thunderbird to its lowest levels since the lake was created. Approximately two-thirds of Norman's water came from Lake Thunderbird, one-third was drawn from wells in the Garber-Wellington aquifer, and a small amount of water was purchased from Oklahoma City. In 2005 new federal limits on arsenic in drinking water began to be enforced, lowering the limit from 50 parts per billion to 10. Arsenic occurs naturally in the Garber-Wellington aquifer, and Norman shut down sixteen of its thirty-one wells. Around this time, due to ongoing drought, restrictions were tightened on Norman's ability to draw from Lake Thunderbird, and Norman was forced to dig more wells and institute various conservation measures. Mattingly described Norman's current weather patterns as swinging between a "big rain" and a "big dry." 2015 was the wettest year in recorded history, and Norman has generally been in a "big rain" phase since. Increased rainfall meant that Mattingly did not anticipate water shortages until at least 2030, but that could change with shifting weather patterns.

The 2040 Strategic Water Supply Plan, which was released in 2001, recommended expanding Norman's well field in the Garber-Wellington aquifer and partnering with other cities to build a pipeline to carry water from southeast Oklahoma, the portion of the state with the highest rainfall. However, changes in arsenic regulations and anticipated changes to chromium regulations made an expansion of the well field challenging. Under the leadership of Mayor Cindy Rosenthal (2007–2016), Norman began revising its plans for water. Planning meant lots of meetings at city hall with a mostly older, middle-class white audience. In 2010 a series of eight, two-hour-long public water forum meetings were held as a first step in educating the public and developing a 2060 Strategic Water Supply Plan. Norman residents patiently engaged with presentations from engineers and city staff on topics like state water policy and financing water infrastructure. Participating in such meetings is a form of privilege that depends on access to time. Attendees were repeatedly told that the "community" would be making decisions about the future of water in Norman, and it seemed that they were the "community."

A committee was formed in 2012 to recommend a plan for meeting Norman's long-term water needs. The committee included former and future city council members, OU professors, local leaders of environmental organizations, bankers, and real estate developers. A consulting company led the committee through exercises intended to help them select from different proposals for securing future water. In addition to channeling reclaimed wastewater into the lake, proposals included diverting water from the Canadian River, constructing a new reservoir, injecting water from the Water Reclamation Facility into the aquifer, capturing stormwater that flows into the Canadian River, and bringing water from Southeast Oklahoma with a shared pipeline. At an estimated $138 million, augmenting the lake with treated wastewater was the cheapest option. Stormwater capture was estimated to be the most expensive at $1.2 billion.

I find the proposals striking in their scale and cost. Implicit in these plans is that massive investments must be made to secure future water. All plans assumed a future of growth and increased water use that closes off the possibility of radically shifting the way Norman residents consume water. In many ways these plans are contemporary equivalents of the investments the United States made in dams during the mid-twentieth century. As daunting as injecting stormwater into the aquifer seems, it is nothing compared to the fracking for oil and gas that occurs every day in Oklahoma. Augmenting the lake with wastewater was ultimately selected, because it was relatively inexpensive, provided local control that would have been absent if Norman had collaborated on a water pipeline with Oklahoma City, and fit with local values supporting conservation.[36] Reviewing minutes from committee meetings I never had the sense that wastewater augmentation was a predetermined conclusion. As the conversations progressed, what at first seemed almost impossible emerged as a viable plan, in part due to changes in state regulations governing wastewater. In June 2014 Norman's City Council voted unanimously to approve the adoption of the plan for wastewater augmentation coupled with the expansion of the city's wellfields in the Garber-Wellington aquifer. A few weeks later the full 2060 Strategic Water Supply Plan was released, and the City of Norman had a roadmap for the future.

Planning is one thing; implementation is another, especially when the plan involves drinking treated sewage. In February 2020 I returned to the WRF, this time with a public tour sponsored by the City of Norman. The WRF lobby was crowded with people bundled in heavy coats to ward off the brisk morning wind. Mayor Breea Clark was there to kick off the tour and introduce Ken Komiske, who was Norman's director of Utilities at the time. Mayor Clark was not yet on the city council when the 2060 SWSP was developed, but now she was responsible for pushing plans forward. She announced that Norman had received funds to support a three-year pilot project to research technologies that would filter wastewater before it is directed into Lake Thunderbird. Someone else is already drinking our wastewater, so why shouldn't we drink it ourselves, Clark asked. Reclaimed wastewater may be safe to drink, in many ways cleaner than the stormwater runoff that flows into Lake Thunderbird from the Little River, but it's hard for people to get past the idea that they're drinking sewage. A member of a University of Oklahoma research team was at the tour, distributing surveys regarding attitudes about drinking wastewater and the impact of the tour on the "yuck" factor. The researchers found that tours like this increased the likelihood that participants would support wastewater reuse. Political affiliation also influenced wastewater reuse with liberals being more willing to consume recycled water.[37]

The tour split in two, and I joined the group led by Ken Komiske. Near the end of the tour, I asked Komiske about "contaminants of emerging concern" (CECs). These are substances that may be hazardous for human health and are not currently regulated. They include many pharmaceuticals, PFAS, plastic components, fire retardants, and personal care products. Komiske explained that the Wastewater Reclamation Facility was experimenting with ozone and bacteria to remove these contaminants. Currently 85 percent of CECs are removed and the city hoped to get that number up to 95 percent. Tests are done in parts per trillion, Komiske emphasized, meaning that quantities of CECs are extremely minute. 1000 parts per trillion is the equivalent of only ten minutes in thirty-seven years. It is an extremely small number, and yet I have no sense of its significance. Ten minutes of sitting in an electric chair is still ten too many, even if it only happens once every thirty-seven years. Despite Komiske's attempts to ease emerging concerns about contaminants, trust is not easily built. The vast majority of the city's population will not tour the WRF. As Norman slowly moves toward wastewater reuse, city officials will continually face the challenge of convincing residents that their water is safe to drink.

Voting down the 2022 water rate increase and denying funds for Norman's water infrastructure was a move away from nourishing growth, but it created uncertainty and instability that may exacerbate growth's self-destructive consequences. Augmenting Lake Thunderbird with treated wastewater would provide water for a growing population and secure water for the present. The alternative to wastewater reuse is most likely purchasing water from Oklahoma City. Oklahoma City pipes water hundreds of miles from southeast Oklahoma to the metro area where it is stored in reservoirs. This process materially and symbolically decouples water from growth. Oklahoma City need not worry about the runoff from well-fertilized lawns and ever-expanding seas of asphalt, because in contrast to Norman, its residents do not drink the city's runoff. Oklahoma City's water is pulled from a part of the state where lawns, asphalt, and concrete are not so common. In directly provisioning its own drinking water, Norman must deal with its waste and confront the consequences of growth. Norman cannot simply buy more water. It must access that water through technologies of reclamation. This is a very different reclamation of waste than burning trash to generate energy.[38] Norman residents will directly consume their waste, meaning they have a strong interest in removing as many toxins as possible. The waste produced by growth is easily forgotten when wastewater is simply channeled into the Canadian River to eventually make its way into the Gulf of Mexico. Drinking reclaimed wastewater forces us to acknowledge what we put in our water—pharmaceuticals, plastics, hormones, and everything else in the broad category of contaminants of emerging concern. Reuse does not limit growth, but it does force us to take growth's consequences seriously.

The City of Norman is currently working with OU professor Dr. Robert Nairn on a pilot study exploring the potential for engineered wetlands to remove contaminants from treated wastewater. Nairn has engineered wetlands to remove toxins from mining waste at the Tar Creek Superfund Site in Northeast Oklahoma.[39] Creating a wetland where key tributaries like Dave Blue Creek enter Lake Thunderbird would be expensive, but it would directly confront the consequences of growth by reducing the pollutants that are causing eutrophication in the lake.

Chromium-6 and the Problem of Trust

Norman's wells draw water from the Garber-Wellington aquifer, which Ken Komiske called "a heavy metal aquifer" because of its high levels of naturally occurring arsenic and chromium. Erin Brockovich made chromium famous in her fight with Pacific Gas and Electric in Hinkley, California. PG&E paid a settlement of more than $300 million, at the time the largest settlement in a class-action lawsuit in the United States. In 2010 an Environmental Working Group (EWG) study found that of thirty-five cities it sampled, Norman's tap water had the highest levels of what the EWG referred to as the "Erin

Brockovich chemical."[40] Based on EWG sampling, Norman's water had nearly thirteen parts per billion of hexavalent chromium (chromium 6), more than six times the level of the second-most contaminated city in their study.[41]

When I asked Mayor Breea Clark in 2019 about chromium, her first response was to make clear that "It's not Erin Brockovich chromium." In contrast to the EWG's "Erin Brockovich chemical," Mayor Clark claimed that Norman's chromium is not caused by industrial pollution. "It's a different chromium," she explained, "it's naturally occurring."[42] Tinker Air Force Base, however, is just fifteen miles north of downtown Norman. Tinker is a superfund site. In the process of refurbishing airplanes, hexavalent chromium made its way into the same Garber-Wellington aquifer that Norman draws from. Connections like this create mistrust, but I spoke to experts at the University of Oklahoma who study chromium, aquifers, and water filtration. They assured me that it is highly unlikely that chromium from Tinker could make its way into the portion of the aquifer that Norman draws from. Although I trust these experts, a superfund site so close to the city is difficult to ignore.

I met with Ken Komiske in his City Hall office in 2019. At that time Komiske had been the director of Utilities for more than fifteen years. He speaks with a slight New York accent, and like me, he loves to talk water and infrastructure. We were discussing arsenic in the Garber-Wellington aquifer and Komiske shifted to chromium. "I want to emphasize that I am really editorializing here," Komiske noted, indicating that he was speaking only for himself, not the City of Norman. "The chromium is a little on the political side . . . the Hinkley thing with the chromium . . . whatever that movie was." "*Erin Brockovich*," I remind him. Komiske continued, "That was really air related . . . chromium 6 is very bad if you inhale it. If you drink it, chromium 6, your digestive system can turn it to a chromium 3, and that's in your multi-vitamin. You have chromium 3s in your multi-vitamin. It helps with your metabolism." Like his comments on contaminants of emerging concern, Komiske was creating uncertainty about the dangers of chromium.[43] It's not accurate that the chromium in the Hinkley case was only airborne, water borne chromium was a major source of residents' complaints. Komiske is correct that human bodies transform some, but not all, of the cancerous chromium 6 into the harmless chromium 3, but the impacts of chromium 6 when consumed in drinking water are not completely understood.[44]

"I think there should be a tighter connection to the cost of things," Komiske explained. "If you ask anybody if they want cleaner water, they will say sure . . . The EPA makes a rule and four years later we implement that rule and then we need to charge people money . . . They should have had a better connection there. Your chances of developing a cancer in seventy years will go from 1/100,000 to 1/50,000. Is that worth five bucks a month?" I asked about the possibility of filtering chromium-6 from drinking water and Komiske responded, "As an engineer, I can do anything you're willing to pay for."

Like Mayor Clark and Ken Komiske, when I spoke to the manager of Norman's water treatment plant, she emphasized that Norman meets all EPA regulations. Chromium 6 is below one hundred parts per billion in all of Norman's active wells. This fact was also repeatedly stated in City of Norman responses to the EWG report. Komiske told me that EPA regulations are highly conservative. They are based on the likelihood of encountering health problems after seventy years of drinking two liters of water daily, "regardless of whether you smoke, eat potato chips, or drink beer." EPA regulations provide a firm foundation that allows the city to bypass many of the more slippery ambiguities described earlier. From the perspective of city leaders, the federal government develops the rules and Norman follows those rules; any further questions should be addressed to the EPA.

EPA standards are not, however, as firm as they might appear. The EPA began enforcing new limits on arsenic in drinking water in 2005, and Norman reworked its plans for water security as a result. Norman's 2060 Strategic Water Supply Plan anticipated that by 2018 the EPA would also lower permitted chromium levels to ten parts per billion. At that level, Norman would be forced to take all but three of its wells offline or begin filtering for chromium.[45] The 2060 plan was to wait until the EPA lowered its limits and then begin consolidating well water in a single location to simultaneously filter for arsenic and chromium. This would allow Norman to bring its high arsenic wells back online and increase the city's reliance on groundwater.

Plans are based on assumptions that are often incorrect. The 2060 plan did not assume that Donald Trump would be elected president of the United

States in 2016 and appoint Oklahoma's attorney general, Scott Pruitt, as head of the EPA. Running for the office of attorney general, Pruitt accepted significant campaign donations from the oil and gas and poultry industries. As attorney general, Pruitt supported the interests of these industries and protected their profits from regulations intended to preserve public health. Pruitt sued the federal EPA fourteen times and consistently protected large corporations from lawsuits related to environmental destruction and pollution.[46] This is a variation on the conspiracy of developers. Industry uses its financial power to influence government in ways that enable profits at the public's expense. Pruitt ultimately resigned from his position heading the EPA after less than two years, when he came under attack for numerous instances of corruption, both small and large. No changes to EPA regulations on chromium 6 in drinking water occurred during the first term of Trump's presidency, and in 2024 the limit on chromium 6 in drinking water still stood at one hundred parts per billion. Prior to Trump's reelection, the City of Norman expected the EPA to update its chromium regulations in 2027.

If drinking tap water is an act of trust, what to make of the case of chromium? The City of Norman will not step away from the firm standards for water quality provided by the EPA. A powerful federal regulating agency is a key actor in this story and for many experts, like Komiske and scholars I spoke to at the University of Oklahoma, the EPA should be trusted. It was partially my faith in water quality experts at OU that led me to abandon my reverse osmosis water filter. If they drink tap water, then why shouldn't I? There is, however, ample evidence that particularly under President Trump the goal of the EPA has not been to protect the environment but to protect companies that can afford to hire influential lobbyists and donate large amounts of money to election campaigns. Why should I believe the EPA is acting in my interests? The City of Norman tells residents they can trust that tap water is safe because it meets EPA standards, but the city expected these standards to change. It is quite possible that standards have not been tightened only because of a corrupt federal EPA that prides itself on dismantling regulations.

The deeper I explored Norman's chromium 6 issues the more complex the story became. Despite the superfund site on Norman's borders, it does not appear that the chromium in Norman's water is a result of industrial pollution. The science of chromium 6 in drinking water is hazy, and much is unknown about the implications of chromium for human health.[47] If I cannot trust the EPA, how can I respond to chromium 6 in my drinking water? Residents and city officials are left with a high degree of uncertainty. Making a plan is one thing, following through on it is another. Parts of the 2060 water plan are in a holding pattern, waiting for new EPA regulations that may or may not ever arrive. California has moved forward and created its own limit of ten parts per billion for chromium 6 in drinking water, but Norman hesitates to do the same without guidance from the EPA. The city is hopeful that if EPA chromium regulations do change, the federal government will help with the cost of meeting these new standards.

Technologies like wastewater reclamation and chromium filtration are a reminder that there are different ways of investing the surplus generated by growth. Quantitative growth is based on adding more people, tax dollars, and homes. Recall the cycle of self-devouring growth discussed in earlier chapters. In Norman growth has polluted Lake Thunderbird and caused eutrophication. Growth has increased impervious surfaces that exacerbate flooding and contribute to the destruction of backyards at creek side homes. Solutions to these problems, like removing the unpleasant taste and smell from Norman's drinking water, cost money, and one way of generating those funds is through further growth. Nourishing growth by maintaining low connection fees or changing zoning regulations to facilitate development is a strategy for generating funds for the city. That growth, however, creates more impervious surfaces, more stormwater washing pollutants into the lake, and more problems for the city. Such growth also depends on a sort of trickle-down effect. The sale of new houses generates large profits for a few people that are then redistributed through taxes. The cycle is quantitative in the sense that it depends on continual increase. Growth creates a problem that is solved with funds generated by further growth, which in turn creates additional problems for the city.

Filtering chromium and arsenic from drinking water is a different form of growth that invests public funds in qualitatively improving the lives of the numerous Norman residents who cannot afford individualized technologies, like a household reverse osmosis water filter. Resources are distributed to benefit everyone who drinks Norman's tap water. Filtration of carcinogens is expensive and does not directly increase city revenue from taxes or utility fees, but what are the costs of doing nothing? Ken Komiske was correct that the costs and benefits of filtering hexavalent chromium are difficult to assess—we don't know exactly how many cases of cancer, if any, are likely to be produced by the chromium in our drinking water. But, what is the alternative to investing in water filtration? Why are we willing to invest so much in research for cancer treatment, but not prevention? Rather than a cycle of self-devouring growth that creates problems to be solved with further growth, filtration creates a very different future. Filtration may not stimulate economic growth, but by reducing the risk of cancer for all water drinkers, it is less likely people's lives will be turned upside down with cancer treatment, medical debt, and premature death. Investing in filtration technologies may support growth without destruction.

The failed water rate increase in 2022 does not doom this project, but it demonstrates the difficulty of planning. Without the trust necessary to pass a water rate increase, how can the city access the funds needed for filtering chromium and arsenic from drinking water? The City of Norman is well staffed and is in a good position to win grants to bridge gaps in funding.[48] Long term failure to enact plans, however, will ultimately create a chasm between residents who can afford to provision safe drinking water for themselves, and those who cannot.

Mistrust and Growth

In his book *Mistrust: An Ethnographic Theory*, Matthew Carey explores the value of mistrust in terms of its power to separate people and lead them to act as individuals who cannot rely on others. Carey explains that mistrust contributes to "a philosophy of rugged autonomy and moral equality that assumes other people to be both free and fundamentally uncontrollable."[49] Mistrust supports questioning authority and hierarchies of power that place some people above others. It has a levelling effect that can erode the power of the conspiracy of developers. Mistrust can function as a barrier to collective action and an antidote to policies that nourish growth and its self-destructive consequences. That was the case in the 1970s when NCCR took advantage of widespread mistrust associated with Watergate and the Vietnam War to prevent development in the Little River watershed. NCCR's political reforms expanded everyone's formal rights, giving all Norman residents a direct voice in determining city policy.

We live in a world, however, in which we must grapple with the destructive consequences of growth. Wastewater reuse appears to be the most cost-effective and least destructive path forward to provide Norman's residents with a sustainable water supply. Norman also depends on an aquifer with high levels of carcinogenic heavy metals. Filtering chromium and arsenic is expensive, but it would protect residents' health and secure water for the future. The failed 2022 water rate increase would have supported around $40 million in new projects. Wastewater augmentation was estimated to cost nearly $140 million in 2012. Chromium and arsenic filtration were estimated at $150 million in 2022. Combined these two projects that have the potential to address the consequences of self-destructive growth would cost well over seven times as much as the rate increase that voters refused to support in 2022. The City of Norman cannot plan for future water security without trust that binds people together in a way that allows for collaborative planning and action.

There is a fundamental contradiction in the arguments I have advanced in this book. On one hand, I have argued that from Norman's history as a sundown town to the ongoing conspiracy of developers there are numerous reasons to mistrust local government. Mistrust and self-devouring growth result in part from excluding some from an expansive substantive citizenship and empowering a few to have an outsized impact on policy. One solution is to give people equal voices in making the policy decisions that will impact their lives.[50] On the other hand, addressing the consequences of growth requires trust and coordinated action. Expanding citizenship through measures like voting on utility rate increases does not create an urban utopia of equity and individual autonomy. In an era of extreme mistrust and the absence of a shared vision for future community, empowering individuals often means that the only coordinated action is one of opposition. Mistrust can be leveraged to achieve limited goals like increasing connection fees and purchasing an armored vehicle for the police, but each of these victories creates pushback from the other side. Transformative projects like wastewater reuse cannot be achieved without trust. In this sense Norman is a microcosm of the nation. The United States faces enormous challenges that demand creative solutions, but the possibility of a unified response seems highly unlikely.

After the failed 2022 water rate increase Norman residents emphatically rejected a change to the city's charter that would have allowed the city council to increase utility rates without a vote. In 2023 the City of Norman once again tried to pass a water rate increase. An organization linked with a long-time conservative political consultant sent mailers to Norman residents encouraging a "no" vote on the water rate increase.[51] Many people assumed this was backlash from developers who were angry that the city had increased connection fees in 2022. Stephen Ellis continued to oppose the rate increase, arguing that connection fees were inadequate. Despite this opposition, Norman residents voted "yes" on a rate increase that would fund around $50 million of new projects.[52] At least for the moment, divisions were put aside. Although the connection fee issue was raised, in 2023 the city council was not setting new fees and the level of public discourse on the topic was far less than in 2022. Memories of the 2020 battles over police funding were fading, and Mayor Heikkila was likely correct that for some his leadership and investing in an armored vehicle for the police restored a degree of trust in city government. The City of Norman also scheduled the water rate increase vote separately from other votes, meaning that unlike 2022 when it coincided with the vote for mayor, in 2023 it was difficult to connect partisan issues with the water rate increase. Division and mistrust were not eradicated, rather they were temporarily suppressed to fund improvements to Norman's water system.

Conclusion

ALTHOUGH IT IS JANUARY, the afternoon is warm enough to be comfortable walking at Lake Thunderbird without a jacket. Together with Alise and the kids, I wander southwest along the lakeshore from West Sentinel parking lot. This is the same place where I saw people swimming in the murky water on my first visit to Lake Thunderbird more than a decade ago, and it has become a favorite destination for walks or paddleboarding. Alise does not like to go on a Thunderbird walk without the trash grabber that she bought at an estate sale. It doesn't take long for her to fill a bag of trash that she leaves on the bank to be retrieved when we return.

As we walk Gus talks to me about a video game he is deep into. I am only half listening as I try to absorb the landscape, looking at the eroded red banks. When the water is higher after the late spring rains, boats push waves into the banks and gradually wash away more and more soil. We pass a pipeline that transports crude oil under the lake.

We only meet a couple people on our walk, a woman with tresses of pink dyed hair walking a dog and later a man with four or five dogs. The man has a long gray beard and a Jimi Hendrix and The Experience t-shirt. He gives us an enthusiastic greeting and exclaims that it's a great time to get outside before tomorrow's cold weather sets in.

We pass around a point and encounter the large inlet where the Dave Blue and Jim Blue Creeks enter the lake. This is where treated sewage may eventually flow into the lake. We are blasted by wind here, and large pieces of trash are scattered in the forest on the inlet. I even see a household water heater. It seems too far from roads for intentional trash dumping and I wonder if a creek carried it here after a heavy rain.

As we approach the mouth of Dave Blue Creek, we notice that there are fist-sized rose rocks poking out of the wet sand near the water's edge. We aren't the first people to find this. Someone has made small piles of the rose rock crystals. For the most part, rose rocks are unique to Oklahoma. They have a slightly darker red color than the sandy dirt of the shore. Rose rocks are formed from an interaction between barite crystals, sandstone, and groundwater that causes disk shaped barite crystals to make circular petals on the rocks.

Rose rocks played a curious role in the latest battle over eutrophication, the conspiracy of developers, and citizenship. In 2022 the Oklahoma Turnpike Authority (OTA) announced plans to construct a turnpike that would run north/south, parallel to the western edge of Lake Thunderbird, very close to where we were walking. One of the arguments against the turnpike was that it would impact these unique rose rock geological formations.[1] The road was planned to connect with another new turnpike, running east/west through northern Norman to accommodate growth and ease traffic congestion. Perhaps even more than water infrastructure, roads nourish growth as they support more cars, homes, and businesses. City of Norman officials claimed the city could only grow in one direction, east toward Lake Thunderbird. The turnpike would likely cause zoning regulations in east Norman to shift from agricultural to residential.[2] Once again, the Lake Thunderbird watershed was a site of battles about growth. More houses would bring more runoff flowing into Lake Thunderbird, and a multilane road would also mean high amounts of stormwater washing oil and other car-related pollutants into the lake. Those who benefit from growth often avoid its destructive consequences. If the OTA builds a turnpike along Lake Thunderbird, it is unlikely to take responsibility for dealing with polluted water. The challenge of paying for upgrades to the water treatment plant would fall to the residents of Norman.

And so Norman residents argued that in many ways the turnpike was another conspiracy of developers. A participant on the Neighbors 4 Norman Facebook page provided a list of Governor Stitt's appointments to the Oklahoma Transportation Commission.[3] The appointments, all men, included an automobile dealer, a member of the oil and gas industry, a president of a construction company and former member of the Oklahoma Turnpike Authority, an owner of a trucking company, and Gene McKown as the at-large appointment.[4] Recall that Gene McKown had been battling to develop land in the Lake Thunderbird watershed for decades. All of Governor Stitt's appointments were well-positioned to profit from a new turnpike. Like my description of nourishing growth with water infrastructure, critics of the OTA described a process in which public money subsidizes private interests. The OTA borrows money to build turnpikes and then borrows more money when those turnpikes are not profitable. This ultimately leads to escalating fees for road tolls.[5] Lack of transparency and corruption within the OTA is further evidence of a conspiracy of developers that is an essential dimension of capitalism, a system that depends on growth nourished with public resources.[6]

Citizenship was key in the OTA conflict. People like the wealthy men that Governor Stitt appointed to the Oklahoma Transportation Commission benefit immensely from growth, while others, often people like me, are well-positioned to protect themselves from growth's destructive consequences. Norman residents sprang into action filing lawsuits and creating organizations such as Pike Off OTA to oppose the turnpike. Some of the initial resistance to the turnpike came in the form of classic nimbyism, people protecting their rural backyards from new roads and urban growth, but Pike Off OTA's critiques of the OTA went beyond nimbyism to highlight how public funds are used to subsidize the work of the OTA in ways that benefit private investors and nourish growth. Resistance to the OTA is based in part on the privilege of expansive citizenship. Pike Off OTA's leaders include university professors and experienced lawyers from across the political spectrum. They are certainly concerned about corruption but are also motivated by the turnpike's threats to their own land. They are doing exactly what I would do, using their expansive citizenship—skills, wealth, experience, and connections—to protect their property. But, it's unlikely that many of these people would have thrown themselves into fighting a turnpike elsewhere in the state. One of Oklahoma City's historic African American neighborhoods, the Deep Deuce, was ripped apart by a freeway decades earlier, with little resistance from outside activists. When resisting self-devouring growth depends on the expansive citizenship of a few, it necessarily creates inequalities that erode trust. That said, when organizations like Pike Off OTA fight to reform road construction at the state level, it represents a shift from protecting one's own backyard to protecting all backyards.

The fight over turnpikes is the issue of the day in Norman, but I have no doubts that other battles about growth are coming. The cases I have discussed demonstrate that using public funds to nourish growth that benefits a narrow set of private interests suffocates life, in part because those who benefit from growth are protected from the consequences of their actions.

Policy debates in the United States are often about what kind of growth should be subsidized. Do we subsidize the oil industry or electric cars? Both options assume public support for private interests will somehow benefit all. The case of water infrastructure in Norman demonstrates that we need to be wary of solutions to climate change that depend on subsidizing growth through consumption. More growth is not always the answer.

In some ways the solution to the problem of self-destructive growth is simple—stop nourishing growth. If, for example, homeowners in the Lake Thunderbird watershed were to stop fertilizing their lawns it would be a major step toward preventing eutrophication. Holding owners of impervious surfaces responsible for the damage their property does downstream is another way to stop nourishing growth. More broadly, removing government subsidies and tax breaks for oil companies would slow down the growth that suffocates life. There are many ways to stop nourishing growth, but political will is needed to enact these seemingly simple solutions. This is where eutrophication encounters the conspiracy of developers. Oil companies, for example, exert intense pressure on lawmakers to subsidize their businesses. Developers in Norman donate money to politicians or support campaigns related to changes in utility rates. The 2016 fight to stop a stormwater utility was in some ways a fight to continue subsidizing growth.

The power of the conspiracy of developers is compounded by differences in substantive citizenship. Some benefit enormously from growth, while others are well-positioned to protect themselves from its destructive consequences. Wealth brings political influence and the power to hire an experienced attorney to represent one's interests. Even those who lack the capital to donate thousands of dollars to political campaigns can organize with their neighbors to influence policymaking, often pursuing different forms of nimbyism. Success depends on the educational and professional experience to articulate arguments in ways that will be heard by city staff and elected officials. Clear differences in substantive citizenship breed mistrust.

Eutrophication cannot be stopped without addressing citizenship. When NCCR expanded the formal power of citizenship in the 1970s, this was a direct attempt to stop nourishing self-devouring growth. Norman's experiment with giving citizens direct control over utility rates is one way to combat the conspiracy of developers that supports eutrophication, but it comes with problems of its own. Division and mistrust mean that expanding citizenship often leads to inaction. "No" is the only consensus that can be reached, and other interventions are needed. Placing limits on the power of wealth to influence elections is one way to undermine the substantive citizenship of a few and rebuild trust.

Identity and substantive citizenship are inseparable. Racism continues to limit participation in city policy making. Norman's residents have never elected a Black city council member.[7] Norman has a sizable Native American community, and yet Indigenous perspectives are rarely incorporated into policymaking. Since Cindy Rosenthal's election as mayor in 2007, Norman has elected many women to leadership positions, but they often face misogynistic attacks. The upper-level city staff that run the city are almost all men. Perhaps the greatest barriers to substantive citizenship, however, are class and education. In a university town like Norman, it is not difficult to find highly educated people who are able to join committees, participate in meetings, and articulate their ideas to city leaders. It is far more difficult to bring those without significant formal education into the decision-making process. There is no simple solution to this problem. The city needs to perform targeted outreach to gather the perspectives of those who are less likely to participate in civic life. These are just some of the battles that must be fought to expand substantive citizenship for all and prevent the nourishing of growth that suffocates life.

Seeing Urban Growth through Creeks

Water infrastructure is such an effective tool for the conspiracy of developers because it hides in plain sight. It redistributes wealth in ways that are often unseen. Norman is unusual in that NCCR's activism in the 1970s made infrastructure visible. Giving residents control over the funding of water infrastructure expanded the scope of citizenship in ways that compounded the challenge of trust, at times creating barriers to needed upgrades in water infrastructure. But perhaps more importantly, it created continual conversations about the distribution of the benefits of urban growth.

When Norman residents learned that the OTA was planning to build a turnpike in rural Norman, they quickly recognized connections between infrastructure, growth, water, and the interests of developers. Something similar happened during yet another major debate over lift stations, water, and growth in the Lake Thunderbird watershed during the early 2000s.[8] Each of these battles increases the visibility of infrastructure and brings more people into the discussion. Many who are currently active in Norman politics were pulled in by the early 2000s lift station debates. Visibility does not solve the problems I have discussed, but it is a necessary step in the process.

Creeks make connections within the city visible. When I am tired of work or frustrated with the state of the world, I often take evening bike rides to Eastwood Park and Bishop Creek. In early April the setting sun lights up the deep pink flowers of a red bud tree. The mulberry trees are filling out with light green leaves and the tart black berries will soon arrive. It's a nice time of year in Norman. This weekend tens of thousands of people in armor and cloaks poured into Reaves Park for the annual Medieval Fair. In a few weeks a different crowd, more tattoos and tank tops than tunics, will arrive for the Norman Music Festival. This evening, a few people wander through Eastwood Park. A young man who looks to be in his late teens walks near the creek with headphones on. His shaggy hair is bleached on one side and black on the other. He seems lost in his music and the spring foliage. Something about his presence reminds me that many locals refer to Eastwood as Hobbit Park, because of the little creatures they saw emerging from the landscape when they experimented with hallucinogenic substances here during their youth.

Eastwood Park is unique in Norman with its canopy of large trees, rolling hills, and most importantly, Bishop Creek flowing through the park. The creek takes its name from James Bishop, who claimed land on its banks in the 1889 land run.[9] Where most Norman parks center around a sports field, Eastwood simply offers a pleasant environment for passing time. In 2014 my family and I started meeting others in Eastwood Park on Sunday mornings. The adults stood in the shade drinking coffee and the kids gravitated toward the creek, where they splashed in a riffle, caught crawfish and gambusia, and explored upstream. There was trash in the creek to be sure, but it did not deter the kids.

One Sunday we noticed signs around the creek labeled "Friends of Bishop Creek" and announcing a "no-mow zone." Friends of Bishop Creek was a small organization that had convinced the City of Norman to stop mowing up to the creek's edge. Long grasses, bushes, and small trees began to emerge. A few letters to the editor appeared in the *Norman Transcript* from concerned residents, worried that the tall grass would be perfect tick and snake habitat, but the no-mow zone persisted. The no-mow zone was a different way to nourish growth, which only required people to sit back and do nothing rather than intervene with fertilizers. Another Sunday there were people clearing space near the creek for what turned out to be a pollinator garden. They filled a small garden with flowering plants that do well in Oklahoma's climate that alternates between heavy rain and periods of intense heat and drought. Second graders from Lincoln Elementary, located across the street, use the pollinator garden as an outdoor classroom.

One of the leaders behind developing and maintaining the pollinator garden explained that her efforts grew out of interests in activism and social justice that emerged decades earlier. She noted that she is a member of the Chickasaw and Choctaw tribes and with encouragement from an aunt she got involved in tribal governance at the age of twelve. The pollinator garden is an extension of this work and is intended to educate students about creek ecology and the importance of riparian plants in preventing erosion and maintaining water quality. This is just one part of her activism. She also organizes forums to teach communities about their water rights.

Another of the "Friends of Bishop Creek" is Karen Chapman. I often run into Karen in Eastwood Park, as she walks through the tall grass with a sturdy walking stick in hand and a large camera around her neck. Karen is a talented nature photographer, and she shares her photographs on the Friends of Bishop Creek Facebook site. Karen also shares photos of the trash she pulls out of the creek. Nearly every week from 2012 to 2022, Karen put on her waterproof coveralls and waded through the creek, picking up trash. Karen usually pulled between six and eight bags of trash out of the section of the creek that runs through the park, perhaps a little less than two city blocks. Between April and November 2022 she removed more than fifteen hundred pounds of trash from the creek.

Karen and a group of women began monitoring Bishop Creek for Blue Thumb in 2012. Most of the people closely engaged with water in Norman, including volunteers and city employees, are women. I monitor Bishop Creek at Eastwood Park and for many years Karen monitored a site further downstream. I initially wanted to monitor Imhoff Creek, closer to my house, but Imhoff does not meet Blue Thumb's requirement of having flowing water the entire year. It is not only Norman's residents who increasingly perceive Imhoff as a drainage channel; conservation organizations also do not categorize it as a creek. It would be difficult to advocate for a no-mow zone on a drainage canal.

In a time of epistemological crises, when truth and trust seem almost impossible, creeks offer a valuable way of knowing the world. I enjoy the rhythm of a monthly visit to the creek to collect a water sample. When rains are scarce the creek reduces to a trickle, grasses grow in the creek bed, and dissolved oxygen in the water falls to a level that is not sustainable for aquatic life. When the rain returns in the spring, water rushes through the creek and oxygen levels increase. There is something comforting about collecting data at a specific place and time. After Norman's roads were salted during a rare winter snow, I detected ammonia in the creek for the first time. So many traces of the city are found in creeks. Creeks are like a line that connects dots to form a comprehensible image. Like all connections, they are partially imagined, but they are also rooted in material processes.

If creeks are a way of knowing, they are full of surprises. Around each bend in the creek is something new that wakes my mind to a different way of thinking. I never know what I will find at the riffle where I collect my

Fig. 8. (*top*) Turtles in Bishop Creek. Photo by Karen Chapman.

Fig. 9. (*bottom*) Trash in Bishop Creek. Photo by Karen Chapman.

monthly water sample. In August a brilliantly colored longear sunfish was chasing smaller fish away from a circle of rocks and sand in a small pool just upstream from the riffle. Male longear sunfish make these circular nests and then they guard them after their mates lay eggs. On a warm September day there was a whole grocery store chicken carcass rotting in the creek. In October a red tent was pitched near the riffle, surrounded by a grocery cart, lawnmower, and small ladder. In November I noticed that chicken wire had been wrapped around many of the trees, presumably to protect them from the beavers that had been gnawing at their trunks.

In June 2020 Karen and I met with Blue Thumb's volunteer coordinator, Cheryl Cheadle, at Eastwood Park to discuss our vision for Bishop Creek. It was a typical warm sunny June Oklahoma day, comfortable for standing in the shade, but not much more than that. It was the third month of the COVID-19 pandemic, and we were still figuring out how to gather safely. Although we were outside and standing far apart, we wore face masks.

We talked about different possibilities for the creek. Cheryl noted the value of people connecting with nature. How could we convince children to spend more time in the creek? After some brainstorming, Karen departed, and I led Cheryl on a short walk around the creek. Cheryl and I took off our masks. It felt good to breathe freely as the heat and humidity increased. We put on our rubber boots and waded into the creek, beginning at the little riffle where I collect my water samples. Walking around a small bend in the creek we met a heron perched on a bank. Small fish flitted through the warm shallow pools. We exited the creek near the deeper pools and continued walking along the banks, making a short loop through the park. Near the end of the walk, we spotted a soft-shelled turtle sunning itself on the banks. We were only a few feet away when it noticed us and scuttled off into the creek. It was my first time seeing this long turtle with a distinctive pointed nose.

Cheryl is full of energy and optimism. She chattered throughout the walk, identifying species like the kingbird that I can never seem to remember. Cheryl had recently read that two of three people say that COVID-19 has changed the way they look at the world. She wondered if we were experiencing an opportunity for a spiritual reconnection with nature. I don't know exactly what a spiritual connection is, but I wanted people to see the

Fig. 10. Yellow-crowned night heron at Bishop Creek. Photo by Karen Chapman.

creek—a yellow-crowned night heron, a soft-shelled turtle, and kingbirds. Unlike my walks through Imhoff and Merkel Creeks, Bishop does not feel like stormwater infrastructure. It feels like a creek. I wanted people to know that this habitat exists in the middle of the city and that it is connected to their homes, roads, and parking lots. I wanted people to see that asphalt and riparian forests are part of the same system.

Karen and I obtained financial support from Blue Thumb and the City of Norman to produce and install an informative sign near the pollinator garden in Eastwood Park. The sign summarizes our monitoring results and features some of Karen's photographs of animals and trash. The goal was to help park visitors see the creek as an ecosystem that is connected to their homes and the rest of the city. This, I believe, is the ultimate result of Blue Thumb's statewide creek monitoring program. It is a form of citizen science that generates data, but more than those numbers and reports, it produces citizens who care about creeks, people who see how creeks bring together landscapes, economies, and politics.

Creeks expand our vision of the city. The creek and its eroding banks are inseparable from the new strip mall upstream. A shift in perception will not solve the problem of self-devouring growth, but it is a start. It sparks a conversation. Economic growth produces wealth, but it also generates destruction. Progress and growth create futures that eat themselves, transforming what was once desired into a world where life is suffocated. We cannot address environmental destruction and inequality unless we are willing to think seriously about the destructive consequences of growth. Creeks are one path to this realization.

Growth and destruction are connected, but Bishop Creek is also a reminder that nourishing growth does not inevitably suffocate life. The turtles, fish, and herons in Bishop Creek persist despite a habitat that has been thoroughly marginalized by the city's growth. The abundance of life in this little riparian pocket of the city is astonishing. Even with the no-mow zone the banks continue to erode and Styrofoam cups float in the water, but in the spring, songbirds will migrate north, and in the fall monarch butterflies will pass through on their long journey south. The temporality of creeks is not one of progress, but of change. Creeks help us see that we are constantly shaping change.[10] Our actions shape creeks and creeks shape us. Just as urban creeks clarify the destructive consequences of growth, their persistence brings hope.

NOTES

INTRODUCTION

1. Livability, "Norman, OK, Is One of the Best Cities to Live in America," accessed July 1, 2024, https://livability.com/best-places/2023-top-100-best-places-to-live-in-the-us/norman-ok/.
2. Whitney, "Living Lawns, Dying Waters"; Robbins and Sharp, "Producing and Consuming Chemicals."
3. An EPA impact study on Lake Thunderbird from the 1970s describes a "musty odor" associated with blue-green algae blooms and the scent of "freshly turned earth" as a result of a "mold-like bacteria" in the water. EPA, Draft Environmental Impact Statement, 50–51.
4. National Geographic, Encyclopedia Entry: Dead Zone, accessed July 30, 2024, https://education.nationalgeographic.org/resource/dead-zone/.
5. Livingston, *Self-Devouring Growth*. I was fortunate to encounter Julie Livingston's book about Botswana early in my research for this project, and her concept of self-devouring growth is highly useful for understanding Norman and other cities in the United States.
6. *Frontier*, "Federal Regulations, Coal Phase Outs Mostly Responsible for Decreasing Carbon Output in Oklahoma, March 12, 2021," https://www.readfrontier.org/stories/federal-regulations-coal-phase-outs-mostly-responsible-for-decreasing-carbon-output-in-oklahoma/.
7. Holston, *Insurgent Citizenship*. In her work on African migrants in the United States, Cati Coe offers a useful discussion of political belonging, a concept that resonates with substantive citizenship. Coe, *The New American Servitude*.
8. Dave Blue Creek is named for a man who lived on the creek and ran a trading post where he sold provisions to railroad survey crews in the 1870s. John Womack describes him as "a Cherokee Indian, buffalo exterminator, trapper, trader and alleged cattle rustler." Womack, *Cleveland Country, Oklahoma*, 197.
9. EPA, "Contaminants of Emerging Concern Including Pharmaceuticals and Personal Care Products," accessed July 1, 2023, https://www.epa.gov/wqc/contaminants-emerging-concern-including-pharmaceuticals-and-personal-care-products.

10. Spending time in urban rivers like the Los Angeles River can also reshape our vision of cities. Gandy, *The Fabric of Space*; Sayd Randle, "Aqueduct-Walking in the Mojave Desert," *Sage Magazine*, September 26, 2016, https://sagemagazine.org/aqueduct-walking-in-the-mojave-desert/.
11. On nature that flourishes in marginalized urban spaces see Gandy, *Natura Urbana*.
12. Like Anna Tsing's analysis of matsutake mushrooms in degraded forests, urban creeks help us see the surprising possibilities that can emerge from damaged ecologies. Tsing, *Mushroom at the End of the World*.
13. Drought.gov: National Integrated Drought Information System, "Oklahoma," accessed July 1, 2024, https://www.drought.gov/states/oklahoma.
14. NBC News, "How a Debate Over Police Funding Escalated in Norman, Oklahoma—and Divided the Town," September 22, 2020, https://www.nbcnews.com/news/us-news/how-debate-over-police-funding-escalated-norman-oklahoma-divided-town-n1240661.
15. Star, "Ethnography of Infrastructure."
16. New federal legislation like the creation of the Environmental Protection Agency gave residents an increasing number of tools for resisting local growth: Sabin, *Public Citizens*.
17. Larry Hill, "Letter to the Editor: Utilities, Lift Station Issues 'Linked,'" *Norman Transcript*, September 1, 1974.
18. This process can also happen in rural areas. Pilgeram, *Pushed Out*.
19. Harvey, *Urban Experience*. Critics of conspiracy theories sometimes argue that they distract from structural inequalities, but structural inequalities are in part reproduced by conspiracies between owners of capital and political power.
20. Sobo, "Conspiracy Theories in Political-Economic Context"; Kendzior, *They Knew*; Parker, "Human Science as Conspiracy Theory."
21. Masco and Wedeen explain that "a paranoid style of thought might just be for many a necessary skill set—even a basic survival strategy—for those living in political orders committed to maintaining extreme inequalities." Masco and Wedeen, "Introduction: Conspiracy/Theory," 17. The challenge in analyzing conspiracy is that even conspiracy theories that deviate radically from reality are often still generated by a sense of paranoia that is well grounded in the current political order.
22. Ewing, Reid, and Shima Hamidi, "Compactness versus Sprawl," 413–32.
23. Jackson, *Crabgrass Frontier*.
24. Bagstad, Stapleton, and D'Agostino, "Taxes, Subsidies, and Insurance," 285–98.
25. ARIA Development, "Team," accessed July 1, 2024, https://www.ariadevelopmentok.com/team#team-1.
26. Switzer, Stoops, and Keith supported local businessman Sam Talley in Ward 3. Talley also happened to be Sassan Moghadam's son-in-law, but Unite Norman endorsed Kelly Lynn. Despite receiving significant support from established Ward 3 leaders and numerous members of the development community, Talley finished

third of three candidates in the initial round of voting, just behind Lynn. Lynn went on to beat incumbent, and Unite Norman recall target, Alison Petrone, in the runoff election.

27. Max Bryan, "Council Divisions Highlighted During Mayor's State of the City Address," *Norman Transcript*, September 28, 2022.
28. The survey conducted after the failed water rate increase vote indicated that distrust was far higher among Republicans and Independents than Democrats, and this translated to a largely partisan vote with Republicans and Independents voting "no" and 66 percent of Democrats surveyed voting "yes" on the rate increase. Mindy Ragan Wood, "Survey: Rate Increase Failure Is Economic, Partisan, Referendum," *Norman Transcript*, June 8, 2022.
29. Minor conflicts over masking occurred throughout the meeting. The city council was masked, although some councilmembers removed their masks to speak. For the most part the police officers in the audience did not wear masks, despite continued requests from some of the audience members.
30. The Oklahoma Supreme Court ruled that Norman's City Council had violated the Open Meetings Act by not including the amendments to reallocate police funds on the meeting agenda. The lawsuit was brought by Norman's Fraternal Order of Police. Minday Ragan Wood, "Oklahoma Supreme Court Sides with Norman FOP in City's Appeal of Suit," *Norman Transcript*, April 13, 2021.
31. Holston, *Insurgent Citizenship*.
32. Holston, *Insurgent Citizenship*.
33. Kelly Weill, "Did Doxxing of an Oklahoma Councilwoman Lead to a Neighbor Being Raped?" *Daily Beast*, July 7, 2020, https://www.thedailybeast.com/norman-oklahoma-councilwoman-alexandra-scott-fears-police-doxxing-led-to-neighbor-being-raped.
34. Ari Fife, "'Encourage Women to Empower Other Women': Female Politicians in Norman Discuss Complexities of Life in Office," *OU Daily*, February 11, 2022, https://www.oudaily.com/news/encourage-women-to-empower-other-women-female-politicians-in-norman-discuss-complexities-of-life-in/article_a98d3f64–8aac-11ec-8ee2–7f093681f1cd.html. Even before the June 16, 2020, city council meeting, in regards to Mayor Clark, a police officer in a neighboring town posted on Facebook, "Mayor dipshit needs to be pulled out of office and tried on the courthouse lawn . . . the problem with politicians, they don't get hung in public anymore . . . #bringbackpublichangings!" Beth Wallis, "Norman: A Town Divided," *OU Daily*, October 14, 2020, https://www.oudaily.com/crimson_quarterly/norman-a-town-divided/article_4773c97a-0e38-11eb-805f-47b79598e57b.html.
35. On citizenship and water infrastructure see Anand, *Hydraulic City*; Bakker, *Privatizing Water*; von Schnitzler, *Democracy's Infrastructure*.
36. NIMBY = Not In My BackYard.

HISTORICAL INTERLUDE

1. Russell Cobb describes the state's past and present as "the great Oklahoma swindle." Like Cobb, I argue that the state's foundations are rooted in racism, but I articulate a more specific relationship between citizenship, capitalism, and the environment. Cobb, *Great Swindle*.
2. Baird and Goble, *Oklahoma*, 142.
3. Historically they were referred to as the "Five Civilized Tribes," and some Five Tribes institutions retain this title.
4. Baird and Goble, *Oklahoma*.
5. Hightower, *1889*, 10.
6. Howard, "Rush to Oklahoma," 391–94.
7. *Boom Town* is also the story of the Oklahoma City Thunder and their rapid rise to contenders for an NBA championship under the leadership of Kevin Durant, Russel Westbrook, and James Harden. As I write in 2024, the Oklahoma City Thunder have passed through the bust that often follows a boom. After years of "tanking," intentionally fielding teams that are unlikely to win many games in the hopes of landing top draft picks, the Thunder are once again competing at a high level. They are led by a young core of Shai Gilgeous-Alexander, Jalen Williams, and Chet Holmgren. In the NBA a bust can sometimes open the way for a boom. Perhaps similarly, Oklahoma City has become one of the most popular locations in the U.S. for members of "Gen Z" to purchase their first home. The urban blight that plagued Oklahoma City in earlier decades led to real estate affordable enough to attract young people who are revitalizing the city and rents are beginning to rise rapidly.
8. Anderson, *Boom Town*, 88.
9. Anderson, *Boom Town*, 65.
10. Anderson, *Boom Town*, 102.
11. Anderson, *Boom Town*.
12. Womack, *Norman*, 11.
13. Womack, *Norman*, 13.
14. Hightower, *1889*, 11.
15. Womack, *Norman*, 17–19.
16. Womack, *Norman*, 19.
17. Womack, *Norman*, 25.
18. Mosteller, "Place, Politics, and Property."
19. Baird and Goble, *Oklahoma*; Chang, "Enclosures of Land and Sovereignty."
20. Helton and Robertson, "Foundations of Federal Indian Law."
21. Dispossession of land is an essential dimension of settler colonialism. See Voyles, *Settler Sea*; Arvin, Tuck, and Morrill, "Decolonizing Feminism."
22. Helton and Robertson, "Foundations of Federal Indian Law," 37.
23. Hightower, *1889*, 12–13; Mosteller, "Cultural Politics of Land."
24. Chang, "Enclosures of Land and Sovereignty"; Hightower, *1889*, 11; LaDuke and Cowen, "Beyond Wiindigo Infrastructure."

25. Worster, *Dust Bowl*. The depletion of the Ogallala aquifer is another case of self-devouring growth in the Great Plains. Bessire, *Running Out*.
26. This is not to say that deception was not also a tool of dispossession. The case of the Osage is one well-documented case of murder, deception, and theft of land. Grann, *Killers of the Flower Moon*.
27. Baird and Goble, *Oklahoma*; Mosteller, "The Cultural Politics of Land" explains that accepting allotments prior to the passage of the Dawes Act was a strategic act of agency that allowed the Citizen Potawatomi to struggle for security in a context of forced removals.
28. Baird and Goble, *Oklahoma*, 158.
29. Levy, *University of Oklahoma: A History*, vol. 1, 15–16.
30. *Norman Transcript*, December 27, 1890; quoted in Levy, *University of Oklahoma: A History*, vol. 1, 18–19.
31. Womack, *Norman*, 35.
32. Womack, *Norman*, 43.
33. Boyd, "Oklahoma Oil," 98.
34. Legacy.com, "Logan Wickliffe "Wick" Cary Jr.," accessed July 22, 2024, https://www.legacy.com/us/obituaries/nola/name/logan-cary-obituary?id=14426092.
35. Ricky Marathon, "Students Seek Change to Honors College Name," *OU Daily*, April 23, 2009, https://www.oudaily.com/news/students-seek-change-to-honors-college-name/article_5fa3bada-dac6–5ae2-a817–66357c4061cf.html. McClendon's parents' names were dropped from the Honors College name in 2024. Ana Barboza and Shelby Emery, "OU Board of Regents Approves Tuition, Housing Increase," *OU Daily*, June 21, 2024, https://www.oudaily.com/news/ou-board-of-regents-approves-tuition-housing-increase/article_a0a4c760–3003–11ef-9dcb-6baaeb6cfca8.html.
36. Bryan Gruley, Joe Carroll, and Asjylyn Loder, "The Incredible Rise and Final Hours of Fracking King Aubrey McClendon," *Bloomberg Businessweek*, March 10, 2016, https://www.bloomberg.com/features/2016-aubrey-mcclendon/.

1. TASTING GROWTH AND WHITE SUPREMACY

1. Truden, "Absentee Shawnees."
2. Truden, "Absentee Shawnees."
3. Traci Brynne Voyles explains, it is not just that "environmental problems compound social inequities . . . social inequities also cause vast environmental problems." Voyles, *Settler Sea*, 7. On watersheds, eutrophication, and colonial legacies see Todd, "From a Fishy Place." Trombley, "Watershed Encounters."
4. Oklahoma does have playa and oxbow lakes.
5. Joe Wertz, "Mapped: Oklahoma's Dams and the Potential Hazards They Pose," *StateImpact Oklahoma*, December 12, 2014, https://stateimpact.npr.org/oklahoma/2014/12/12/mapped-oklahomas-dams-and-the-potential-hazards-they-pose/.

6. Allan Cromley, "Rate 'Rider' Muddies Little River Bill," *Daily Oklahoman*, May 29, 1960.
7. Public Law 86–529, June 27, 1960.
8. Allan Cromley, "Rate 'Rider' Muddies Little River Bill," *Daily Oklahoman*, May 29, 1960.
9. Marx, *Capital*.
10. Donald Worster described the American West as a "hydraulic society . . . ruled by a power elite based on the ownership of capital and expertise." Worster, *Rivers of Empire*, 7.
11. Reisner, *Cadillac Desert*, 111.
12. Reisner, *Cadillac Desert*, 142.
13. Henry Fountain, "How Bad Is the Western Drought? Worst in 12 Centuries, Study Finds," *New York Times*, February 14, 2022, https://www.nytimes.com/2022/02/14/climate/western-drought-megadrought.html; Elizabeth Kolbert, "The Lost Canyon Under Lake Powell," *New Yorker*, August 9, 2021, https://www.newyorker.com/magazine/2021/08/16/the-lost-canyon-under-lake-powell.
14. Rebecca Solnit, "Letter from a Drowned Canyon," *California Sunday Magazine*, March 30, 2017, https://story.californiasunday.com/drowned-canyon/.
15. Central Arizona Project, "Colorado River Reductions," accessed July 3, 2024, https://www.cap-az.com/water/water-supply/adapting-to-drought/colorado-river-reductions/.
16. Hundley, *Great Thirst*; Kahrl, *Water and Power*.
17. Mains, *Under Construction*; Fisher, *Toward Sustainable Development*.
18. Scientists have argued that climate change is pushing the line dividing the humid east from the arid western plains further east. The 98th meridian, just east of Norman, may be the new dividing line between wet and dry climates. Harvey Leifert, "Dividing Line: The Past, Present and Future of the 100th Meridian," *EARTH*, January 9, 2018, https://www.earthmagazine.org/article/dividing-line-past-present-and-future-100th-meridian.
19. Sabin, *Public Citizens*, 5.
20. Jack Bagby, "10 Years Bring Great Changes in Norman," *Norman Transcript*, May 22, 1960.
21. Douglas McKay, "Plan of Development for Norman Project, Oklahoma," U.S. Department of the Interior, December 1954, Carl Albert Center, University of Oklahoma, Tom Steed Collection; Joe Simonds, "Norman Project," Bureau of Reclamation, 1999.
22. Simonds, "Norman Project."
23. Tom Steed, letter to a constituent, February 14, 1955, Carl Albert Center, University of Oklahoma, Tom Steed Collection.
24. "Water Projects May Bring City New Potential," *Norman Transcript*, September 14, 1958.
25. Carolyn Hart, "Kerr Predicts Canal by '70," *Oklahoma City Times*, July 10, 1958.

26. Paid announcement from Interested Citizens and Taxpayers, "Norman Has 'Staked Its Claim' to the Little River Reservoir Let's 'Prove It Up' Tomorrow at the Polls!" *Norman Transcript*, May 22, 1961.
27. Paid announcement from Interested Citizens and Taxpayers, "Norman Has 'Staked Its Claim' to the Little River Reservoir Let's 'Prove It Up' Tomorrow at the Polls!" *Norman Transcript*, May 22, 1961.
28. Celilo Falls on the Columbia River was another case in which narratives of orderly growth and trust supported dam construction and the displacement of Native Americans in the mid-twentieth century. Barber, *Death of Celilo Falls*.
29. Open Letter from Mayor and City Council, *Norman Transcript*, May 17, 1961.
30. "Need of Project Cited by Downing," *Norman Transcript*, May 16, 1961.
31. Jack Bagby, "Norman Gives Reservoir Project Approval in Landslide Vote," *Norman Transcript*, May 24, 1961.
32. "Work Begins on Reservoir Project," *Norman Transcript*, August 1, 1962.
33. In the mid-twentieth century dams often displaced Indigenous people and disrupted cultural practices. Lawrence, "Damming Rivers, Damning Cultures."
34. Joy Hampton, "Locals Stand with Standing Rock Sioux," *Norman Transcript*, November 21, 2016. The Dakota Access Pipeline was in many ways a continuation of struggles over dams in the mid-twentieth century and what Nick Estes and Jaskiron Dhillon (in "Black Snake," 5) call the "Indian wars of extermination."
35. Lake Thunderbird's name continued this erasure. "Lake Thunderbird" was selected from over five thousand entries from Norman residents in a contest to determine the new name for what had been called the Little River Reservoir. Comments from the committee approving the name change noted that "it is an Indian name and captures the heritage of the area," and "The Thunderbird is the Indian God of rain which ties in with the body of water." Such comments lump all Native Americans together to evoke an imagined past. They ignore the beliefs and experiences of the Absentee Shawnee and the numerous other tribes who relied on the Little River watershed. Quotes above are from: Joe Burke, letter to the commissioner of the Bureau of Reclamation on behalf of the committee to select a permanent name for the Little River Reservoir, September 13, 1965. Carl Albert Center, University of Oklahoma, Fred R. Harris Collection.
36. Peggy O'Rear, "Forced Move Brings Heartbreak for Indian Families," *Daily Oklahoman*, March 25, 1962.
37. Sugden, *Tecumseh*.
38. Sugden, *Tecumseh*.
39. Blanchard, "They Came One at a Time."
40. Blanchard, "They Came One at a Time."
41. Mosteller, "Place, Politics, and Property."
42. Blanchard, "They Came One at a Time," 162; Mosteller, "Place, Politics, and Property," 162.
43. Mosteller, "Place, Politics, and Property," 163.

44. Mosteller, "Place, Politics, and Property," 167; Kelli Mosteller demonstrates the diversity of Native American experiences with allotment and removal. Mosteller convincingly argues that because the Citizen Potawatomi tribe accepted allotments relatively early, in 1861, they were better prepared to negotiate with the U.S. government regarding their conflict with the Absentee Shawnee over access to land in the Little River Valley. Mosteller, "Cultural Politics of Land."
45. Quoted in Mosteller, "Place, Politics, and Property," 169.
46. Alford, *Civilization*, 151.
47. Alford, *Civilization*, 152.
48. Blanchard, "They Came One at a Time." Absentee Shawnee Tribe, "About Us," accessed July 3, 2024, https://www.astribe.com/about-us.
49. Doris Duke Collection, "Interview with Webb Little Jim, Conducted by Julia Jordan," February 2, 1969, Western History Collection, University of Oklahoma.
50. Doris Duke Collection, "Interview with Clifton Blanchard, Conducted by David Jones," April 15, 1968, Western History Collection, University of Oklahoma.
51. Truden, "Absentee Shawnees," 15.
52. Doris Duke Collection, "Interview with Clifton Blanchard, Conducted by David Jones," April 15, 1968, Western History Collection, University of Oklahoma.
53. Doris Duke Collection, "Interview with Clifton Blanchard."
54. LaDuke and Cowen, "Beyond Wiindigo Infrastructure."
55. LaDuke and Cowen, "Beyond Wiindigo Infrastructure," 252–53.
56. Randell and Curley, "Dams and Tribal Land Loss in the United States."
57. Livingston, *Self-Devouring Growth*.
58. Mains, *Under Construction*.
59. Fostvedt, Tullos, and Tilt, "Institutional Analysis of Small Dam Removals."
60. Voyles, *Settler Sea*, 145.
61. Henderson, *Race and the University*, 226.
62. Henderson, *Race and the University*, 10.
63. Henderson, *Race and the University*, 197 and 226.
64. Loewen, *Sundown Towns*, 4.
65. Loewen, *Sundown Towns*, 169.
66. Loewen, *Sundown Towns*, 238. Womack, *Norman*, 215–17. John Womack explains that because local laborers were unable to finish the job, George Rogan was eventually offered the protection he needed to complete the roof and other Main Street roofs before returning home, weeks later. Womack takes this as evidence that Norman city officials did have the power to protect African Americans, but with few exceptions chose not to do so.
67. Loewen, *Sundown Towns*, 245.
68. Levy, *University of Oklahoma: A History*, vol. 2, 68.
69. Levy, *University of Oklahoma*, vol. 2, 69–71. Levy estimates that in the 1920s one in ten eligible Oklahoma men were members of the Ku Klux Klan (65).
70. Levy, *University of Oklahoma*, vol. 2, 72.

71. Dana Branham, "Confronting History," *OU Daily*, accessed July 3, 2024, http://projects.oudaily.com/debarr/.
72. Mack Burke, "Unanimous Approval: DeBarr to Be Renamed Dean's Row," *Norman Transcript*, December 19, 2017, https://www.normantranscript.com/news/unanimous-approval-debarr-to-be-renamed-deans-row-avenue/article_13f99394-e529-11e7-be74-8fdc684c0a85.html.
73. Henderson, *Race and the University*, 11–14.
74. Henderson, *Race and the University*, 13.
75. Henderson, *Race and the University*, 185.
76. Henderson, *Race and the University*, 18.
77. Ferguson, *Presence and Social Obligation*; Widlock, *Anthropology and the Economy of Sharing*.
78. Widlock, *Anthropology and the Economy of Sharing*.
79. "Farmers Protesting Norman Growth," *Oklahoman*, October 24, 1961.
80. Jack Bagby, "Another 60 Square Miles Annexed to Protect Reservoir," *Norman Transcript*, October 22, 1961.
81. Earl Sneed, "Norman Beat Oklahoma City by Days on Annexation," *Norman Transcript*, February 22, 1962.
82. Sneed, "Norman Beat Oklahoma City."
83. Sneed, "Norman Beat Oklahoma City."
84. "Test Promised on Annexation, Commission Action Draws Boyd Blast," *Norman Transcript*, October 20, 1961.
85. Jeff Cox, "Letter to the Editor: Annexation Complaint," *Norman Transcript*, October 24, 1961.
86. "City, Landowners Will Both Benefit," *Norman Transcript*, October 19, 1961.
87. "City, Landowners Will Both Benefit."
88. "Well Done, City Officials," *Norman Transcript*, October 20, 1961.
89. "Editorial: Our Point of View: City's Objective above Reproach," *Norman Transcript*, October 22, 1961.
90. "Editorial: Our Point of View: City's Objective above Reproach."
91. "De-Annexation Suit against Norman Filed," *Norman Transcript*, February 8, 1962.
92. "Foes of Annexation Urged Not to Vote, Tax Protest Backed," *Norman Transcript*, February 11, 1962.
93. "Foes of Annexation Urged Not to Vote, Tax Protest Backed."
94. "Foes of Annexation Urged Not to Vote, Tax Protest Backed."
95. Scott, *Seeing Like a State*.
96. "Indian Graves Pose Problem for Bureau," *Norman Transcript*, February 20, 1962.
97. COMCD, Regular Meeting Minutes, February 1, 2007.
98. COMCD vs. ODEQ, Filed in the District Court of Oklahoma Country, Oklahoma, CV-2011–2251, December 12, 2011, 4.
99. COMCD vs. ODEQ, Filed in the District Court of Oklahoma Country, Oklahoma, CV-2011–2251, December 12, 2011, 4.

100. Oklahoma Water Resources Board, Lake Thunderbird Water Quality 2021 Final Report, April 29, 2022.
101. "Turnover at Lake Thunderbird Affects Taste and Odor of Water," *Norman Transcript*, September 5, 2017, https://www.normantranscript.com/news/turnover-at-lake-thunderbird-affects-taste-and-odor-of-drinking-water/article_2fad9150-927a-11e7-8d7c-4b2e35483bac.html.
102. In regards to the TMDL for the Chesapeake Bay Watershed, Jeffrey Trombley writes, "Restoration does not require us to rethink our relationship to the watershed or the estuary nor does it challenge the social conditions that give rise to ecological destruction." Trombley, "Watershed Encounters," 124.
103. Flint, Michigan, and Jackson, Mississippi, are examples of communities that lacked the government support to protect their drinking water.
104. Livingston, *Self-Devouring Growth*.
105. Lipsitz, *Possessive Investment in Whiteness*.

2. EXPANDING CITIZENSHIP AND DEBATING GROWTH

1. The City of Norman was able to secure a FEMA grant that was used to renovate The Vineyard's retention pond. The renovations were completed in 2023 and when I spoke to Scanlon in 2024, he said that although there had not yet been heavy enough rains to put the new stormwater infrastructure to the test, he was hopeful that his flooding problems were solved.
2. Logan Layden, "Why Norman Is the Only Oklahoma Town Where Citizens Control the Price of Water," *StateImpact Oklahoma*, June 26, 2014, https://stateimpact.npr.org/oklahoma/2014/06/26/why-norman-is-the-only-oklahoma-town-where-citizens-control-the-price-of-water/.
3. Layden, "Why Norman Is the Only Oklahoma Town."
4. Larry Hill, "Letter to the Editor: 2 Sewer Lift Stations 'Spell Growth' for Norman," *Norman Transcript*, July 9, 1974.
5. Sue Holmes, "City Trustees Okay Bids Allowing Population Hike," *Norman Transcript*, July 10, 1974.
6. "Money City's Biggest Problem, Dunn Says," *Norman Transcript*, September 22, 1974.
7. Jim Bross, "City Due Growing Pains: Environmental Board Fearful," *Norman Transcript*, July 16, 1974; Sue Holmes, "Construction Halt Sought Until Environment Studied," *Norman Transcript*, July 22, 1974.
8. Andrea Chancellor, "Environmental Study Must for Lift Stations Project," *Norman Transcript*, August 23, 1974.
9. EPA, Draft Environmental Impact Statement.
10. Linda Dobkins, "Opinions Varied on EPA's Report on Lift Stations," *Norman Transcript*, February 2, 1977.
11. Canter, *Environmental Impact Assessment*.
12. Larry A. Wood went on to lead many successful political campaigns in Oklahoma. He took the model of using citizen's petitions to the state level, where citizen's

petitions led to votes that overturned laws that prevented the sale of liquor by the drink in Oklahoma bars.

13. "Editorial: Our Point of View: Speaking Up for Norman," *Norman Transcript*, July 24, 1974.
14. Jess Speer, "Letter to the Editor: Utility Hike Editorial Criticized," *Norman Transcript*, July 29, 1974.
15. "Utilities Hike Petition Protest Hearing Opens," *Norman Transcript*, October 15, 1974.
16. Jane Glenn, "Anderhub, Wesner Win; Other Posts in Runoff," *Norman Transcript*, March 19, 1975.
17. "Editorial: Our Point of View: Utility Rate Proposal," *Norman Transcript*, November 14, 1975.
18. Andrea Chancellor, "City Manager Backs Utility Cutback to Minimum of $11," *Norman Transcript*, December 24, 1974; Chancellor, "Consultant Reports after Study City Water System in Trouble," *Norman Transcript*, January 19, 1975.
19. Newspaper clippings from John Wood's NCCR collection.
20. "Who Pays for Growth," draft with annotations in hand, no date, header of "hancock," five pages, author's archive.
21. Coffman, "Trailwoods Neighborhood Best Management Practices."
22. City of Norman, Affordable Housing Town Hall, October 19, 2022.
23. Karvoven, *Politics of Urban Runoff*.
24. Jane Glenn, "Plat in Watershed Approved," *Norman Transcript*, April 11, 1975.
25. Dobkins, "Opinions Varied."
26. Mack Burke, "'No One More Deserving': Gene McKown Wins Norman Human Rights Award," *Norman Transcript*, December 6, 2017.
27. Tom Blakey, "Council Oks Northside Lift Station Contract," *Norman Transcript*, February 14, 2007.
28. City of Norman, Text File, File Number: PP-1213–8.
29. "Editorial: Our Point of View: The Ward System 1," *Norman Transcript*, November 12, 1975.
30. "Editorial: Our Point of View: Tuesday's Election," *Norman Transcript*, November 17, 1975.
31. Jeanne Crabtree, "Letter to the Editor: City 'Should Change' to Ward System," *Norman Transcript*, November 16, 1975.
32. Ruth Vanwinkle, "Letter to the Editor: Ward System Hit," *Norman Transcript*, November 16, 1975.
33. "Editorial: Our Point of View: More about Wards," *Norman Transcript*, July 17, 1975.
34. Unsigned letter draft from Larry Woods personal archive, no date.
35. Caleb Slinkard, "James Chappel Appointed to Norman Council Seat after Two Tie Votes, 4–4," *Norman Transcript*, July 6, 2016, https://www.normantranscript.com/news/local_news/james-chappel-appointed-to-norman-council-seat-after-two-tie-votes-4-4/article_7bb5687d-c57c-5bd3-a56a-14bb269eca86.html.

36. Candidate Committee and Expenditures Report for Rarchar Tortorello for Norman 2021, 1st Quarter Report, January 25, 2021–March 31, 2021; Candidate Committee and Expenditures Report for Michael Nash for Norman 2021, First Quarter Report, January 24, 2021–April 30, 2021.
37. The plan was approved and my son and I were happy to receive gift cards and free tacos when we got a round of shots in November.
38. Jane Glenn, "Police Getting Free Drinks Being Checked," *Norman Transcript*, August 5, 1975.
39. Jane Glenn, "Three Patrolmen Asked to Quit, after Free-Drink Police Probe," *Norman Transcript*, August 20, 1975.
40. "Henslee Position New in City," *Norman Transcript*, August 15, 1975.
41. D. M. Graves, "Letter to the Editor: Gray Ouster," *Norman Transcript*, August 22, 1975.
42. Linda Dobkins, "NCCR Accuses Dick Gray of 'Wrist-Slapping' Police," *Norman Transcript*, August 17, 1975, 5.
43. "Tempers Flair over Motion by Councilman," *Norman Transcript*, August 20, 1975.
44. Margaret Milliken, "Letter to the Editor: Haas' Approach Called Arrogant," *Norman Transcript*, August 21, 1975; June Allen, "Letter to the Editor: Haas' Manner," *Norman Transcript*, August 22, 1975.
45. Alan Bromley, "Norman City Counsel Quits," *Oklahoma Daily*, August 31, 1975.
46. Fielding Haas also attacked NCCR members as radicals in a letter to the editor of the Oklahoma Daily. In response, an NCCR member sued Haas for libel. The Oklahoma Supreme court ruled in Haas's favor. JUSTIA, "Wright v. Haas," accessed July 5, 2024, https://law.justia.com/cases/oklahoma/supreme-court/1978/47877.html.
47. Linda Dobkins, "With FBI from 1969 to March 1975, Neal Former Undercover Agent," *Norman Transcript*, September 25, 1975.
48. One-page typed document signed by John Neal, from Larry Wood Archive.
49. "Obituary, Clark Hetherington," *Norman Transcript*, February 19, 2012, https://obituaries.normantranscript.com/obituary/clark-hetherington-745017962.
50. University of Oklahoma, "Part of the Legacy, the Hetheringtons," accessed July 5, 2024, https://www.ou.edu/web/news_events/articles/news_2013/hetheringtonfamily.
51. "Investigation of Police Set: Alien Policy Prompts Check," *Norman Transcript*, July 2, 1975.
52. "Gray Cites 'Errors in Judgment' in Eagerly Awaited Report on Police," *Norman Transcript*, August 27, 1975.
53. "Illegal Alien Arrested Here," *Norman Transcript*, July 17, 1975; Linda Dobkins and Jane Glenn, "Bill Henslee Quits as Police Chief: Council Gets Report in Closed Session," *Norman Transcript*, August 14, 1975.
54. Dobkins and Glenn, "Bill Henslee Quits as Police Chief."

55. "Police Chief Ordering End to Stopping Young Blacks," *Norman Transcript*, September 19, 1974.
56. "Editorial: Our Point of View: Shifting of Power," *Norman Transcript*, November 23, 1975.
57. "City's Election on Propositions Gratifies NCCR," *Norman Transcript*, November 20, 1975.
58. Mindy Ragan Wood, "Looking toward Nov., Most City Charter Amendments Pass," *Norman Transcript*, August 24, 2022.

3. URBAN CREEKS AND THE COMMONS

1. Channelization that prioritizes urban development over green space that absorbs stormwater is a common dynamic with urban rivers and creeks. The Los Angeles River is a key example. Gandy, *Fabric of Space*; Gumprecht, *Los Angeles River*.
2. Ben-Joseph, *ReThinking a Lot*, 32.
3. Linda Dobkins, "Yard Falling Away," *Norman Transcript*, March 1, 1977.
4. Livingston, *Self-Devouring Growth*.
5. Ben-Joseph, *ReThinking a Lot*.
6. For a discussion of the application of the circulation of blood in bodies as a metaphor for the circulation of water in cites see Illich, *H2O and the Waters of Forgetfulness*.
7. Hardin, "Tragedy of the Commons," 1244.
8. Hardin's primary argument was for limiting human reproduction, a claim that ignores the massive differences in resource use among human populations. The case of urban creeks demonstrates the flaws in associating population growth with destruction of the commons. It is not the number of people that destroys urban creeks, rather it is their consumer lifestyles, specifically their reliance on impervious surfaces.
9. MacLellan, "Tragedy of Limitless Growth."
10. Ostrom, *Governing the Commons*.
11. MacLellan, "Tragedy of Limitless Growth." Karen Bakker explains that Hardin's tragedy is one of "open access, in which no property-rights systems are in place." Bakker, *Privatizing Water*, 172.
12. Andy Rieger, "A Legacy to Remember," *Norman Transcript*, March 18, 2018.
13. Joy Hampton, "Residents along Imhoff Creek Say Property Is Slowly Washing Away," *Norman Transcript*, May 26, 2016.
14. Marcia Miller, "Letter to the Editor: Does Anyone Care about Imhoff Creek?" *Norman Transcript*, September 2, 2007.
15. As I write in 2024, the City of Norman had assigned $3 million in funds from the American Rescue Act Plan to be used for restoration on Imhoff Creek downstream from the bridge. The City of Norman is moving forward with grant applications to support additional restoration upstream from Imhoff Bridge that is estimated to cost more than $4.7 million. If the city secures grant funds this

project could be completed before 2030. City of Norman Staff Report, "Consideration of Approval, Acceptance, Rejection, Amendment, and/or Postponement of Amendment Two to Contract K-1415/-134," February 27, 2024.

16. Facebook, Ward 3 Public Page, March 31, 2019.
17. Karvoven, *Politics of Urban Runoff*.
18. City of Norman, "Imhoff Creek Watershed: Percentage of Impervious Surfaces," May 26, 2017.
19. In regard to Austin, Texas, Karvoven, *Politics of Urban Runoff*, 67, writes that creeks "have been used primarily as conduits for wastewater and as repositories for urban detritus, notably transients and trash." That's certainly true in Norman, but they also provide a space of escape from parental supervision and access to trees, water, and wildlife.
20. Mesonet, "Monthly Rainfall Tables," Norman, accessed July 7, 2024, https://www.mesonet.org/index.php/weather/monthly_rainfall_table.
21. Riley, *Restoring Neighborhood Streams*.
22. Facebook, "Unite Norman Media Outreach," October 17, 2021.
23. Mondy Ragan Wood, "Hearing Set in Shaz vs City of Norman," *Norman Transcript*, January 11, 2022.
24. Mindy Ragan Wood, "Judge Sides with Homebuilder in Lawsuit against City," *Norman Transcript*, February 21, 2023.
25. Mindy Ragan Wood, "Council Approves Shaz Application, Ends Legal Dispute with 5–4 Vote," *Norman Transcript*, June 29, 2023.
26. City of Norman, "Ward 7—Steven Tyler Holman," accessed July 7, 2024, https://www.normanok.gov/your-government/city-council/ward-7-stephen-tyler-holman.
27. Mack Burke, "State Supreme Court Orders Return of Friendly Market Property," *Norman Transcript*, September 12, 2017.
28. City of Norman Council Meeting, June 8, 2021.
29. NIMBY: Not In My Backyard.
30. The Vineyard resident was no longer a city council member when the City of Norman approved funding to pair with the FEMA grant.

4. FACEBOOK, STORMWATER, AND DIGITAL EUTROPHICATION

1. Facebook, Ward 5 Public Page, August 24, 2016.
2. Facebook, Ward 5 Public Page, August 24, 2016.
3. Joy Hampton, "Answering Common Questions Regarding City's Stormwater Proposal," *Norman Transcript*, August 18, 2016, https://www.normantranscript.com/news/government/answering-common-questions-regarding-citys-stormwater-proposal/article_435b313f-0ca8–5fbe-b6aa-1c10b7b3194e.html.
4. Hampton, "Answering Common Questions."
5. Joy Hampton, "A Storm of Dissent," *Norman Transcript*, May 22, 2016, https://www.normantranscript.com/news/government/a-storm-of-dissent/article_dc9f60e3–035e-5e5c-8cd5–4cd11acd5db0.html.

6. Cynthia Rogers, "Letter to the Editor: Silence Is Not Golden for The Transcript," *Norman Transcript*, August 14, 2016.
7. John Woods, "Letter to the Editor: We Can Do Better," *Norman Transcript*, August 20, 2016, https://www.normantranscript.com/opinion/letters_to_the_editor/we-can-do-better/article_2ebad7d3-d3be-58b3-b52f-ed555982a9fb.html.
8. "Editorial: Residents Can Ask for Better Plan," *Norman Transcript*, August 17, 2016. https://www.normantranscript.com/opinion/editorials/editorial-residents-can-ask-for-better-plan/article_5caf7014-b761–5f7a-b09d-912e14964bdc.html.
9. Emma Keith, "Saying Goodbye to Journalism, In All Its Highs and Lows," *Norman Transcript*, August 18, 2022.
10. Flood, "Responding to 'Fake News.'"
11. Richard Hasen, "How to Keep the Rising Tide of Fake News from Drowning Our Democracy," *New York Times*, March 7, 2022, https://www.nytimes.com/2022/03/07/opinion/cheap-speech-fake-news-democracy.html?searchResultPosition=10.
12. The relationship between social media use and anxiety and depression among U.S. teens, especially young women, can also be conceptualized as self-devouring growth. Social media apps like Instagram have fueled economic growth but have also destroyed young people's mental health.
13. Michelle Goldberg, "Loneliness Is Breaking America," *New York Times*, July 19, 2021, https://www.nytimes.com/2021/07/19/opinion/trump-covid-extremism-loneliness.html.
14. Sabrina Tavernise, "First They Fought about Masks. Then over the Soul of the City," *New York Times*, December 26, 2021, https://www.nytimes.com/2021/12/26/us/oklahoma-masks.html.
15. Yuval Noah Harari, "When the World Seems Like One Big Conspiracy," *New York Times*, November 20, 2020, https://www.nytimes.com/2020/11/20/opinion/sunday/global-cabal-conspiracy-theories.html.
16. Reid Epstein, "Where Facts Were No Match for Fear," *New York Times*, October 24, 2021, https://www.nytimes.com/2021/10/24/us/politics/montana-misinformation-national-heritage.html.
17. Facebook, Ward 5 Public Page, August 24, 2016.
18. Tim Farley, "Lawsuit Settled against Former Councilman," *Norman Transcript*, February 1, 2020, https://www.normantranscript.com/news/lawsuit-settled-against-former-councilman/article_73dafd0e-44b6–11ea-bfc4-cb22acdecf16.html.
19. Mack Burke, "Stormwater Utility Vote by the Numbers," *Norman Transcript*, August 26, 2016, https://www.normantranscript.com/news/local_news/stormwater-utility-vote-by-the-numbers/image_abafd99e-6b1f-11e6-b005–53445422e0b4.html.
20. Facebook, Ward 5 Public Page, July 28, 2016.
21. Sobo, "Playing with Conspiracy Theories."
22. Tufekci, "How Social Media Took Us from Tahrir Square to Donald Trump."

23. Facebook, Ward 5 Public Page, June 19, 2016.
24. The contrast between Black Cat and Cattle Rancher resonates with common themes in anthropological studies of international development. International development practitioners often assume that models developed through scientific testing can be applied universally regardless of conditions on the ground. Scott, *Seeing Like a State*.
25. Westermeyer, "Stigmatized Identity Motivating Right-Wing Populism."
26. Joy Hampton, "City's Little River Proposal Seen as Land Grab by Rural Residents," *Norman Transcript*, September 13, 2016, https://www.normantranscript.com/news/government/city-s-little-river-proposal-seen-as-land-grab-by-rural-residents/article_77997e2c-7a19–11e6–9b9e-4728b949ea58.html.
27. Facebook, Ward 5 Public Page, December 26, 2019.
28. Cindy Rosenthal, "Letter to the Editor: Waiting Would Be a Mistake," *Norman Transcript*, August 21, 2016, https://www.normantranscript.com/opinion/letters_to_the_editor/waiting-would-be-a-mistake/article_1be247cc-d1de-5cfb-b236–75aed8f8844e.html.
29. Ed Cocker, "Letter to the Editor: Stormwater Bond: A Tangled Web," *Norman Transcript* March 8, 2019; Cocker, "Letter to the Editor: 'No' on Proposition 2: Stormwater Bond," *Norman Transcript*, February 22, 2019.
30. MAGA Hat's profile pic was the iconic red hat with four capital letters: MAGA (Make America Great Again).
31. Facebook, Ward 5 Public Page, April 18, 2019.
32. Facebook, Ward 5 Public Page, March 29, 2019.
33. Facebook, Ward 5 Public Page, March 29, 2019.
34. Facebook, Ward 5 Public Page, January 21, 2019.
35. This was before Wilson faced a recall effort in 2020, ostensibly due to her voting not to give the Norman Police Department the full amount of its requested budget increase.
36. POLAR: Political and Legal Anthropology Review, "Fake News and Anthropology: A Conversation on Technology, Trust, and Publics in an Age of Mass Disinformation Part 1," February 16, 2020, https://polarjournal.org/2020/02/16/anthropology-and-fake-news-a-conversation-on-technology-trust-and-publics-in-an-age-of-mass-disinformation/.
37. Jonathan Haidt and Tobias Rose-Stockwell, "The Dark Psychology of Social Networks," *Atlantic*, December 2019, https://www.theatlantic.com/magazine/archive/2019/12/social-media-democracy/600763/.

5. PLANNING FOR FUTURE WATER

1. Broch-Due and Ystanes, "Introducing Ethnographies of Trusting."
2. Norman Utilities Authority, *2060 Strategic Water Supply Plan* (Norman, Oklahoma, 2014), 2–16.
3. Carey, *Mistrust*, 98.

4. Mindy Ragan Wood, "Water Rate Increase Fails: What's Next for Norman," *Norman Transcript*, April 17, 2022, https://www.normantranscript.com/news/water-rate-increase-fails-whats-next-for-norman/article_90c39f18-bcf8–11ec-b70f-bb14627862a2.html.
5. City of Norman Public Meeting, February 21, 2022.
6. Facebook, Unite Norman Media Outreach Page, August 28, 2021.
7. Facebook, Neighbors 4 Norman Public Page, February 28, 2022, 2.
8. Norman City Council Meeting, March 22, 2022.
9. This was a rare case of Ellis and Rogers splitting their votes. After the connection fee increase, Rogers publicly announced that she would vote in favor of the water rate increase.
10. Mindy Ragan Wood, "Survey: Rate Increase Failure Is Economic, Partisan, Referendum," *Norman Transcript*, June 8, 2022.
11. The survey conducted after the failed water rate increase vote indicated that distrust was far higher among Republicans and Independents than Democrats, and this translated to a largely partisan vote with Republicans and Independents voting "no" and 66 percent of Democrats surveyed voting "yes" on the rate increase (Wood, "Survey: Rate Increase Failure").
12. City of Norman, "Mayor," accessed July 28, 2024, https://www.normanok.gov/your-government/mayor.
13. YouTube, "City of Norman Study Session and Special Session," June 16, 2020, https://www.youtube.com/watch?v=X-ZqaVuN_Fc.
14. District Attorney Greg Mashburn cleared Officer Glazier of any wrongdoing. See Jane Glenn Cannon, "Norman Officer's Actions Deemed Justifiable in Shooting," *Oklahoman*, December 31, 2014, https://www.oklahoman.com/story/news/2014/12/31/norman-officers-actions-deemed-justifiable-in-shooting/60774776007/. Although I was living in Norman at the time, I don't recall the incident, and there was limited news coverage of Sanchez-Juarez's death.
15. Hochschild, *Strangers in Their Own Land*.
16. Facebook, The Office of Ward 3 Councilman Kelly Lynn Public Page, January 11, 2023.
17. Mindy Ragan Wood, "'Scoreboard': Lynn Takes Ward 3, Provides One-Word Statement," *Norman Transcript*, April 6, 2021.
18. Norman City Council Meeting, March 22, 2022.
19. Norman City Council Study Session, August 16, 2022.
20. Merriam-Webster, "Word of the Year 2022," accessed July 28, 2024, https://www.merriam-webster.com/wordplay/word-of-the-year-2022.
21. Mindy Ragan Wood, "Take Two: Council to Again Debate SRO Property," *Norman Transcript*, August 16, 2022, https://www.normantranscript.com/news/take-two-council-to-again-debate-sro-property/article_552b9a92–1cfb-11ed-9655–539b59beec74.html.
22. Max Bryan, "NPD Identifies Suspect in Thursday Night Shooting near Down-

town," *Norman Transcript*, January 24, 2022, https://www.normantranscript.com/news/npd-identifies-suspect-in-thursday-night-shooting-near-downtown-norman/article_6f233940-7d7e-11ec-8018-2bfd3b6f484f.html.

23. Mindy Ragan Wood, "Three Residents File Petition to Vote on All Homeless Shelters," *Norman Transcript*, February 22, 2022, https://www.normantranscript.com/news/three-residents-file-petitions-to-vote-on-all-homeless-shelters/article_9143daa0-9379-11ec-86e6-37708da6856b.html.
24. "Editorial: Family, Public Deserve Transparency in Euwins Case," *Norman Transcript*, May 4, 2022, https://www.normantranscript.com/opinion/editorial-family-public-deserve-transparency-in-euwins-case/article_e3fdb5a8-cb29-11ec-aee9-8b9b4c0d3643.html.
25. Max Bryan, "Cleveland County DA Agrees to Meet with Shed Euwins' Family," *Norman Transcript*, April 27, 2022, https://www.normantranscript.com/news/cleveland-county-da-agrees-to-meet-with-shed-euwins-family/article_2c791b4c-c64d-11ec-bd0b-73c9650c1ed8.html.
26. Jonathan Kyncl, "Demonstrators Rally for Euwins amid Lack of Criminal Charges and Case 'Inconsistencies,'" *Norman Transcript*, May 7, 2022, https://www.normantranscript.com/news/demonstrators-rally-for-euwins-amid-lack-of-criminal-charges-and-case-inconsistencies/article_58662e80-ce44-11ec-8ccb-2f8d01e1c54c.html.
27. Tim Willert, "Authorities Investigating Jail Death of Popular Business Owner, Mental Health Advocate," *Norman Transcript*, December 9, 2022, https://www.normantranscript.com/news/authorities-investigating-jail-death-of-popular-business-owner-mental-health-advocate/article_958a6468-77fc-11ed-8107-33f41df74923.html.
28. Willert, "Authorities Investigating."
29. Tim Willert, "Second Woman Dies in Cleveland County Custody," *Norman Transcript*, January 7, 2023, https://www.normantranscript.com/news/second-woman-dies-in-cleveland-county-custody/article_0def0a94-8d33-11ed-a5d0-333175a983d0.html.
30. Mindy Ragan Wood, "City Council Reacts to Hanchett's Death; Incarceration Draws Policy Questions," *Norman Transcript*, December 14, 2022, https://www.normantranscript.com/news/city-council-reacts-to-hanchetts-death-incarceration-draws-policy-questions/article_4f7f02f8-7c07-11ed-8b52-073a891323a8.html.
31. As Sarah Kendzior explains, "A rise in conspiracy theories is inevitable when collective trauma is combined with a lack of transparency and a history of state abuse." Kendzior, *They Knew*, 29.
32. Ormerod and Scott, "Drinking Wastewater."
33. Annin, *Purified*.
34. There is a rich anthropological literature on waste and reuse. Works that I have found particularly useful include Ahmann, "Waste to Energy"; Chalfin, *Waste*

Works; Doherty, *Waste Worlds*; Millar, *Reclaiming the Discarded*; Reno, "Waste and Waste Management."

35. Annin, *Purified*.
36. Norman Utilities Authority, *2060 Strategic Water Supply Plan*.
37. Wade, Peppler and Person, "Community Education and Perceptions of Water Reuse."
38. Ahmann, "Waste to Energy."
39. Chip Minty, "New Hope for Tar Creek," *Sooner Magazine* 41, no. 4 (Summer 2021), https://soonermag.oufoundation.org/stories/new-hope-for-tar-creek.
40. Environmental Working Group, "Chromium-6 in U.S. Tap Water," December 20, 2010, https://www.ewg.org/research/chromium-6-us-tap-water.
41. Environmental Working Group, "Chromium-6 in U.S. Tap Water." Many of Norman's wells have higher levels than this, but they are blended with lake water and water purchased from Oklahoma City.
42. Mayor Clark also stated that Norman has closed wells because of high chromium levels, but this is not accurate. Norman closed wells because of arsenic, but none of the remaining wells exceeded the EPA's standard of 100 ppb for chromium, and no wells have been closed due to high chromium levels.
43. Auyero and Swistun, "Social Production of Toxic Uncertainty."
44. Environmental Protection Agency, *IRIS Toxicological Review of Hexavalent Chromium*.
45. Norman Utilities Authority, *2060 Strategic Water Supply Plan*, appendix D-5.
46. Eric Lipton and Coral Davenport, "Scott Pruitt, Trump's E.P.A. Pick, Backed Industry Donors over Regulators," *New York Times*, January 14, 2017.
47. The case against PG&E in Hinkley, California, was based in part on a study from China where a community was exposed to large amounts of hexavalent chromium in its drinking water. The author of that study later published a follow-up study that questioned the original conclusions. This follow-up, however, was retracted after PG&E's undisclosed financial support for the study came to light. Peter Waldman, "Study Tied Pollutants to Cancer; Then Consultants Got Hold of It," *Wall Street Journal*, December 23, 2005; Smith, "Commentary."
48. Mindy Ragan Wood, "City Water Projects Delayed," *Norman Transcript*, May 18, 2022, https://www.normantranscript.com/news/city-water-projects-delayed/article_c48cbe36-d645-11ec-a605-cf1b1f93a93b.html.
49. Carey, *Mistrust*, 25.
50. Norman's policy to require a vote for utility rate increases could solve problems like the case of Georgia Power, where electricity users are on the hook for a fourteen billion dollar expansion of a nuclear power plant that they never approved. Phillips, "Southern Politics, Southern Power Prices."
51. Mindy Ragan Wood, "Vote No on Water Rate Mailer Misleading, Officials Say," *Norman Transcript*, June 8, 2023.
52. Mindy Ragan Wood, "What's Next for City Water Improvements?" *Norman*

Transcript, June 25, 2023.

CONCLUSION

1. Oklahoma Geological Society, "Rose Rocks," accessed July 28, 2024, https://www.ou.edu/ogs/generalinterest/rose_rocks.
2. Mindy Wood Ragan, "'We Have to Get It Right': City Land Use, Stormwater, Transportation in Question with OTA Plans," *Norman Transcript*, July 31, 2022, https://www.normantranscript.com/news/we-have-to-get-it-right/article_4e8b9b4e-0f98-11ed-9e57-37e535d006f3.html.
3. Facebook, Neighbors 4 Norman Public Page, March 1, 2022.
4. Governor Stitt replaced Gene McKown with Michael Junk as the at-large member in January 2023. Michael Junk leads Public Relations for the QuikTrip Corporation. QuikTrips are roadside convenience stores and gas stations. Oklahoma Department of Transportation, "Michael Junk," April 11, 2023, https://oklahoma.gov/odot/about/transportation-commission/michael-junk.html.
5. Katherine Hirschfeld, "Viewpoint: When It Comes to Turnpikes, Is Oklahoma on the Way to Being Like Pennsylvania?" *Oklahoman*, May 22, 2022, https://www.oklahoman.com/story/opinion/2022/05/22/turnpikes-oklahoma-way-pennsylvania/9793819002/.
6. Pike Off OTA, "Oklahoma, Take Your Eyes off the Road," December 2022, https://pikeoffota.com/oklahoma-take-your-eyes-off-the-road-part-3-of-the-oklahoma-you-have-a-turnpike-problem-series/.
7. James Chappel served as a city councilmember, but he was appointed, not elected.
8. Carol Cole-Frowe, "Wastewater 'Solution' Won't Cross Little River," *Norman Transcript*, January 17, 2008, https://www.normantranscript.com/news/local_news/wastewater-solution-wont-cross-little-river/article_a4914b18-c29d-50a6-a081-1ddc53091b21.html; Carol Cole, "More Wastewater Options Presented at Conference," *Norman Transcript*, May 10, 2006, https://www.normantranscript.com/news/local_news/more-wastewater-options-presented-at-conference/article_9784c351-795b-5681-b86e-2aa0837aa9a1.html.
9. Womack, *Cleveland Country, Oklahoma*, 13–14.
10. Butler, *Parable of the Sower*.

BIBLIOGRAPHY

Ahmann, Chloe. "Waste to Energy: Garbage Prospects and Subjunctive Politics in Late-Industrial Baltimore." *American Ethnologist* 46, no. 3 (2019): 328–42.

Alford, Thomas Wildcat. *Civilization, and the Story of the Absentee Shawnees*. Norman: University of Oklahoma Press, 1979.

Anand, Nikhil. *Hydraulic City: Water and the Infrastructures of Citizenship in Mumbai*. Durham: Duke University Press, 2017.

Anderson, Sam. *Boom Town: The Fantastical Saga of Oklahoma City, Its Chaotic Founding . . . Its Purloined Basketball Team, and the Dream of Becoming a World-Class Metropolis*. New York: Penguin Random House, 2019.

Annin, Peter. *Purified: How Recycled Sewage Is Transforming Our Water*. Washington DC: Island Press, 2023.

Arvin, Maile, Eve Tuck, and Angie Morrill. "Decolonizing Feminism: Challenging Connections between Settler Colonialism and Hetereopatriarchy." *Feminist Formations* 25, no. 1 (2013): 8–34.

Auyero, Javier, and Debora Swistun. "The Social Production of Toxic Uncertainty." *American Sociological Review* 73, no. 3 (2008): 357–79.

Bagstad, Kenneth J., Kevin Stapleton, and John R. D'Agostino. "Taxes, Subsidies, and Insurance as Drivers of United States Coastal Development." *Ecological Economics* 63, no. 2–3 (2007): 285–98.

Baird, W. David, and Danney Goble. *Oklahoma: A History*. Norman: University of Oklahoma Press, 2008.

Bakker, Karen. *Privatizing Water: Governance Failure and the World's Urban Water Crisis*. Ithaca: Cornell University Press, 2013.

Barber, Katrine. *Death of Celilo Falls*. Seattle: University of Washington Press, 2005.

Ben-Joseph, Eran. *ReThinking a Lot: The Design and Culture of Parking*. Cambridge MA: MIT Press, 2015.

Bessire, Lucas. *Running Out: In Search of Water on the High Plains*. Princeton: Princeton University Press, 2021.

Blanchard, Jessica. "'They Came One at a Time': Native-Led Church Planting and Growing the Body of Christ from the Margins of Culture." PhD diss., University of Oklahoma, 2019.

Boyd, Dan. "Oklahoma Oil: Past, Present, and Future." *Oklahoma Geology Notes* 62, no. 3 (2002): 97–106.

Broch-Due, Vigdis, and Margit Ystanes. "Introducing Ethnographies of Trusting." In *Trusting and Its Tribulations: Interdisciplinary Engagements with Intimacy, Sociality, and Trust*, edited by Vigdis Broch-Due and Margit Ystanes, 1–36. New York: Berghahn, 2016.

Butler, Octavia. *Parable of the Sower*. New York: Grand Central Publishing, 2019 [1993].

Canter, Larry. *Environmental Impact Assessment*. New York: McGraw-Hill, 1977.

Carey, Matthew. *Mistrust: An Ethnographic Theory*. Chicago: HAU Books, 2017.

Chalfin, Brenda. *Waste Works: Vital Politics in Urban Ghana*. Durham: Duke University Press, 2023.

Chang, David. "Enclosures of Land and Sovereignty: The Allotment of American Indian Lands." *Radical History Review* 109 (2011): 108–19.

Cobb, Russell. *The Great Swindle: Race, Religion, and Lies in America's Weirdest State*. Lincoln: University of Nebraska Press, 2020.

Coe, Cati. *The New American Servitude: Political Belonging among African Immigrant Home Care Workers*. New York: NYU Press 2019.

Coffman, Reid. "Trailwoods Neighborhood Best Management Practices." Prepared for United States Environmental Protection Agency and Oklahoma Conservation Commission, 2014.

Doherty, Jacob. *Waste Worlds: Inhabiting Kampala's Infrastructures of Disposability*. Oakland: University of California Press, 2021.

Environmental Protection Agency. Draft Environmental Impact Statement. Norman, Oklahoma. Project No. WPC-OKLA-505. U.S. Environmental Protection Agency, Dallas, Texas, 1977.

Environmental Protection Agency, *IRIS Toxicological Review of Hexavalent Chromium: CASRN 18540-29-9*. US Environmental Protection Agency: Washington DC, 2024.

Estes, Nick, and Jaskiron Dhillon. "The Black Snake, #NoDAPL, and the Rise of a People's Movement." In *Standing with Standing Rock: Voices from the #NoDAPL Movement*, edited by Nick Estes and Jaskiron Dhillon, 1–10. Minneapolis: University of Minnesota Press, 2019.

Ewing, Reid, and Shima Hamidi. "Compactness versus Sprawl: A Review of Recent Evidence from the United States." *Journal of Planning Literature* 30, no. 4 (2015): 413–32.

Ferguson, James. *Presence and Social Obligation: An Essay on the Share*. Chicago: Prickly Paradigm Press, 2021.

Fisher, William, ed. *Toward Sustainable Development: Struggling over India's Narmada River*. Armonk NY: M. E. Sharpe, 1995.

Flood, David. "Responding to 'Fake News' in an Era of Hashtag Leftism." *Anthropology-News* website, January 29, 2019.

Fostvedt, Mattias P., Desiree D. Tullos, and Bryan Tilt. "Institutional Analysis of Small

Dam Removals: A Comparison of Non-Federal Dam Removals in Washington and Oregon." *Water Alternatives* 13, no. 2 (2020): 369–92.

Gandy, Matthew. *The Fabric of Space: Water, Modernity, and the Urban Imagination*. Cambridge MA: MIT Press, 2014.

———. *Natura Urbana: Ecological Constellations in Urban Space*. Cambridge MA: MIT Press, 2022.

Grann, David. *Killers of the Flower Moon: The Osage Murders and the Birth of the FBI*. New York: Vintage Books, 2018.

Gumprecht, Blake. *The Los Angeles River: Its Life, Death, and Possible Rebirth*. Baltimore: Johns Hopkins University Press, 2001.

Hardin, Garrett. "The Tragedy of the Commons." *Science* 162 (1968): 1243–48.

Harvey, David. *The Urban Experience*. Baltimore: Johns Hopkins Press, 1989.

Helton, Taiawagi, and Lindsay Robertson. "The Foundations of Federal Indian Law and Its Application in the Twentieth Century." In *Beyond Red Power: American Indian Politics and Activism since 1900*, edited by Daniel Cobb and Loretta Fowler, 33–56. Santa Fe: SAR Press, 2007.

Henderson, George. *Race and the University*. Norman: University of Oklahoma Press, 2010.

Hightower, Michael. *1889: The Boomer Movement, the Land Run, and Early Oklahoma*. Norman: University of Oklahoma Press, 2018.

Hochschild, Arlie. *Strangers in Their Own Land: Anger and Mourning on the American Right*. New York: New Press, 2018.

Holston, James. *Insurgent Citizenship: Disjunctions of Democracy and Modernity in Brazil*. Princeton: Princeton University Press 2008.

Howard, William Willard. "The Rush to Oklahoma." *Harper's Weekly*, May 18, 1889, 391–94.

Hundley, Norris. *The Great Thirst: Californians and Water—A History*. Berkeley: University of California Press, 2001.

Illich, Ivan. *H2O and the Waters of Forgetfulness*. Sheffield UK: Equinox, 1986.

Kahrl, William. *Water and Power: The Conflict over Los Angeles' Water Supply in the Owens Valley*. Berkeley: University of California Press, 1982.

Karvoven, Andrew. *The Politics of Urban Runoff: Nature, Technology, and the Sustainable City*. Cambridge MA: MIT Press, 2011.

Kendzior, Sarah. *They Knew: How a Culture of Conspiracy Keeps America Complacent*. New York City: Flat Iron Books, 2022.

Jackson, Kenneth. *Crabgrass Frontier: The Suburbanization of the United States*. New York: Oxford University Press, 1985.

LaDuke, Winona, and Deborah Cowen. "Beyond Wiindigo Infrastructure." *South Atlantic Quarterly* 119, no. 2 (2020): 243–68.

Lawrence, Michael. "Damming Rivers, Damning Cultures." *American Indian Law Review* 30, no. 1 (2005/2006): 247–89.

Levy, David. *The University of Oklahoma: A History*. Volume 1, *1890–1917*. Norman: University of Oklahoma Press, 2008.
———. *The University of Oklahoma: A History*. Volume 2, *1917–1950*. Norman: University of Oklahoma Press, 2015.
Lipsitz, George. *The Possessive Investment in Whiteness: How White People Profit from Identity Politics*. Philadelphia: Temple University Press, 1998.
Livingston, Julie. *Self-Devouring Growth: A Planetary Parable as Told from Southern Africa*. Durham: Duke University Press, 2019.
Loewen, James. *Sundown Towns: A Hidden Dimension of American Racism*. New York: New Press, 2005.
MacLellan, Matthew. "The Tragedy of Limitless Growth: Re-interpreting the Tragedy of the Commons for a Century of Climate Change." *Environmental Humanities* 7, no. 1 (2016): 41–58.
Mains, Daniel. *Under Construction: Technologies of Development in Urban Ethiopia*. Durham: Duke University Press, 2019.
Marx, Karl. *Capital: A Critique of Political Economy*. Volume 1. London: Penguin Books, [1867] 1976.
Masco, Joseph, and Lisa Wedeen. "Introduction: Conspiracy/Theory." In *Conspiracy/Theory*, edited by Joseph Masco and Lisa Wedeen, 1–33. Durham: Duke University Press, 2023.
Millar, Kathleen. *Reclaiming the Discarded: Life and Labor on Rio's Garbage Dump*. Durham: Duke University Press, 2018
Mosteller, Kelli. "The Cultural Politics of Land: Potawatomi Allotment and Citizenship in Kansas and Indian Territory, 1861–1891." *Trans-Scripts 1* (2011): 82–101.
Mosteller, Kelli Jean. "Place, Politics, and Property: Negotiating Allotment and Citizenship for the Citizen Potawatomi, 1861–1891." PhD diss., University of Texas at Austin, 2013.
Ormerod, Kerri Jean, and Christopher Scott. "Drinking Wastewater: Public Trust in Potable Reuse." *Science, Technology, and Human Values* 38, no. 3 (2013): 351–73.
Ostrom, Elinor. *Governing the Commons: The Evolution of Institutions for Collective Action*. Cambridge: Cambridge University Press, 1990.
Parker, Martin. "Human Science as Conspiracy Theory." *Sociological Review* 48, no. 2 (2000): 191–207.
Phillips, Kristin D. "Southern Politics, Southern Power Prices: Race, Utility Regulation, and the Value of Energy." *Economic Anthropology* 10, no. 2 (2023): 197–212.
Pilgeram, Ryanne. *Pushed Out: Contested Development and Rural Gentrification in the US West*. Seattle: University of Washington Press, 2021.
Randell, Heather, and Andrew Curley. "Dams and Tribal Land Loss in the United States." *Environmental Research Letters* 18, no. 9 (2023): 1–10.
Reisner, Mark. *Cadillac Desert: The American West and Its Disappearing Water*. Penguin: New York City, 1986.

Reno, Joshua. "Waste and Waste Management." *Annual Review of Anthropology* 44 (2015): 557–72.
Riley, Ann. *Restoring Neighborhood Streams: Planning, Design, and Construction*. Washington DC: Island Press, 2016.
Robbins, Paul, and Julie Sharp. "Producing and Consuming Chemicals: The Moral Economy of the American Lawn." *Economic Geography* 79, no. 4 (2003): 425–51.
Sabin, Paul. *Public Citizens: The Attack on Big Government and the Remaking of American Liberalism*. New York City: W. W. Norton, 2021.
Scott, James. *Seeing Like a State: How Certain Schemes to Improve the Human Condition Have Failed*. New Haven: Yale University Press, 1998.
Simonds, Joe. *The Norman Project*. Bureau of Reclamation, 1999.
Smith, Allan. "Commentary: Hexavalent Chromium, Yellow Water, and Cancer: A Convoluted Saga." *Epidemiology* 19, no. 1 (2008): 24–26.
Sobo, Elisa. "Conspiracy Theories in Political-Economic Context: Lessons from Parents with Vaccine and Other Pharmaceutical Concerns." *Journal for Cultural Research* 25, no. 1 (2021): 51–68.
———. "Playing with Conspiracy Theories." *AnthropologyNews* website, July 31, 2019.
Star, Susan Leigh. "The Ethnography of Infrastructure." *American Behavioral Scientist* 43, no. 3 (1999): 377–91.
Sugden, John. *Tecumseh: A Life*. New York: Henry Holt, 1997.
Todd, Zoe. "From a Fishy Place: Examining Canadian State Law Applied in the Daniels Decision from the Perspective of Metis Legal Orders." *TOPIA* 36 (2016): 43–57.
Trombley, Jeffrey. "Watershed Encounters." *Environmental Humanities* 10, no. 1 (2018): 107–28.
Truden, John. "The Absentee Shawnees and the True Story of Lake Thunderbird." *Oklahoma Humanities* 14, no. 2 (2021): 12–16.
Tsing, Anna. *The Mushroom at the End of the World: On the Possibility of Life in Capitalist Ruins*. Princeton: Princeton University Press, 2015.
Tufekci, Zeynep. "How Social Media Took Us from Tahrir Square to Donald Trump." *MIT Technology Review*, September/October 2018.
von Schnitzler, Antina. *Democracy's Infrastructure: Techno-Politics and Protest after Apartheid*. Princeton: Princeton University Press, 2016.
Voyles, Traci Brynne. *The Settler Sea: California's Salton Sea and the Consequences of Colonialism*. Lincoln: University of Nebraska Press, 2021.
Wade, Madeline, Randy Peppler, and Angela Person. "Community Education and Perceptions of Water Reuse: A Case Study in Norman, Oklahoma." *Journal of Environmental Studies and Sciences* 11 (2021): 266–73.
Westermeyer, William. "Stigmatized Identity Motivating Right-Wing Populism: How the Tea Party Learned to Love Donald Trump." In *The Anthropology of Donald Trump: Culture and the Exceptional Moment*, edited by Jack David Eller, 21–39. London: Routledge, 2022.

Whitney, Kristoffer. "Living Lawns, Dying Waters: The Suburban Boom, Nitrogenous Fertilizers, and the Nonpoint Source Pollution Dilemma." *Technology and Culture* 51, no. 3 (2010): 652–74.

Widlock, Thomas. *Anthropology and the Economy of Sharing*. London: Routledge, 2017.

Womack, John. *Cleveland Country, Oklahoma: Historical Highlights*. John Womack: Noble, Oklahoma 1983.

———. *Norman: An Early History, 1820–1900*. Norman: John Womack, 1976.

Worster, Donald. *The Dust Bowl: The Southern Plains in the 1930s*. New York: Oxford University Press, 2004.

———. *Rivers of Empire: Water, Aridity, and the Growth of the American West*. Oxford: Oxford University Press, 1992.

INDEX

Page locators in italics indicate figures.

www.ingramcontent.com/pod-product-compliance
Lightning Source LLC
Chambersburg PA
CBHW030714040825

30551CB00007BA/16

* 9 7 8 1 4 9 6 2 4 0 1 9 4 *